200
FARMHOUSE
& COUNTRY HOME PLANS

Classic And Modern Farmhouses
From 1,299 To 4,890 Square Feet

HOME PLANNERS
TUCSON, ARIZONA

Published by Home Planners
A Division of Hanley-Wood, Inc.
Editorial and Corporate Offices:
3275 West Ina Road, Suite 110
Tucson, Arizona 85741

Distribution Center:
29333 Lorie Lane
Wixom, Michigan 48393

Rickard D. Bailey, CEO and Publisher
Cindy Coatsworth Lewis, Publications Manager
Paulette Mulvin, Editor
Paul D. Fitzgerald, Book Designer

Photo Credits
Front Cover: © John R. Dillon, Photographer
Back Cover: © Carl Socolow

10   9   8   7   6

Printed in the United States of America.

ISBN: 1-881955-41-9

On the front cover: A beautifully configured Classic Farmhouse, Design Q9242,
the home of Rick and Kathy Slivka, was built by Christopher Semenza of
Semenza Homes. For additional information about this design, see page 20.

On the back cover: Classic Farmhouse design at its best! Our Design Q2774, the
home of John and Janie Deardorff, is a popular and practical family plan. For
more information about this design, see page 7.

TABLE OF CONTENTS

Editor's Note
Everyone loves Farmhouse design-maybe because it evokes such a sense of warmth and security. From rustic exterior to cozy interior, the country style is a favorite from Mid-West plains to East and West Coast urban centers. This collection draws its inspiration from the simple honesty of country living, while actually providing the most popular features in residential housing. Filled with the spirit of the country life, this book brings together recognizable rural style and efficient, amenity-laden architectural floor planning for a selection of homes that tugs at the heart. For complete cost information, available for many of our designs, see page 214, where we describe our exclusive Quote One® cost-estimating service.

About The Designers

The Blue Ribbon Designer Series™ is a collection of books featuring the home plans of a diverse group of outstanding home designers and architects known as the Blue Ribbon Network of Designers. This group of companies is dedicated to creating and marketing the finest possible plans for home construction on a regional and national basis. Each of the companies exhibits superior work and integrity in all phases of the stock-plan business including modern, trendsetting floor planning, a professionally executed blueprint package and a strong sense of service and commitment to the consumer.

Design Basics, Inc.

For nearly a decade, Design Basics, a nationally recognized home design service located in Omaha, has been developing plans for custom home builders. Since 1987, the firm has consistently appeared in *Builder* magazine, the official magazine of the National Association of Home Builders, as the top-selling designer. The company's plans also regularly appear in numerous other shelter magazines such as *Better Homes and Gardens*, *House Beautiful* and *Home Planner*.

Stephen Fuller/Design Traditions

Design Traditions was established by Stephen S. Fuller with the tenets of innovation, quality, originality and uncompromising architectural techniques in traditional and European homes. Especially popular throughout the Southeast, Design Traditions' plans are known for their extensive detail and thoughtful design. They are widely published in such shelter magazines as *Southern Living* magazine and *Better Homes and Gardens*.

Alan Mascord Design Associates, Inc.

Founded in 1983 as a local supplier to the building community, Mascord Design Associates of Portland, Oregon, began to successfully publish plans nationally in 1985. With plans now drawn exclusively on computer, Mascord Design Associates quickly received a reputation for homes that are easy to build yet meet the rigorous demands of the buyers' market, winning local and national awards. The company's trademark is creating floor plans that work well and exhibit excellent traffic patterns. Their motto is: "Drawn to build, designed to sell."

Larry W. Garnett & Associates, Inc.

Starting as a designer of homes for Houston-area residents, Garnett & Associates has been marketing designs nationally for the past ten years. A well-respected design firm, the company's plans are regularly featured in *House Beautiful, Country Living, Home* and *Professional Builder*. Numerous accolades, including several from the Texas Institute of Building Design and the American Institute of Building Design, have been awarded to the company for excellence in architecture.

Home Planners

Headquartered in Tucson, Arizona, with additional offices in Detroit, Home Planners is one of the longest-running and most successful home design firms in the United States. With over 2,500 designs in its portfolio, the company provides a wide range of styles, sizes and types of homes for the residential builder. All of Home Planners' designs are created with the care and professional expertise that fifty years of experience in the home-planning business affords. Their homes are designed to be built, lived in and enjoyed for years to come.

Donald A. Gardner, Architects, Inc.

The South Carolina firm of Donald A. Gardner was established in response to a growing demand for residential designs that reflect constantly changing lifestyles. The company's specialty is providing homes with refined, custom-style details and unique features such as passive-solar designs and open floor plans. Computer-aided design and drafting technology resulting in trouble-free construction documents places the firm at the leading edge of the home plan industry.

Larry E. Belk Designs

Through the years, Larry E. Belk has worked with individuals and builders alike to provide a quality product. After listening to over 4,000 dreams and watching them become reality all across America, Larry's design philosophy today combines traditional exteriors with upscale interiors designed for contemporary lifestyles. Flowing, open spaces and interesting angles define his interiors. Great emphasis is placed on providing views that showcase the natural environment. Dynamic exteriors reflect Larry's extensive home construction experience, painstaking research and talent as a fine artist.

CLASSIC FARMHOUSES

The Classic American Farmhouse is the very essence of country-style living. It evokes images of Sunday-afternoon picnics on rolling green lawns, cold lemonade served on wide covered porches and gatherings around a cozy fireplace on wintery evenings. Its floor plans cater to family living with roomy living spaces, large kitchens and plenty of bedrooms.

Easily recognizable, the Classic Farmhouse has a number of characteristics that make it a standout. Probably most noticeable is its tall, upright, stately appearance coupled with a covered front porch or wrapping porch. The porch usually has simple, square columns with square, dimensioned railings.

The home itself is almost always two-stories, or at least 1½-stories, with the porch being either raised or at grade. The Classic Farmhouse will support a straight gabled roof that is usually steeply pitched. In some instances, the roof may have cross gables over a garage or a living area extension. It is not unusual to find a cupola or a weathervane at the rooftop or over the garage.

Covered on the exterior with horizontal wood siding, the Classic Farmhouse is trimmed with wood and sports a wood fascia. Other exterior details include a prominent chimney stack at one or both ends of the home and paned, shuttered windows in a symmetrical fenestration. Some versions may have round, half-round or Palladian windows and entry doors with fan lights. Though not common, some Classic Farmhouses have two or three dormer windows at the second floor.

Design Q2774 is the quintessential Classic Farmhouse, bringing together a rustic charm and comfortable livability. The wraparound covered porch, raised-hearth fireplace in the family room and exterior enhancements such as the shuttered, multi-pane windows and the steeply gabled roofline herald its popular interior layout. In two stories, the plan accommodates formal and informal living spaces, four bedrooms and 2½ baths. Attic space on the unfinished third floor makes a great storage area or can be developed into additional bedrooms at a later time.

This home is just one of many in the Classic Farmhouse section that draws design flavor from rustic predecessors, yet provides a comfortable, convenient home for today's family.

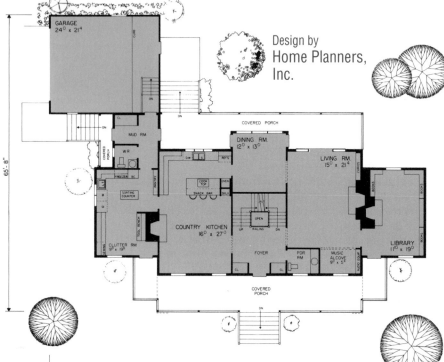

Design Q2694

First Floor: 2,026 square feet
Second Floor: 1,386 square feet
Total: 3,412 square feet

L

Design by
**Home Planners,
Inc.**

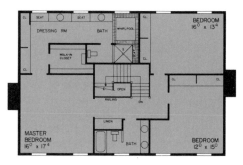

● This two-story design faithfully recalls the 18th-Century homestead of Secretary of Foreign Affairs John Jay. California Engineered Plans and California Stock Plans are available for this home. Call 1-800-521-6797 for more information.

QUOTE ONE™

Cost to build? See page 214 to order complete cost estimate to build this house in your area!

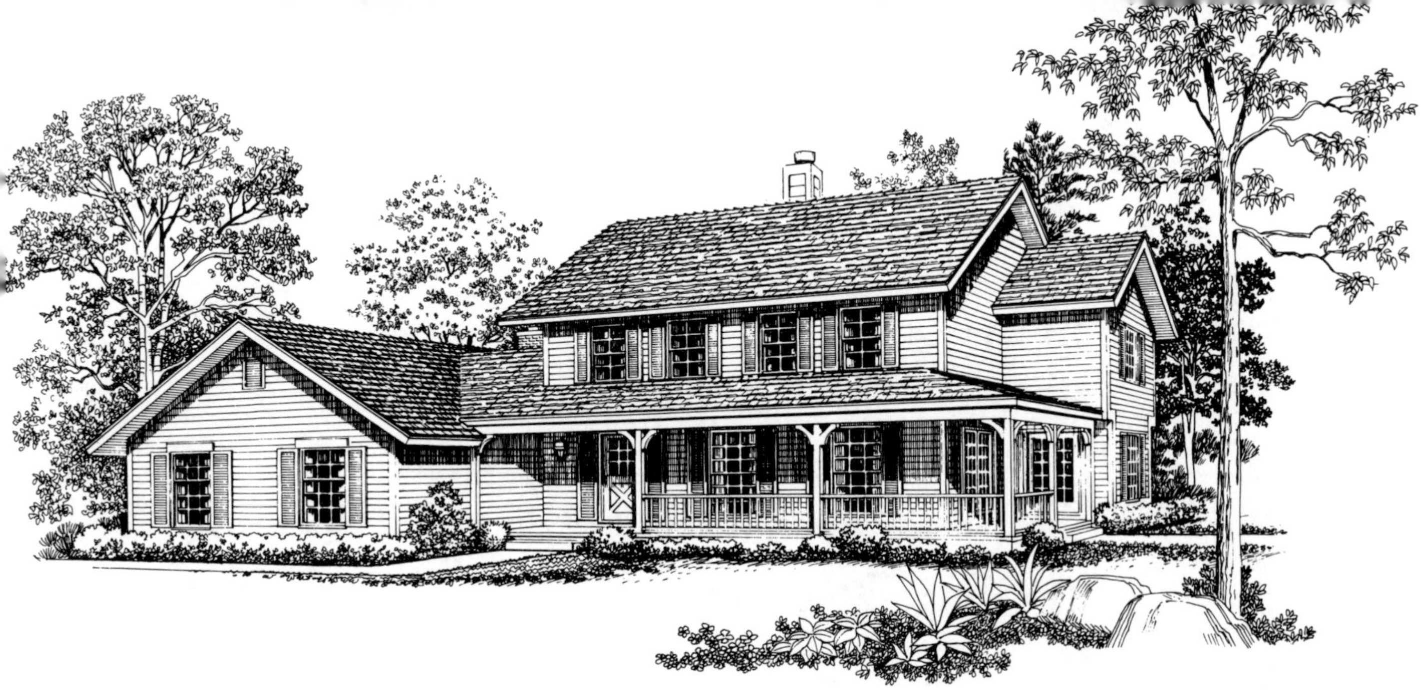

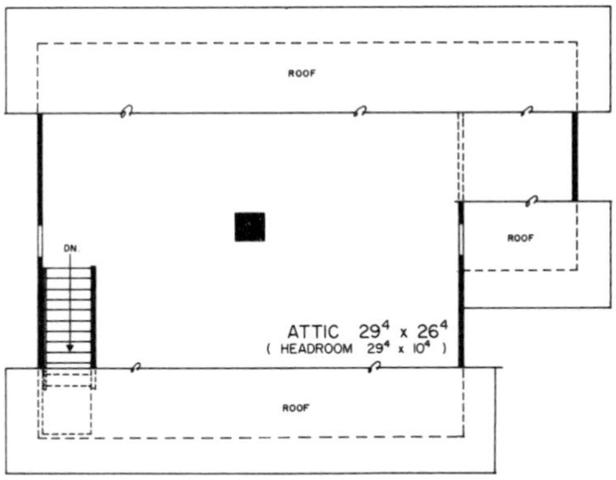

ROOF
DN.
ROOF
ATTIC 29⁴ x 26⁴
(HEADROOM 29⁴ x 10⁴)
ROOF

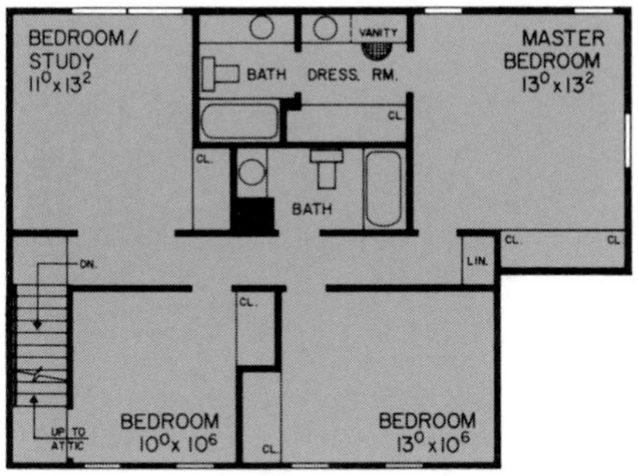

BEDROOM / STUDY 11⁰x13²
VANITY
BATH
DRESS. RM.
MASTER BEDROOM 13⁰x13²
CL.
BATH
DN.
LIN.
BEDROOM 10⁰x10⁶
BEDROOM 13⁰x10⁶
UP TO ATTIC

Width 59'-6"
Depth 46'

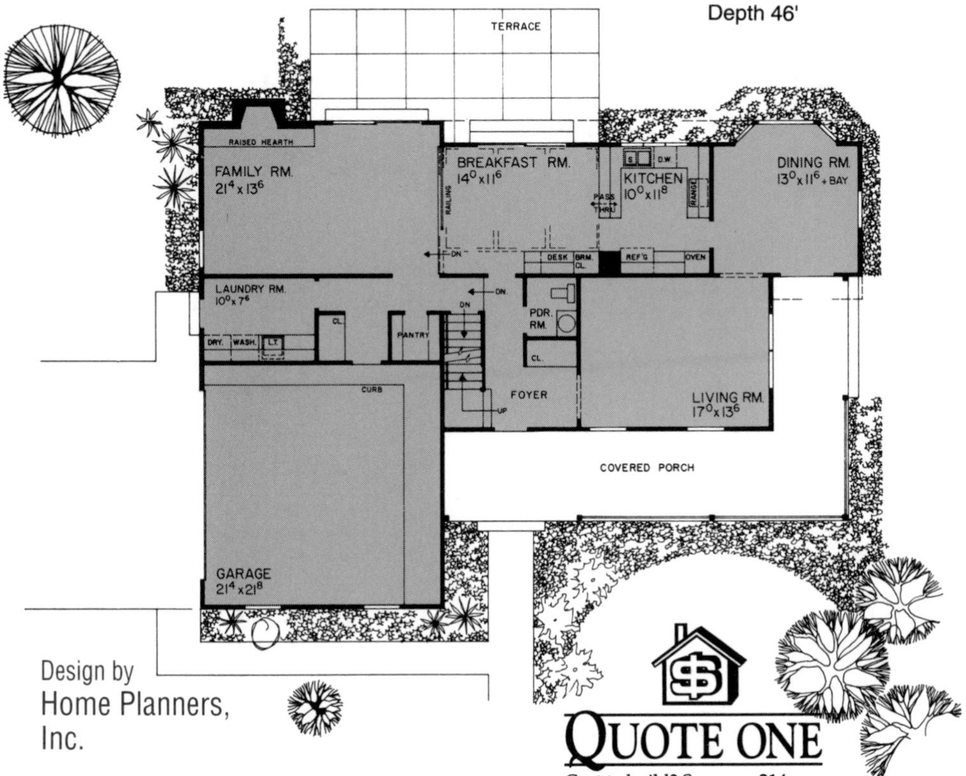

TERRACE
RAISED HEARTH
FAMILY RM. 21⁴x13⁶
BREAKFAST RM. 14⁰x11⁶
KITCHEN 10⁰x11⁸
DINING RM. 13⁰x11⁶ + BAY
RANGE
PASS THRU
DESK
BRM. CL.
REF'G
OVEN
LAUNDRY RM. 10⁰x7⁶
DRY.
WASH.
PANTRY
PDR. RM.
FOYER
LIVING RM. 17⁰x13⁶
COVERED PORCH
CURB
GARAGE 21⁴x21⁸

Design Q2774

First Floor: 1,366 square feet
Second Floor: 969 square feet
Total: 2,335 square feet
Attic: 969 square feet

L **D**

● Another farmhouse adaptation with all the most up-to-date features expected in a new home. Beginning with the formal areas, this design offers pleasures for the entire family. There is the quiet corner living room which has an opening to the sizable dining room. This room will enjoy plenty of natural light from the delightful bay window overlooking the rear yard. It is also conveniently located with the efficient U-shaped kitchen just a step away. The kitchen features many built-ins with pass-through to the beamed-ceiling nook. Sliding glass doors to the terrace are fine attractions in both the sunken family room and nook. The service entrance to the garage has a storage closet on each side. There is extra storage in the large attic, with expansion possibilities there also. Recreational activities and hobbies can be pursued in the basement area, where there is more bulk storage space. Note four bedrooms with two baths upstairs. For information on customizing this design, call 1-800-521-6797, ext. 800. California Engineered Plans and California Stock Plans are available for this home. Call 1-800-521-6797 for more information.

Design by
Home Planners, Inc.

QUOTE ONE

Cost to build? See page 214 to order complete cost estimate to build this house in your area!

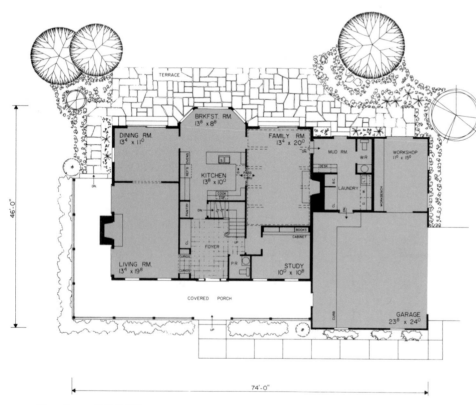

TERRACE

BRKFST. RM.
13⁸ x 8⁸

DINING RM.
13⁴ x 11⁰

FAMILY RM.
13⁴ x 20⁰

MUD RM.

WORKSHOP
11⁰ x 15⁰

W R

KITCHEN
13⁸ x 10⁰

LAUNDRY

PASS THRU

COOK TOP

PANTRY

BOOKS

CABINET

WORKBENCH

CL

FOYER

UP

DN

LIVING RM.
13⁴ x 19⁸

PR

STUDY
10⁰ x 10⁸

GARAGE
23⁸ x 24⁰

CURB

COVERED PORCH

UP

46'-0"

74'-0"

BEDROOM
13⁴ x 14²

BATH

BATH

SEAT

HIS WALK-IN CLOSET

DRESS. RM.

HER WALK-IN CLOSET

TWLS

LIN

VANITY

RAILING

CL

CL

DN

CL

CL

BEDROOM
13⁴ x 14²

BEDROOM
13⁸ x 10⁰

MASTER BEDROOM
13⁴ x 14⁴

Design by
Home Planners,
Inc.

QUOTE ONE™

Cost to build? See page 214
to order complete cost estimate
to build this house in your area!

Design Q2946 First Floor: 1,581 square feet
Second Floor: 1,344 square feet
Total: 2,925 square feet

L **D**

● This traditional farmhouse design is made for hospitality. The star attractions are the large covered porch and rear terrace, perfect gathering points for family and friends. Inside, the design offers much more: separate living room and family room, each with its own fireplace, formal dining room, large kitchen and breakfast area with bay windows, separate study with built-ins for books and other materials, workshop with plenty of room to maneuver, and mud room. The second floor offers a master suite and 3 family bedrooms plus 2 full baths. The master bedroom provides His and Hers closets with double lavatories in the master bath. For information on customizing this design, call 1-800-521-6797, ext. 800.

Design Q3324

First Floor: 1,762 square feet
Second Floor: 1,311 square feet
Total: 3,073 square feet

L **D**

Design by
Home Planners,
Inc.

● This home provides a perfect opportunity to share the comforts of traditional family living with in-home office space. The versatile plan allows for a well-positioned study off the foyer and a combination guest room/office near the laundry room—both with nearby facilities and excellent views. The large kitchen presents many possibilities for dining pleasures: a cozy meal in the breakfast nook; light eating and conversation at the bar; and evening meals in the dining room. The master bedroom provides spacious comfort with His and Hers walk-in closets and an impressive dressing area. The two bedrooms share a large bathroom with plenty of linen space. For information on customizing this design, call 1-800-521-6797, ext. 800.

BEDROOM
13² x 14⁸

BATH

SEAT
HIS

LIN LIN DRESSING HER

WOOD RAILING
DN
SEAT

MASTER
BEDROOM
13⁸ x 19⁶

BEDROOM
13² x 14⁸

WOOD RAILING
OPEN
TO
FOYER BELOW

Width 66'
Depth 47'-6"

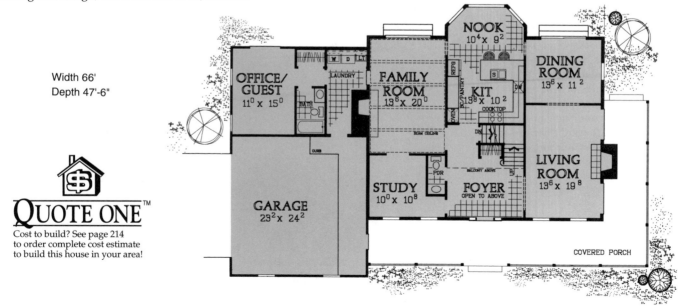

OFFICE/
GUEST
11⁰ x 15⁰

W D
LAUNDRY

BATH

GARAGE
23² x 24²

NOOK
10⁴ x 9²

FAMILY
ROOM
13⁸ x 20⁰

KIT
13⁸ x 10²
COOKTOP

DINING
ROOM
13⁶ x 11²

STUDY
10⁰ x 10⁸

FOYER
OPEN TO ABOVE

LIVING
ROOM
13⁶ x 19⁸

COVERED PORCH

Quote One™

Cost to build? See page 214 to order complete cost estimate to build this house in your area!

Design Q9677

First Floor: 1,584 square feet
Second Floor: 867 square feet
Total: 2,451 square feet

● Flexibility is the key to the appeal of this country-style plan. The dining room/great room can be built as one great room with the dining room relocated to the family room. The master suite has a large walk-in closet, a fireplace and a master bath with shower, whirlpool tub and double-bowl vanity. Both the sun room and master bath have access to a uniquely shaped deck. Note that there is space available on the deck for a hot tub. The screened porch offers the best in outdoor living space. Three bedrooms on the second level are joined by two full baths for convenience. Dormer windows on the second floor project out from two of the bedrooms, allowing room for window seats or storage.

Design by
Donald A.
Gardner,
Architect, Inc.

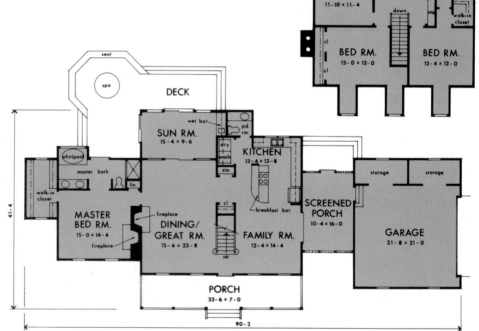

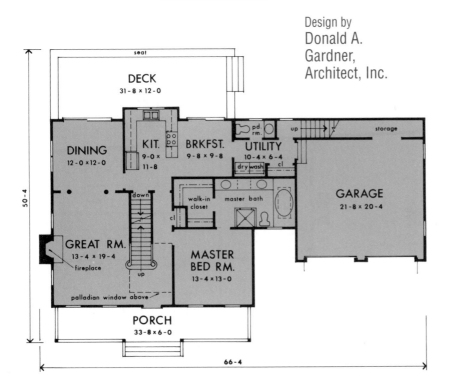

attic storage

bath

BED RM.
13-4 × 10-8

down

BED RM.
17-0 × 10-8

cl   cl   cl   cl

foyer
below

clerestory with palladian window

down

BONUS
RM.
14-4 × 23-8

Design by
Donald A.
Gardner,
Architect, Inc.

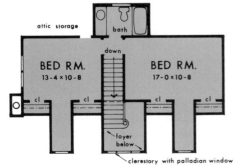

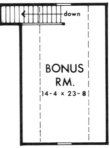

seat

DECK
31-8 × 12-0

DINING
12-0 × 12-0

KIT.
9-0 ×
11-8

BRKFST.
9-8 × 9-8

UTILITY
10-4 × 6-4

pd.
rm.

up

storage

dry wash

cl

down

GREAT RM.
13-4 × 19-4

fireplace

walk-in
closet

master bath

cl

GARAGE
21-8 × 20-4

up

MASTER
BED RM.
13-4 × 13-0

palladian window above

50-4

PORCH
33-8 × 6-0

66-4

Quote One®

Cost to build? See page 214
to order complete cost estimate
to build this house in your area!

Design Q9606

First Floor: 1,289 square feet
Second Floor: 542 square feet
Total: 1,831 square feet

● This cozy country cottage is perfect for the growing family —offering both an unfinished basement
option and a bonus room. Enter
through the two-story foyer with a
Palladian window in a clerestory
dormer above. The master suite is on
the first floor for privacy and accessibility. Its accompanying bath boasts
a whirlpool tub with skylight above
and double-bowl vanity. The second
floor contains two bedrooms, a full
bath, and plenty of storage. Note that
all first-floor rooms except the
kitchen and utility room boast 9-foot
ceilings. For crawl-space foundation,
order Design Q9606; for basement
foundation, order Design Q9606A.

RAILING

VERANDA

GREAT RM
13⁶ X 15⁴

KITCHEN
9¹⁰ X 11⁸

MASTER
BEDROOM
11⁰ X 15⁰

WHIRLPOOL

SNACK BAR

DW SNK

REF

BATH

PDR

LAUNDRY

W. D.

PANTRY

CL.

DN

UP

DINING
ROOM
11⁰ X 11⁰

FOYER

LIVING
ROOM
12⁰ X 13⁴

GARAGE
23⁰ X 24⁸

VERANDA

RAILING

Design by
Home Planners,
Inc.

QUOTE ONE™

Cost to build? See page 214
to order complete cost estimate
to build this house in your area!

Width 53'-8"
Depth 57'

BEDROOM
11⁰ X 13⁰

OPEN BELOW

STORAGE

BATH

DN

LINEN

BEDROOM
12⁸ X 12⁰

DESK

BEDROOM
12⁰ X 14⁴

Design Q3462 First Floor: 1,395 square feet
Second Floor: 813 square feet; Total: 2,208 square feet

L

● Get off to a great start with this handsome
family farmhouse. Covered porches front and rear
assure comfortable outdoor living while varied
roof planes add visual interest. Inside, distinct
formal and informal living zones provide the best
accommodations for any occasion. The columned
foyer opens to both the dining and living rooms.
The central kitchen services the large family room
with an island work counter and snack bar. For
everyday chores, a laundry room is conveniently
located and also provides access to the garage. On
the first floor you'll find the master bedroom
suite. It enjoys complete privacy and luxury with
its double closets and master bath with double-
bowl vanity, whirlpool tub and separate shower.
Upstairs, three family bedrooms extend fabulous
livability.

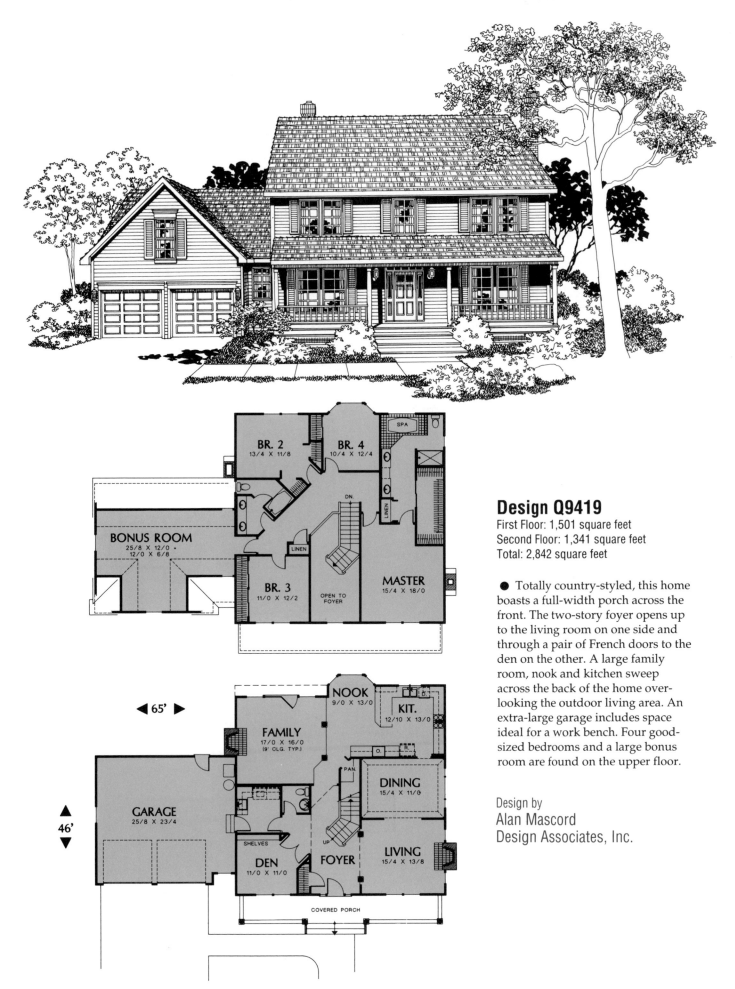

BONUS ROOM
25/8 X 12/0 •
12/0 X 6/8

BR. 2
13/4 X 11/8

BR. 4
10/4 X 12/4

SPA

DN.

LINEN

LINEN

BR. 3
11/0 X 12/2

OPEN TO
FOYER

MASTER
15/4 X 18/0

Design Q9419

First Floor: 1,501 square feet
Second Floor: 1,341 square feet
Total: 2,842 square feet

● Totally country-styled, this home
boasts a full-width porch across the
front. The two-story foyer opens up
to the living room on one side and
through a pair of French doors to the
den on the other. A large family
room, nook and kitchen sweep
across the back of the home overlooking the outdoor living area. An
extra-large garage includes space
ideal for a work bench. Four good-
sized bedrooms and a large bonus
room are found on the upper floor.

Design by
Alan Mascord
Design Associates, Inc.

◀ 65' ▶

NOOK
9/0 X 13/0

KIT.
12/10 X 13/0

FAMILY
17/0 X 16/0
(9' CLG. TYP.)

PAN.

O.

R.

DINING
15/4 X 11/0

▲
46'
▼

GARAGE
25/8 X 23/4

SHELVES

UP

DEN
11/0 X 11/0

FOYER

LIVING
15/4 X 13/8

COVERED PORCH

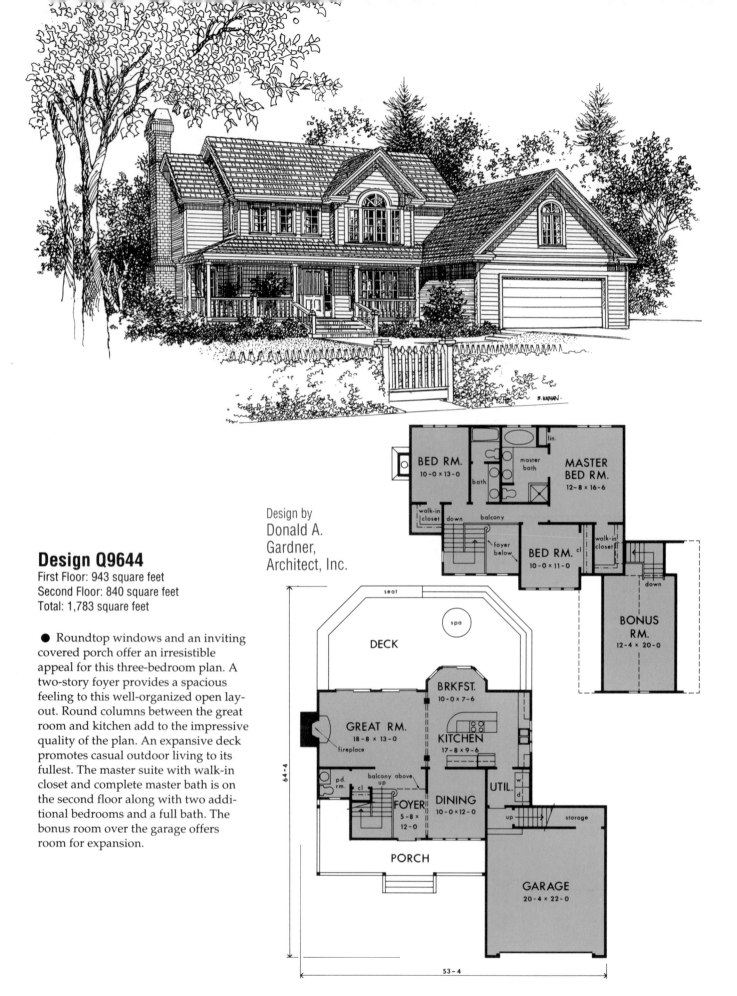

Design Q9644

First Floor: 943 square feet
Second Floor: 840 square feet
Total: 1,783 square feet

● Roundtop windows and an inviting covered porch offer an irresistible appeal for this three-bedroom plan. A two-story foyer provides a spacious feeling to this well-organized open layout. Round columns between the great room and kitchen add to the impressive quality of the plan. An expansive deck promotes casual outdoor living to its fullest. The master suite with walk-in closet and complete master bath is on the second floor along with two additional bedrooms and a full bath. The bonus room over the garage offers room for expansion.

Design by
Donald A. Gardner, Architect, Inc.

BED RM.
10-0 × 13-0

master bath

lin.

MASTER BED RM.
12-8 × 16-6

bath

walk-in closet

down

balcony

foyer below

BED RM.
10-0 × 11-0

cl

walk-in closet

down

BONUS RM.
12-4 × 20-0

seat

spa

DECK

BRKFST.
10-0 × 7-6

GREAT RM.
18-8 × 13-0

fireplace

KITCHEN
17-8 × 9-6

64-4

pd. rm.

cl

balcony above
up

FOYER
5-8 × 12-0

DINING
10-0 × 12-0

UTIL.

w d

up

storage

PORCH

GARAGE
20-4 × 22-0

53-4

B. NATHAN

Design Q9643

First Floor: 1,165 square feet
Second Floor: 1,053 square feet
Total: 2,218 square feet
Bonus Room: 282 square feet

● The beauty of the exterior of
this four-bedroom plan is
enhanced by the use of arched
windows, dormers and a
wraparound front porch. The
entrance foyer is partially open to
the second level, allowing a balcony to pass over the center and
generate visual excitement. Both
the living and family rooms have
fireplaces. The U-shaped kitchen
is centrally located between the
breakfast area and dining room
for maximum efficiency. A large
rear deck enhances outdoor living. A master suite with a generous master bath shares the second floor with three other bedrooms and a bonus room.

Design by
Donald A.
Gardner,
Architects, Inc.

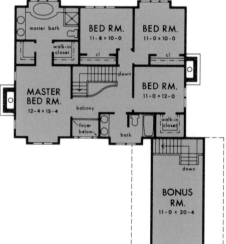

Width 53'
Depth 70'-8"

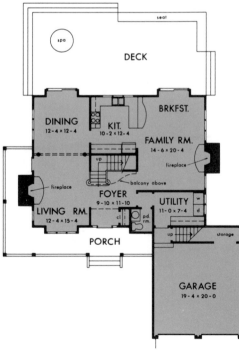

● It's hard to get beyond the covered front porch of this home, but doing so reveals a bright two-story entry open to the central hall. Just to the left, an enticing bay window enlivens the living room, featuring French doors which connect to the family room. The efficient kitchen with snack bar and pantry is open to the bay-windowed breakfast area with planning desk. The salad sink and counter space double as a service for the formal dining room. The master bedroom features a raised ceiling and arched window. Its adjoining bath contains a walk-through closet/transition area and a corner whirlpool.

Design Q9230

First Floor: 1,303 square feet
Second Floor: 1,084 square feet
Total: 2,387 square feet

Design by
Design
Basics,
Inc.

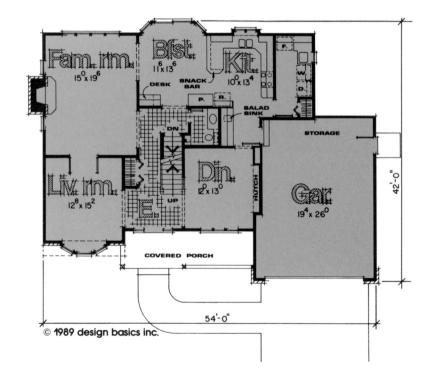

© 1989 design basics inc.

Design Q9214

First Floor: 1,188 square feet
Second Floor: 1,172 square feet
Total: 2,360 square feet

● Beginning with the interest of a wraparound porch, there's a feeling of country charm in this two-story plan. Formal dining and living rooms, visible from the entry, offer ample space for gracious entertaining. The large family room is truly a place of warmth and welcome with its gorgeous bay window, fireplace and French doors to the living room. The kitchen, with island counter, pantry and desk, makes cooking a delight. Upstairs, the secondary bedrooms share an efficient compartmented bath. The expansive master suite has its own luxury bath with double vanity, whirlpool, walk-in closet and dressing area.

Design by
Design
Basics,
Inc.

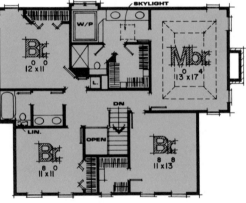

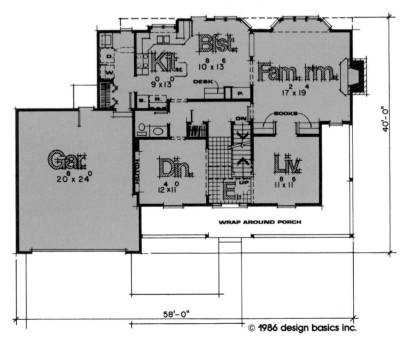

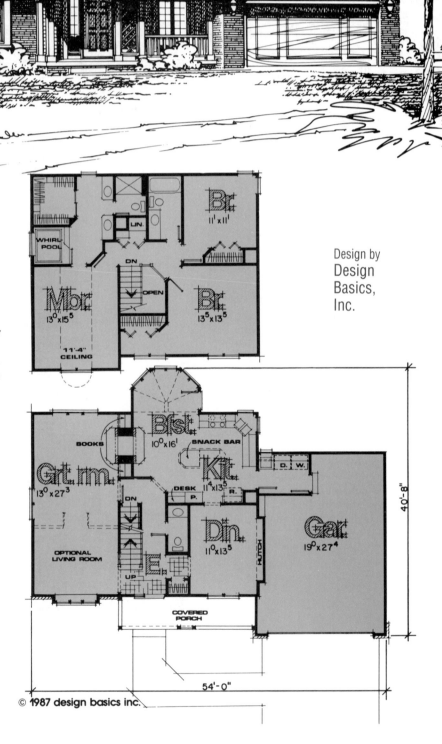

Design Q9212

First Floor: 1,096 square feet
Second Floor: 975 square feet
Total: 2,071 square feet

● "Country charm" is the keynote for this delightful three-bedroom, two-story home. Create a very large great room or place a strategically located wall to provide a living room toward the front. The dining room features extra hutch space. The roomy kitchen is complete with large island counter/snack bar, pantry and desk. The gazebo-shaped breakfast room shares a through-fireplace with the great room. The three-bedroom upstairs includes a master suite which boasts an eye-catching arched transom window and bath with whirlpool.

Design by
Design Basics, Inc.

Design Q9289

First Floor: 927 square feet
Second Floor: 1,163 square feet
Total: 2,090 square feet

● If you've ever dreamed of living in a country home, you'll love the wrapping porch on this four-bedroom, two-story home. Comfortable living begins in the great room with windows and nearby staircase. Just off the entry, a formal dining room was designed to make entertaining a pleasure. The large kitchen includes a pantry, island counter, roll-top desk and Lazy Susan. A private door accesses the wraparound porch from the kitchen. Be sure to take a good look at the bright dinette. Upstairs, secondary bedrooms share a centrally located bath with double vanity. For convenience, the laundry room is located on the same level as the bedrooms. The deluxe master bedroom is accessed by double doors. In the master bath, you'll enjoy the whirlpool, transom window and sloped ceiling.

Design by
Design
Basics,
Inc.

Design Q9242

First Floor: 1,322 square feet
Second Floor: 1,272 square feet
Total: 2,594 square feet

● Here's the luxury you've been looking for—from the wraparound covered front porch to the bright sun room at the rear off the breakfast room. A sunken family room with fireplace serves everyday casual gatherings, while the more formal living and dining rooms are reserved for special entertaining situations. The kitchen has a central island with snack bar and is located most conveniently for serving and cleaning up. Upstairs are four bedrooms, one a lovely master suite with French doors into the master bath and a whirlpool tub in a dramatic bay window. A double vanity in the shared bath easily serves the three family bedrooms.

Design by
Design
Basics,
Inc.

Cost to build? See page 214
to order complete cost estimate
to build this house in your area!

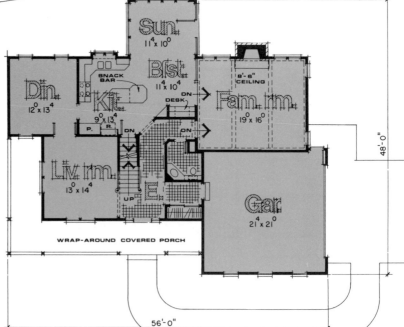

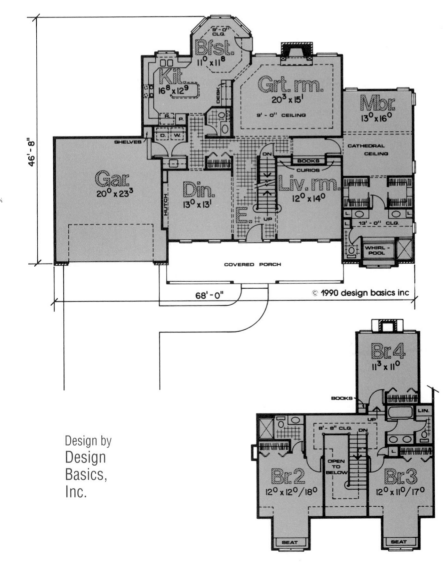

Design Q9274

First Floor: 1,780 square feet
Second Floor: 815 square feet
Total: 2,595 square feet

● A large covered front porch welcomes visitors to this home. The entrance hall opens to a formal dining room with hutch space and a living room with built-in curio cabinets. The volume great room features a handsome fireplace flanked by windows. A large kitchen provides an island counter, pantry, dual Lazy Susans and a desk. A private hall with built-in bookcase leads to the first-floor master suite. The extravagant master bath features two walk-in closets, His and Hers vanities and a whirlpool tub. Upstairs, two of the three bedrooms feature decorator window seats.

Design by
Design
Basics,
Inc.

Design by
Donald A.
Gardner,
Architect, Inc.

● Enjoy outdoor living with a covered front porch at the front of this home and an expansive deck to the rear. The floor plan allows for great livability and features split-bedroom styling with the master suite on the first floor. Upstairs bedrooms share a full bath. There is also bonus space above the garage for a studio, study or play room. For a crawl-space foundation, order Plan Q9654; for a basement foundation, order Q9654-A.

Design Q9654

First Floor: 1,578 square feet
Second Floor: 554 square feet
Total: 2,132 square feet

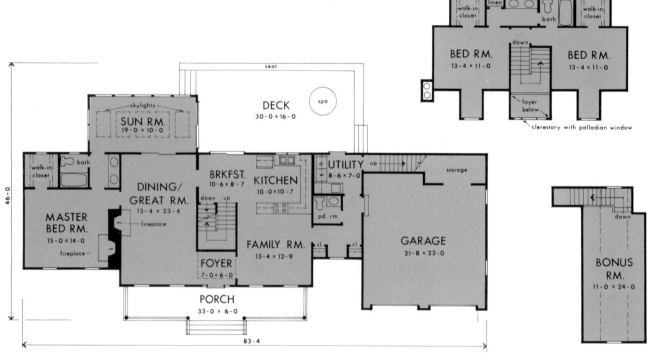

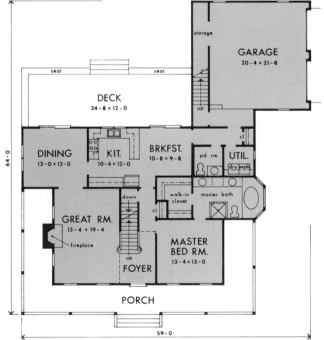

DECK
34-8 x 12-0

seat   seat

storage

GARAGE
20-4 x 21-8

up

cl

DINING
13-0 x 12-0

KIT.
10-4 x 12-0

BRKFST.
10-8 x 9-8

pd. rm.

UTIL.

dry wash

walk-in closet

master bath

cl

down

GREAT RM.
13-4 x 19-4

fireplace

up

FOYER

MASTER BED RM.
13-4 x 13-0

PORCH

64-0

59-0

attic storage   attic storage

bath

down

BED RM.
13-4 x 10-8

BED RM.
17-0 x 10-8

cl   cl   cl   cl

foyer below

clerestory with palladian window

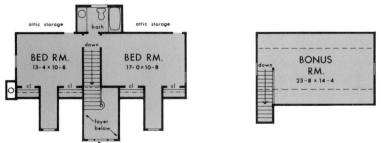

down

BONUS RM.
23-8 x 14-4

Design Q9645

First Floor: 1,356 square feet
Second Floor: 542 square feet
Total: 1,898 square feet

● The welcoming charm of this country farmhouse is expressed by its many windows and its covered wraparound porch. A two-story entrance foyer is enhanced by a Palladian window in a clerestory dormer above to allow natural lighting. A first-floor master suite allows privacy and accessibility. The master bath includes a whirlpool tub, shower, and double-bowl vanity along with a walk-in closet. The first floor features a nine-foot ceiling throughout with the exception of the kitchen area, which features an eight-foot ceiling. The second floor provides two additional bedrooms, a full bath, and plenty of storage space. An unfinished basement and bonus room provide room to grow. Order Design Q9645 for crawl-space foundation; order Design Q9645-A for basement foundation.

Design by
Donald A. Gardner, Architect, Inc.

QUOTE ONE®
Cost to build? See page 214 to order complete cost estimate to build this house in your area!

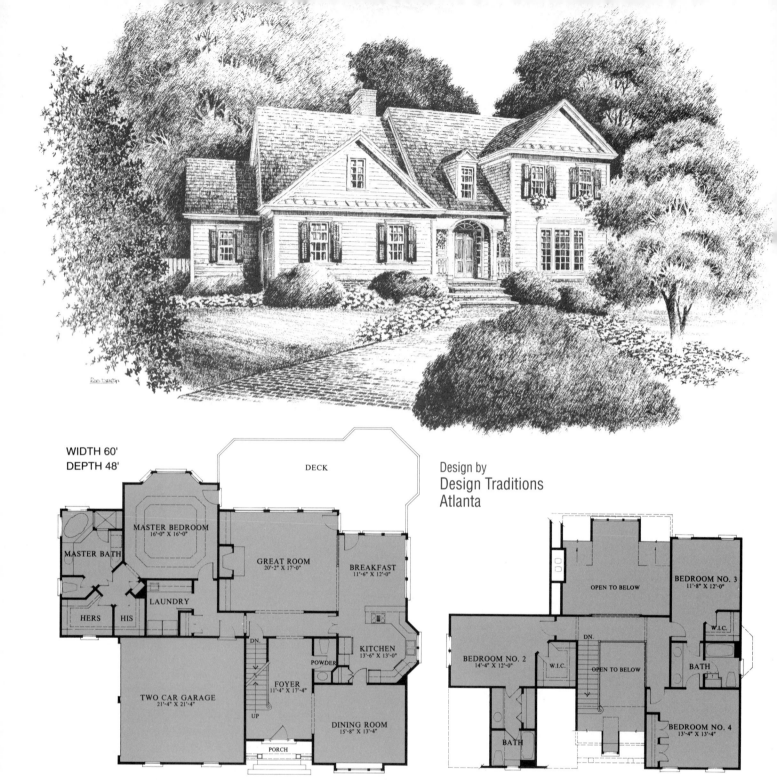

WIDTH 60'
DEPTH 48'

DECK

MASTER BEDROOM
16'-0" X 16'-0"

MASTER BATH

GREAT ROOM
20'-2" X 17'-0"

BREAKFAST
11'-6" X 12'-0"

HERS   HIS

LAUNDRY

DN.

POWDER

KITCHEN
13'-6" X 13'-0"

TWO CAR GARAGE
21'-4" X 21'-4"

FOYER
11'-4" X 17'-4"

UP

DINING ROOM
15'-8" X 13'-4"

PORCH

Design by
Design Traditions
Atlanta

OPEN TO BELOW

BEDROOM NO. 3
11'-8" X 12'-0"

W.I.C.

BEDROOM NO. 2
14'-4" X 12'-0"

W.I.C.

DN.

OPEN TO BELOW

BATH

BATH

BEDROOM NO. 4
13'-4" X 13'-4"

Design Q9863 First Floor: 1,940 square feet
Second Floor: 1,025 square feet
Total: 2,965 square feet

● Some of the most charming features of Traditional design are revealed as one approaches this home. Wood siding, window shutters, flower boxes and a classic elliptical entranceway bring this architectural tradition to life. The open foyer with tray ceiling and powder room leads to the dining room. The adjacent kitchen with

an octagonal counter top gives way to a spacious breakfast area with access to the deck and vaulted great room complete with fireplace. The great room hall leads to a very private master suite with bay window overlooking the back yard and easy access to the out-of-doors. The master bath with separate shower, garden tub, His and

Hers vanities and a spacious walk-in closet completes the master suite. Overlooking the great room, the upper level stairway landing leads to two additional bedrooms that share a full bath. A fourth bedroom offers more privacy, with a walk-in closet and a private bath.

Quote One®

Cost to build? See page 214
to order complete cost estimate
to build this house in your area!

Design by
Design Traditions

Design Q9864
First Floor: 1,395 square feet
Second Floor: 1,210 square feet
Total: 2,605 square feet

WIDTH 47'-0"
DEPTH 47'-6"

● The well-balanced use of stucco and stone combined with box bay window treatments and a covered entry make this English country home especially inviting. The two-story foyer opens on the right to the attractive living and dining rooms with large windows. The step-saving kitchen and breakfast areas flow easily into the two-story great room and a media room with a see-through fireplace. The upper level offers a pleasing combination of open design and privacy. To the right of the foyer stairs, the balcony overlooks the great room. The master bedroom has a modified tray ceiling and is complete with a sitting area. The master bath with a double vanity and separate shower leads to a large walk-in closet. Double vanities are also found in the full bath off the hall. Bedrooms 2 and 3 are ample in size and feature walk-in closets. The unfinished bonus room completes this level and provides further storage space.

25

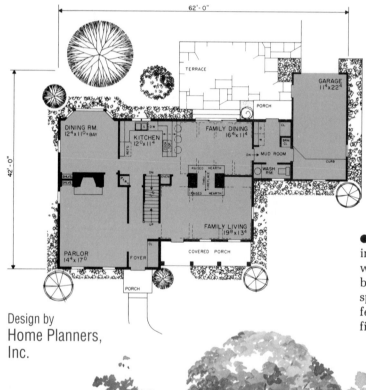

Design by
Home Planners,
Inc.

Design Q2681

First Floor: 1,350 square feet
Second Floor: 1,224 square feet
Total: 2,574 square feet

● The charm of Early America is exemplified in this delightful design. Note the three areas which are highlighted by a fireplace. The three-bedroom second floor is nicely planned. Make special note of the master bedroom's many fine features. Study the rest of this design's many fine qualities.

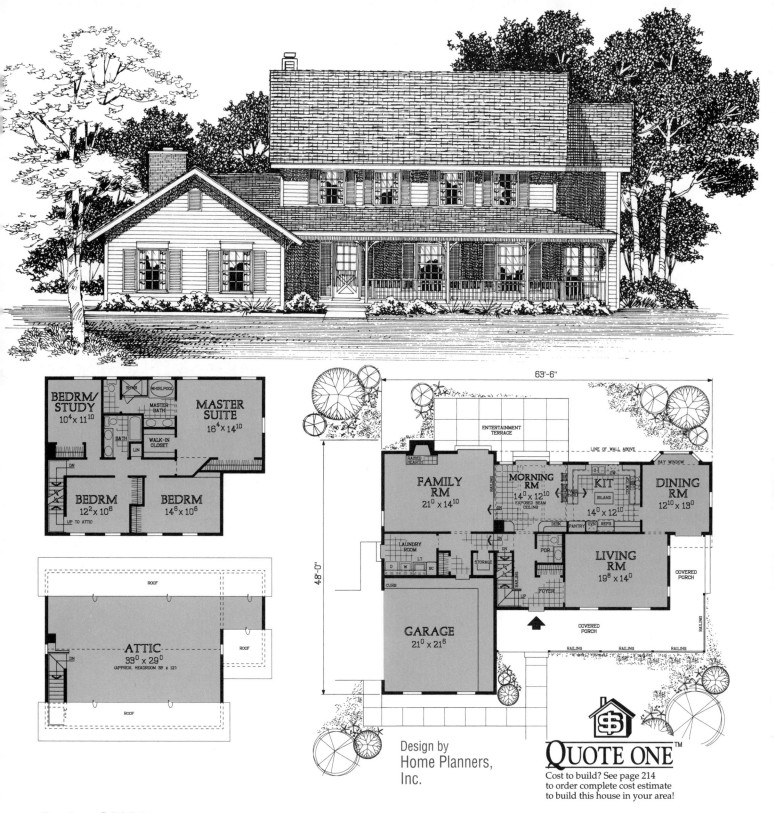

Design by
Home Planners,
Inc.

Quote One™
Cost to build? See page 214
to order complete cost estimate
to build this house in your area!

Design Q3325 First Floor: 1,595 square feet; Second Floor: 1,112 square feet; Total: 2,707 square feet

L **D**

● Horizontal clapboard siding, varying roof planes and finely detailed window treatments set the tone for this delightful family farmhouse. The living and dining rooms function very well together. The spacious family room, with its raised-hearth fireplace, and the morning room extend a wealth of livability. The U-shaped kitchen, with a tile floor, utilizes a work island supplemented by plenty of cabinet, cupboard and counter space. The sleeping

accommodations of this plan include a master bedroom suite with a walk-in closet in addition to a long wardrobe closet. The master bath has a tub plus a stall shower and twin lavatories. For information on customizing this design, call 1-800-521-6797, ext. 800. California Engineered Plans and California Stock Plans are available for this home. Call 1-800-521-6797 for more information.

Design Q9314

First Floor: 1,679 square feet
Second Floor: 1,990 square feet
Total: 3,669 square feet

Design by
**Design
Basics,
Inc.**

● Designed to be a country estate residence, this two-story home combines a sophisticated floor plan with a charming elevation. Throughout the home, beautiful windows bring the outdoors in. From the covered front porch, move inside to view a spectacular two-story entry with curving staircase. French doors lead into the library with a bayed window, built-in desk and bookcases. To the right, note the formal dining room. A great room benefits from the 10-foot spider-beamed ceiling, plus a wet bar and built-in entertainment center. Home owners will relish the combination breakfast/hearth room and kitchen concept. Upstairs, a balcony between the bedrooms overlooks the entry below. Segregation of the secondary bedrooms with walk-in closets provides privacy. Special finishing touches include the formal ceiling and bayed sitting area in the master suite. The master dressing/bath area is enhanced by His and Hers vanities, an oval whirlpool beneath the arched window and a deluxe walk-in closet with windows.

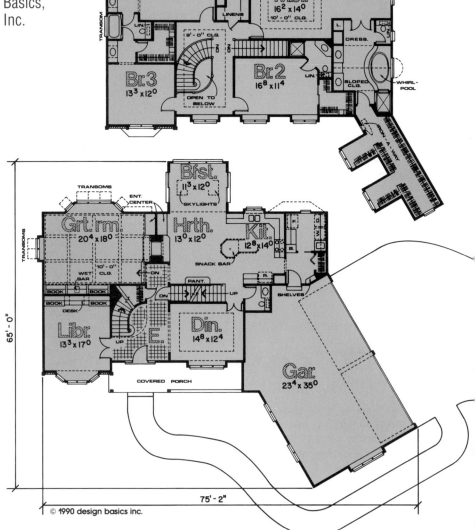

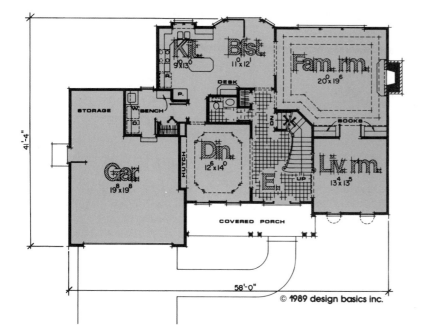

Design by
Design
Basics,
Inc.

SKYLIGHT

WHIRLPOOL

Mbr
13² x 16⁰

8'-4"
CEILING

BOOKS

Br
13⁰ x 11

DN

Br
11⁶ x 12⁷

OPEN TO
BELOW

Br
13³ x 11⁰

Kit
9⁹ x 13⁰

Bfst
11⁰ x 12¹

Fam. rm.
20⁰ x 19⁵

STORAGE

BENCH

P.

DESK

BOOKS

Gar
19⁸ x 19⁸

HUTCH

Dn
12⁶ x 14⁰

Liv. rm.
13⁴ x 13⁵

UP

41'-4"

COVERED PORCH

58'-0"

© 1989 design basics inc.

Design Q9215

First Floor: 1,386 square feet
Second Floor: 1,171 square feet
Total: 2,557 square feet

● Amenities for casual family living and entertaining abound in this attractive Colonial. A charming covered front porch makes for an inviting exterior. Inside, the two-story entry with flared staircase opens into the formal dining and living rooms. French doors connect the living room with the more informal family room for expanded entertaining space. A spacious kitchen handily serves both the family and dining rooms. Also note the bay-windowed breakfast area. The first floor features nine-foot ceilings throughout. Upstairs are four bedrooms, one a master suite with a skylit bath with whirlpool and large walk-in closet.

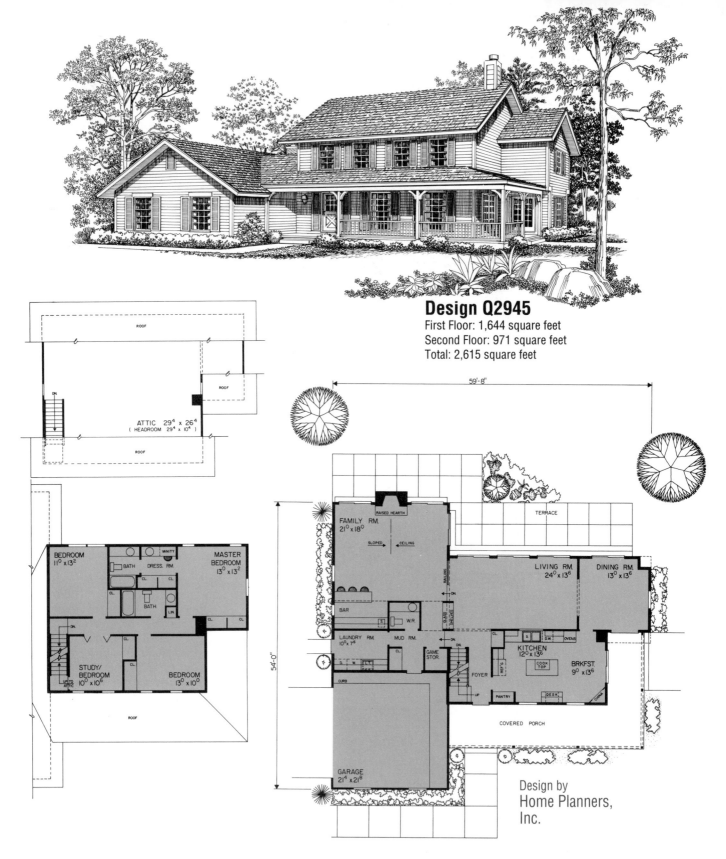

Design Q2945

First Floor: 1,644 square feet
Second Floor: 971 square feet
Total: 2,615 square feet

Design by
Home Planners,
Inc.

● This masterfully affordable farm-house manages to include all the basics— then adds a little more. Note the wraparound covered porch, large family room with raised-hearth fire-place and wet bar, spacious kitchen with island cooktop, formal dining room, and rear terrace and extra stor-age on the first floor. Upstairs, the plan's as flexible as they come: three or four bedrooms (the fourth could easily be a study or playroom) and lots of unfinished attic just waiting to be transformed into living space. This would make a fine sewing room, home office or children's play-room. Special amenities make this home a stand-out from others in its class. Note the many built-ins, the sliding glass doors to the terrace, and the wealth of closets and storage space. For information on customizing this design, call 1-800-521-6797, ext. 800.

PLAINS OR PRAIRIE-TYPE FARMHOUSES

In the days of Western expansion, homes on the plains and prairies were, for the most part, utilitarian structures erected quickly and with little fuss. They were usually built from available materials — often sod or hay — because of the scarcity of wood or brick. Practical in form, though not especially architecturally appealing, these home were constructed to withstand the fierce winds, harsh winters and burning summer sun so prevalent in that part of the country.

Today's versions of the Plains or Prairie Farmhouse take all the best features of those sturdy ancestors and incorporate them into a much more charming and livable rendition. Their tremendous appeal derives from their nostalgic nod to pioneer beginnings and timeless endurance. Maintaining a low-slung, ground-hugging appearance (to shrug off prairie winds), the modern Prairie Farmhouse almost always has a covered front porch that wraps around at least three sides to shield the house from the sun. Some examples carry the covered porch on all four sides. This porch is usually an at-grade-level element, in keeping with the low profile of the whole house. Porch columns and railings are normally square though some turned spindles and other simple decoration may appear, echoing Colonial and Victorian influences.

The roof of these prairie homes is the most obvious design element. The entire structure of the home is dominated by a roof that is double-pitched from gable to porch covering. Looking somewhat like a large hat, these roofs function as sun-deflectors in areas of the country known for warm, dry summer seasons.

Sometimes two-story, more often 1½-story, in nature, the Prairie Farmhouse boasts upper-level dormer windows that protrude from the roof. Two or three dormer windows to a set seems to be the general rule; however, four or even five may appear on some examples. On more dramatic examples, a Palladian window may appear at the center of the second floor. The windows themselves are symmetrically set, paned and often shuttered.

Horizonal wood siding is the facing of choice, with brick and occasionally stone complementing as the exterior detailing. Chimneys generally have no regular placement but may be seen anywhere (or not at all) from the front.

Design Q9004 is a fine example of the Prairie-Type Farmhouse. Its sweeping, wide porch wraps around three sides of an exterior sided in wood and it supports a prominent roofline that is double-pitched. Three dormers grace the facade, while two chimneys (one to the left front and one to the right rear) allow for hearths throughout the house. Like others in this section, this Prairie-Type Farmhouse includes a luxurious floor plan within its rustic, countrified exterior.

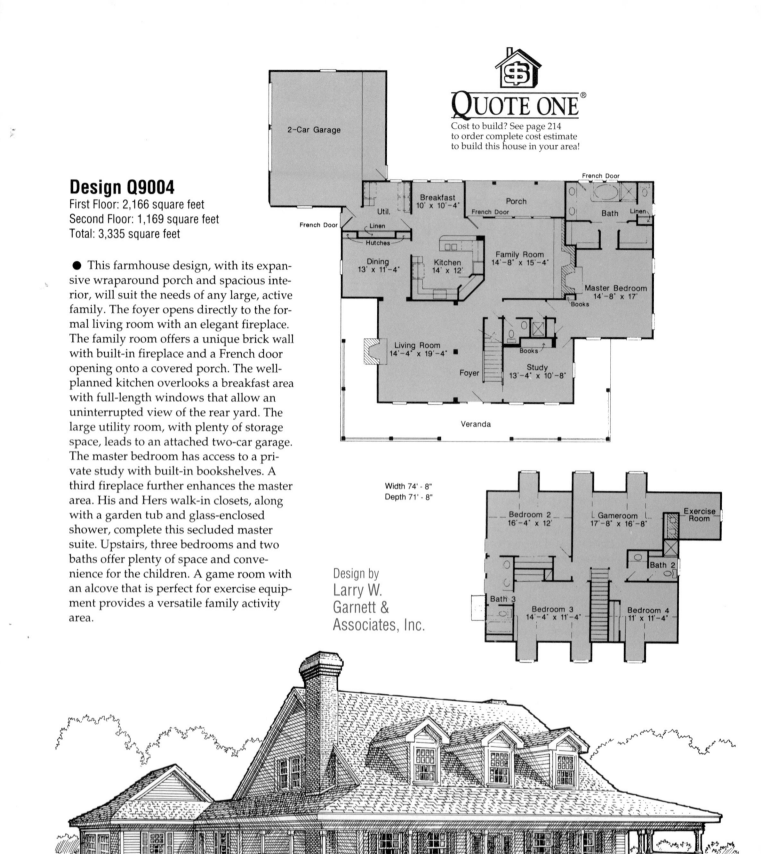

Design Q9004

First Floor: 2,166 square feet
Second Floor: 1,169 square feet
Total: 3,335 square feet

● This farmhouse design, with its expansive wraparound porch and spacious interior, will suit the needs of any large, active family. The foyer opens directly to the formal living room with an elegant fireplace. The family room offers a unique brick wall with built-in fireplace and a French door opening onto a covered porch. The well-planned kitchen overlooks a breakfast area with full-length windows that allow an uninterrupted view of the rear yard. The large utility room, with plenty of storage space, leads to an attached two-car garage. The master bedroom has access to a private study with built-in bookshelves. A third fireplace further enhances the master area. His and Hers walk-in closets, along with a garden tub and glass-enclosed shower, complete this secluded master suite. Upstairs, three bedrooms and two baths offer plenty of space and convenience for the children. A game room with an alcove that is perfect for exercise equipment provides a versatile family activity area.

Design by
Larry W.
Garnett &
Associates, Inc.

Quote One®
Cost to build? See page 214 to order complete cost estimate to build this house in your area!

2-Car Garage

Breakfast 10' x 10'-4"
Porch
French Door
Util.
Linen
French Door
Hutches
Bath
Linen
Dining 13' x 11'-4"
Kitchen 14' x 12'
Family Room 14'-8" x 15'-4"
Master Bedroom 14'-8" x 17'
Books
Living Room 14'-4" x 19'-4"
Books
Foyer
Study 13'-4" x 10'-8"
Veranda

Width 74' - 8"
Depth 71' - 8"

Bedroom 2 16'-4" x 12'
Gameroom 17'-8" x 16'-8"
Exercise Room
Bath 2
Bath 3
Bedroom 3 14'-4" x 11'-4"
Bedroom 4 11' x 11'-4"

Design Q9002

First Floor: 1,504 square feet
Second Floor: 690 square feet
Total: 2,194 square feet

● The symmetry and grace of the turn-of-the-century farmhouse is captured in this design. The veranda provides plenty of shade for outdoor activities. Inside, the kitchen with center-island work counter opens to the breakfast area with a full-length bay window. The master bedroom features a walk-in closet and abundant linen storage. A corner tub and glass-enclosed shower highlight the bath. An optional French door allows access to a swimming pool, or possibly a private spa. Upstairs, the balcony overlooks the living room below. Two bedrooms each have walk-in closets and private dressing areas. Plans for a detached two-car garage are included.

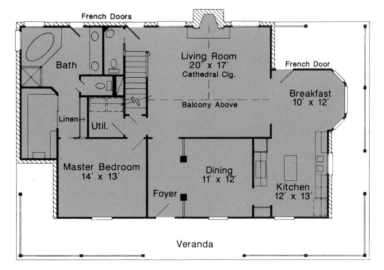

Design by
Larry W.
Garnett &
Associates, Inc.

Width 57' - 4"
Depth 37' - 8"

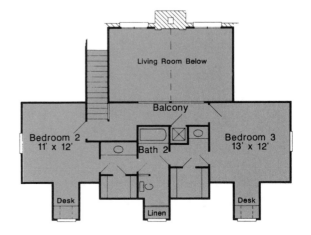

Design Q9000

First Floor: 1,669 square feet
Second Floor: 780 square feet
Total: 2,449 square feet

● The wraparound veranda of this farmhouse design offers a shaded outdoor living area. Inside, an efficient floor plan provides plenty of open living areas. The foyer and formal dining room are separated by a thirty-two-inch-high wall, while the kitchen opens directly to a spacious breakfast area. The convenient utility room has plenty of space for a freezer and extra storage. A small rear porch can be connected by a breezeway to the detached garage (plans included). The highlight of this home is the living room. A center fireplace with tall glass on each side soars to the top of the cathedral ceiling, while a balcony opens from the game room above. A French door opens to the rear porch. Each upstairs bedroom offers a built-in desk or window seat. The master bath features His and Hers walk-in closets and abundant linen storage.

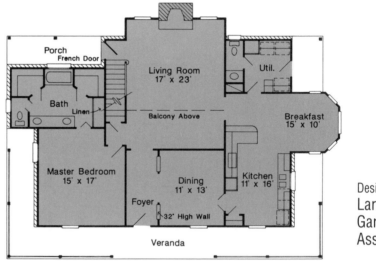

Design by
Larry W. Garnett & Associates, Inc.

Width 59' - 4"
Depth 44' - 4"

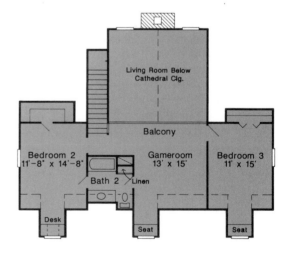

Design Q900

First Floor: 1,995 square
Second Floor: 1,077 square
Total: 3,072 square feet

● A wraparound front porch and dormer windows give this home a casual and comfortable appearance. A leaded-glass transom above the front door, along with the dormer window in the sloped ceiling, fill the foyer with natural light. The large living area features French doors on each side of an elegant fireplace, and a built-in wet bar. An island cooktop, along with a walk-in pantry are part of the well-planned kitchen. The utility room, with extra work space, leads to an attached two-car garage and storage area. The master bedroom has generous closet space and a two-way fireplace opening into the master bath. His and Hers lavatories, an oversized tub and glass-enclosed shower complete this elegant master bath. The balcony has French doors opening into a large game room. Bedroom 3 has a private bath, while Bedroom 2 shares access to a bath with the game room. Each bedroom has a sloped ceiling and a cozy alcove created by the dormer window.

Design by
Larry W.
Garnett &
Associates, Inc.

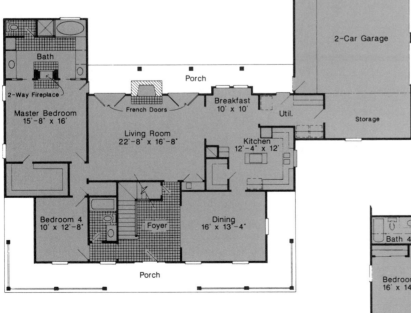

Width 79'
Depth 60' - 6"

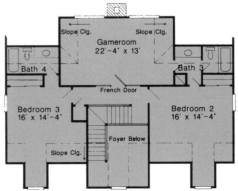

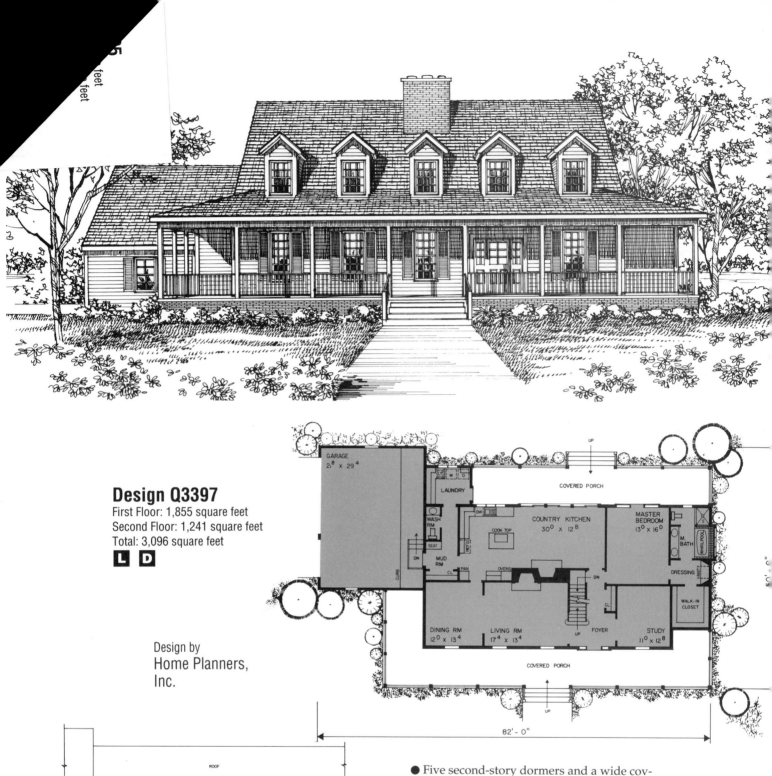

Design Q3397

First Floor: 1,855 square feet
Second Floor: 1,241 square feet
Total: 3,096 square feet

L **D**

Design by
Home Planners,
Inc.

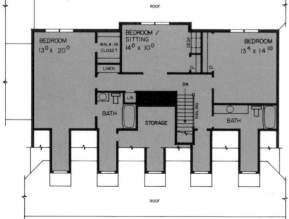

● Five second-story dormers and a wide covered front porch add to the charm of this farmhouse design. Inside, the entry foyer opens to the left to a formal living room with a fireplace and an attached dining room. To the right is a private study. The back of the plan is dominated by a huge country kitchen featuring an island cooktop. On this floor is the master suite with a large walk-in closet. The second floor holds three bedrooms (or two and a sitting room) with two full baths. California Engineered Plans and California Stock Plans are available for this home. Call 1-800-521-6797 for more information.

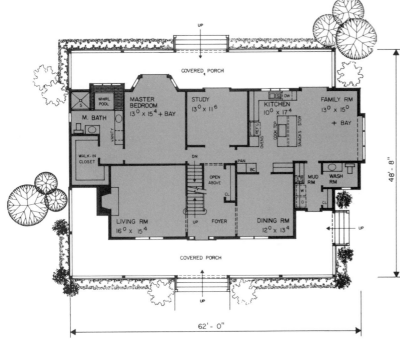

Design Q3396

First Floor: 1,829 square feet
Second Floor: 947 square feet
Total: 2,776 square feet

L **D**

● Rustic charm abounds in this pleasant farmhouse rendition. Covered porches to the front
and rear enclose living potential for the whole
family. Flanking the entrance foyer are the
living and dining rooms. To the rear is the
L-shaped kitchen with island cook top and
snack bar. A small family room/breakfast nook
is attached. A private study is tucked away on
this floor next to the master suite. On the second floor are three bedrooms and a full bath.
Two of the bedrooms have charming dormer
windows.

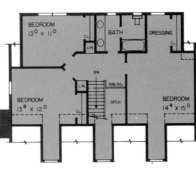

Quote One™

Cost to build? See page 214
to order complete cost estimate
to build this house in your area!

Design by
Home Planners,
Inc.

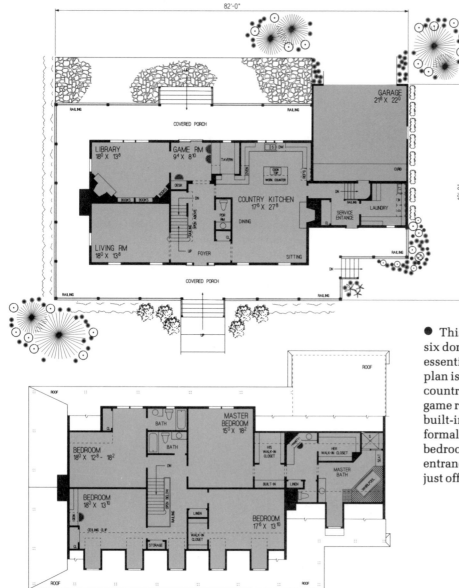

Design Q3399

First Floor: 1,716 square feet
Second Floor: 2,102 square feet
Total: 3,818 square feet

L **D**

Design by
**Home Planners,
Inc.**

● This is the ultimate in farmhouse living — six dormer windows and a porch that stretches essentially around the entire house. Inside, the plan is open and inviting. Besides the large country kitchen with fireplace, there is a small game room with attached tavern, a library with built-in bookshelves and a fireplace, and a formal living room. The second floor has four bedrooms and three full baths. The service entrance features a laundry area conveniently just off the garage.

QUOTE ONE™
Cost to build? See page 214 to order complete cost estimate to build this house in your area!

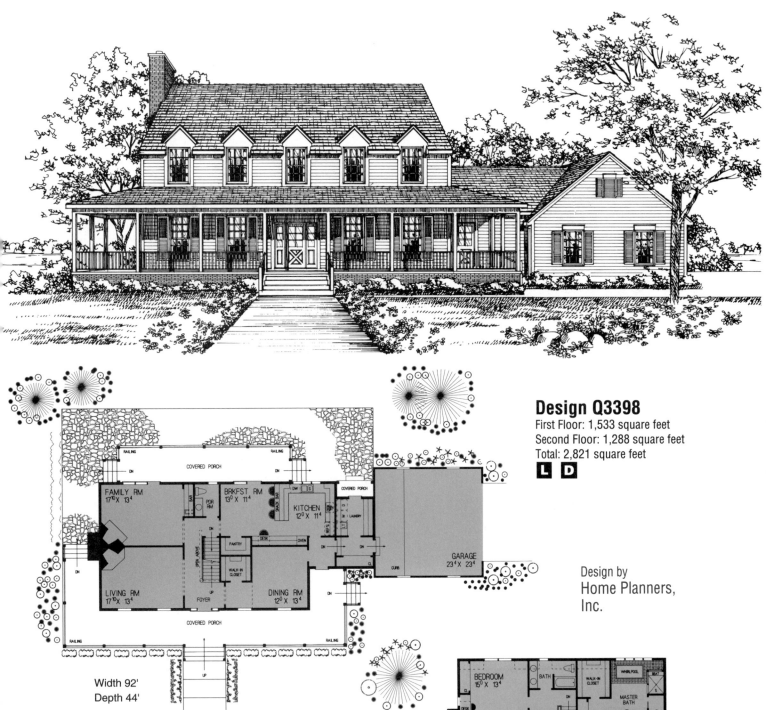

Design Q3398

First Floor: 1,533 square feet
Second Floor: 1,288 square feet
Total: 2,821 square feet

L **D**

Width 92'
Depth 44'

Design by
Home Planners, Inc.

● With its classic farmhouse good-looks and just-right floor plan, this country residence has it all. The wraparound covered porch at the entry gives way to a long foyer with open staircase. To the right and left are the formal dining room and living room. More casual living areas are to the rear: a family room, and U-shaped kitchen with attached breakfast room. The second floor holds sleeping areas — two family bedrooms and a huge master suite with walk-in closet and pampering master bath.

Cost to build? See page 214 to order complete cost estimate to build this house in your area!

Design Q9067

First Floor: 1,999 square feet
Second Floor: 933 square feet
Total: 2,932 square feet

● The wraparound veranda and simple lines give this home an unassuming elegance that is characteristic of its Folk Victorian heritage. Opening directly to the formal dining room, the two-story foyer offers extra space for large dinner parties. Double French doors lead to the study with raised paneling and a cozy fireplace. Built-in bookcases conceal a hidden security vault. The private master suite features a corner garden tub, glass-enclosed shower and a walk-in closet. Overlooking the family room and built-in breakfast nook is the central kitchen. A rear staircase provides convenient access to the second floor from the family room. The balcony provides a view of the foyer below and the Palladian window. Three additional bedrooms complete this exquisite home.

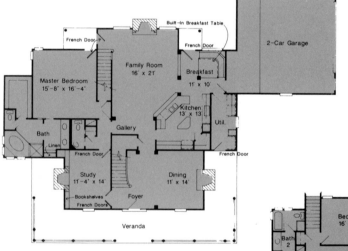

9' Clg. Throughout

Design by
Larry W. Garnett & Associates, Inc.

WIDTH 79' 8"
DEPTH 59'

REAR VIEW

Design by
Home Planners,
Inc.

Design Q2776

First Floor: 1,134 square feet
Second Floor: 874 square feet
Total: 2,008 square feet

L **D**

● This board-and-batten farmhouse design has all of the country charm of New England. The large covered front porch will be appreciated for outdoor enjoyment. Immediately off the front entrance is the delightful corner living room. The dining room with bay window will be easily

served by the U-shaped kitchen. The informal family room features a raised-hearth fireplace, sliding glass doors to the rear terrace and easy access to the powder room, laundry and service entrance. The second floor houses all of the sleeping facilities. There is a master bed-

room with private bath and walk-in closet, as well as two other bedrooms sharing a full bath. This is an excellent one-and-half story design. For information on customizing this design, call 1-800-521-6797, ext. 800.

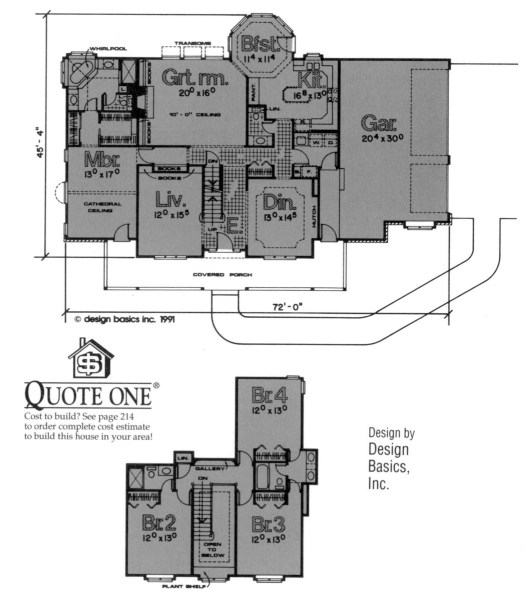

Design Q9298

First Floor: 1,881 square feet
Second Floor: 814 square feet
Total: 2,695 square feet

● Oval windows and an appealing covered porch lend character to this 1½-story home. Inside, a volume entry views the formal living and dining rooms. Three large windows and a raised-hearth fireplace flanked by bookcases highlight a volume great room. An island kitchen with huge pantry and two Lazy Susans serves a captivating gazebo dinette. In the master suite, a cathedral ceiling, corner whirlpool and roomy dressing area deserve careful study. A gallery wall for displaying family mementos and prized heirlooms graces the upstairs corridor. Each secondary bedroom has convenient access to the bathrooms. This home's charm and blend of popular amenities will fit your lifestyle.

QUOTE ONE®

Cost to build? See page 214
to order complete cost estimate
to build this house in your area!

Design by
Design
Basics,
Inc.

© design basics inc. 1991

Floor plan labels (first floor):
WHIRLPOOL
TRANSOMS
Bfst. 11⁴ x 11⁴
Grt. rm. 20⁰ x 16⁰
10' - 0" CEILING
Kit. 16⁸ x 13⁰
PANT.
LIN.
Gar. 20⁴ x 30⁰
W. D.
BOOKS
Mbr. 13⁰ x 17⁰
CATHEDRAL CEILING
Liv. 12⁰ x 15⁵
BOOKS
DN
UP
F.
Din. 13⁰ x 14⁵
HUTCH
COVERED PORCH
45' - 4"
72' - 0"

Floor plan labels (second floor):
Br. 4 12⁰ x 13⁰
LIN.
GALLERY
DN
Br. 2 12⁰ x 13⁰
Br. 3 12⁰ x 13⁰
OPEN TO BELOW
PLANT SHELF

42

Design by
**Design
Basics,
Inc.**

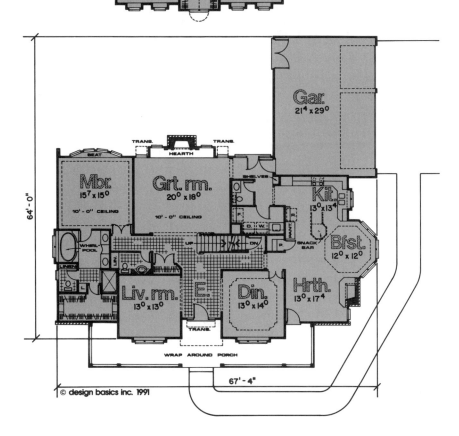

Design Q9297

First Floor: 2,280 square feet
Second Floor: 1,014 square feet
Total: 3,294 square feet

● Bright windows and a wraparound porch enhance the elevation of this four-bedroom, 1½-story home. Formal living and dining rooms are surveyed from the entry. A flush-hearth fireplace and transom windows highlight a volume great room planned for daily living. In the hearth room, catch a glimpse of the decorative fireplace and the convenient access to the front porch. Nearby, a sunny bayed dinette is served by an island kitchen with snack bar and two pantries. The main-floor master bedroom features a 10-foot ceiling and window seat. In the master bath, an oval whirlpool, dual vanities and walk-in closet pamper the home-owners. Upstairs, each secondary bedroom has a walk-in closet. Bedroom 3 has a private bath while Bedrooms 2 and 4 share a Hollywood bath. At 3,294 square feet, this prairie farmhouse adds distinction to any location.

Design Q9603

First Floor: 1,377 square feet
Second Floor: 536 square feet
Total: 1,913 square feet

● One of the most outstanding characteristics of this plan is its flexibility — turn the great room/ dining room combination into one large great room and relocate the dining room to the family room. The cheery sun room with its soothing hot tub provides access through sliding glass doors to the deck and great room and access to the master bedroom through French doors. (Don't overlook the fireplace, walk-in closet and twin vanity in the master suite.) Two second-floor bedrooms share a full bath with twin vanity and linen closet. Both bedrooms have dormer windows and walk-in closets. Other grand features include the screened porch with skylights and the sheltered front porch. For a crawlspace foundation, order plan Q9603, for a basement foundation order Q9603-A.

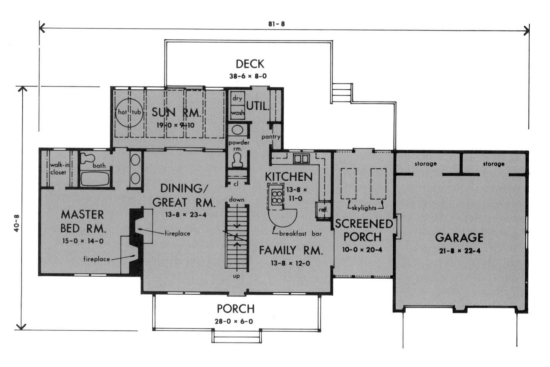

Design by
Donald A.
Gardner,
Architect, Inc.

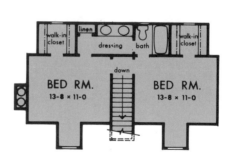

Design Q9625

First Floor: 1,436 square feet
Second Floor: 549 square feet
Sun Room: 145 square feet
Total: 2,130 square feet
Bonus Room: 334 square feet

● Great flexibility is available in this plan—the great room/dining room can be reworked into one large great room with the dining room relocated to the family room. A sun room with cathedral ceiling and sliding glass door to the deck is accessible from both the breakfast and dining rooms. A large kitchen boasts a convenient cooking island. The master bedroom has a fireplace, walk-in closet and spa-cious master bath. Two second-level bedrooms are equal in size and share a full bath with double-bowl vanity. Both bedrooms have a dormer win-dow and a walk-in closet. A large bonus room over the garage is accessi-ble from the utility room below. For a crawl-space foundation order Plan Q9625; for a basement foundation order Plan Q9625-A.

Design by
Donald A. Gardner, Architect, Inc.

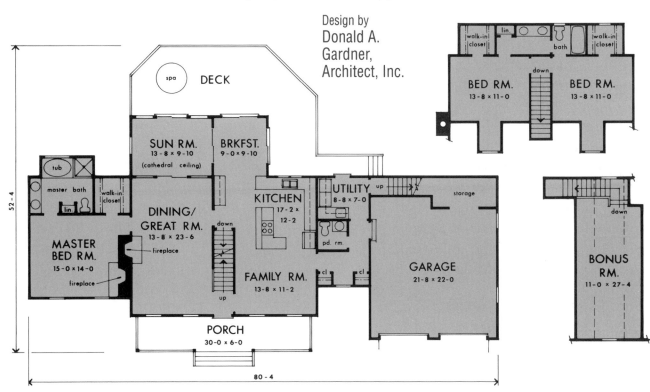

Design Q9001

First Floor: 1,308 square feet
Second Floor: 751 square feet
Total: 2,059 square feet

● A wraparound veranda and simple, uncluttered lines give this home an unassuming elegance that is characteristic of its farmhouse heritage. The kitchen overlooks an octagon-shaped breakfast room with full-length windows. The master bedroom features plenty of closet space and an elegant bath. Located within an oversized bay window is a garden tub with adjacent planter and glass-enclosed shower. Upstairs, two bedrooms share a bath with separate dressing and bathing areas. The balcony sitting area is perfect as a playroom or study. Plans for a detached two-car garage are included.

Design by
Larry W.
Garnett &
Associates, Inc.

Width 53'
Depth 45' - 4"

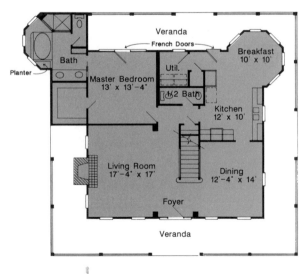

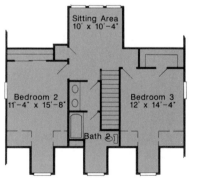

● Outdoor living takes a beautiful turn in this lovely home. The interior is just as great: bay windows in breakfast room and master bath, dormers and arched rear windows, sun room. The spacious great room has a fireplace, cathedral ceiling and clerestory with arched window. The master bath complements the master bedroom with a garden tub, separate shower, double-bowl vanity and walk-in closet. Two bedrooms share the upper level with a study/loft area overlooking the great room. This study area could be converted to a fourth bedroom.

Design Q9624

First Floor: 1,659 square feet (Including Sun Room)
Second Floor: 674 square feet
Total: 2,333 square feet

Design by
Donald A.
Gardner,
Architect, Inc.

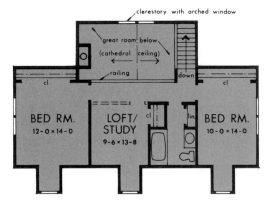

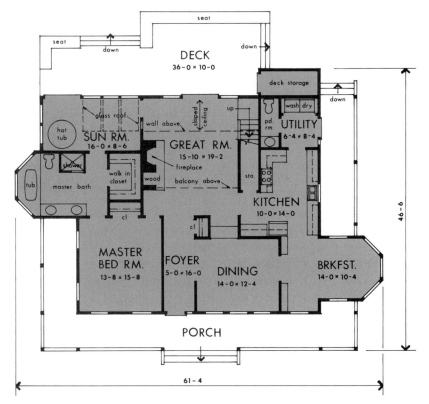

Design Q9003

First Floor: 1,244 square feet
Second Floor: 551 square feet
Total: 1,795 square feet

● The timeless beauty and
practicality of the wraparound
veranda give this farmhouse a
casual, yet distinctive appearance. The efficiently designed
kitchen opens to a light-filled
breakfast area with full-length
windows and a French door
that leads to the veranda. The
master suite offers His and
Hers lavatories and a large
walk-in closet. Upstairs,
optional skylights provide
plenty of natural light to the
balcony. Two bedrooms share
a bath that has separate
bathing and dressing areas.
Plans for a two-car detached
garage are included.

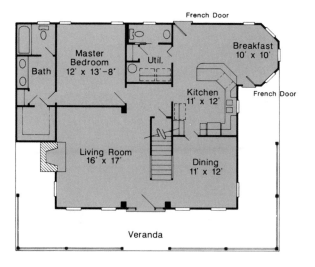

Width 46'
Depth 38' - 8"

Design by
Larry W.
Garnett &
Associates, Inc.

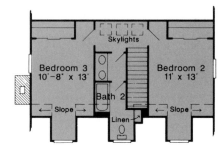

Design Q9605

First Floor: 1,562 square feet
Second Floor: 537 square feet
Total: 2,099 square feet

● Outdoor living is realized in a wraparound covered porch at the front and sides of this house, as well as the open deck with storage to the rear. Also notice how the country feel is updated with arched rear windows and a sun room. Inside find the spacious great room with fireplace, cathedral ceiling and clerestory with arched windows. The kitchen occupies a central location between the dining room and the great room for equally convenient formal and informal occasions. A generous master suite has a fireplace and access to the sun room and covered porch. On the second level are two more bedrooms, a full bath and storage space.

Design by
Donald A.
Gardner,
Architect, Inc.

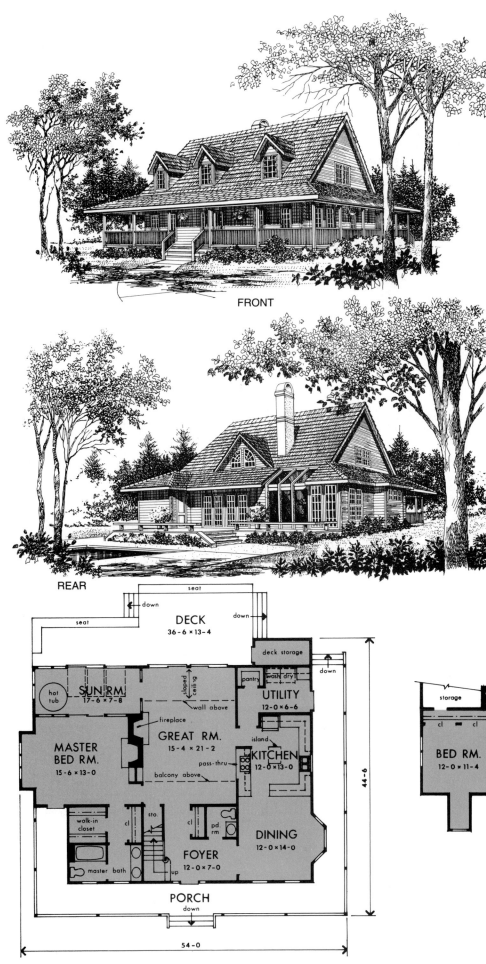

FRONT

REAR

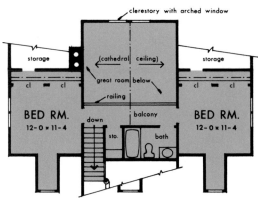

49

B. NATHAN

Design by
**Donald A.
Gardner,
Architect, Inc.**

Design Q9662

First Floor: 1,025 square feet
Second Floor: 911 square feet
Total: 1,936 square feet

● The exterior of this three-bedroom home is enhanced by its many gables, arched windows and wraparound porch. A large great room with impressive fireplace leads to both the dining room and screened porch with access to the deck. An open kitchen offers a country-kitchen atmosphere. The second-level master suite has two walk-in closets and an impressive bath. There is also bonus space over the garage. The plan is available with a crawl-space foundation.

SCREENED PORCH
13-0 × 11-0

spa

DECK

DINING
12-0 × 12-4

KITCHEN
11-4 × 11-4

DECK

fireplace

storage

BRKFST.
11-4 × 8-4

GREAT RM.
13-0 × 22-4

FOYER

balcony above

up

UTILITY
9-0 × 7-4

d
w

cl

pd. rm.

storage

PORCH

GARAGE
20-8 × 24-0

67-8

53-8

master bath

closet   closet   cl

BED RM.
11-0 × 12-4

BED RM.
10-0 × 12-4

MASTER
BED RM.
13-0 × 14-4

down

walk-in closet

sto.   storage

balcony

foyer below

bath

sto.

BONUS
RM.
12-4 × 24-0

SOUTHERN OR PLANTATION-STYLE FARMHOUSES

Catering to a life filled with richness and grace, the historic homes of the Southern plantations were true showpieces. Replete with generous space for dining and entertaining, they mirrored the warm hospitality for which the South became famous. Rooms were large, ornate and filled with amenities geared toward comfort. Kitchens were the focal points around which daily life flowed. Porches, verandas and balconies were plentiful; numerous wide windows were in grand supply to catch any hint of breeze in the stifling Southern summers.

Today's Plantation-Style Farmhouse resembles the Prairie Farmhouse with its double-pitched, sprawling roofline; however, it is overall taller and more upright. The porches on these Southern belles are grand, wrapping structures that are often raised to lift the house out of wet or soggy ground. In fact, in some locations in the South, houses are built on piers to allow water to seep harmlessly beneath the level of the house. Porch columns are often round, in reminiscence of Southern Georgians or columned Colonials. The railings can be square, dimensioned lumber or round, turned spindles.

Plantation-Style homes may be either 1½ or two stories, though the most common examples are 1½-story renditions with secondary living quarters upstairs. Two-story versions may have a full, second-story balcony in the best Southern ante-bellum style. Often, secondary bedrooms are contained on the second floor with the master suite holding court on the first — a split sleeping arrangement agreeable to both children and parents.

Windows are strongly symmetrical with the second-story windows being dormers that protrude from the roof. The center unit is often larger and may have a circle-head on some more modern models. Ornate fan lights may flank entry doors.

Other exterior details include horizontal wood siding and strong, tall chimney stacks often capped with a curved masonry piece to protect the hearth from rain and spark-summoning wind. This once-only-practical design item has grown to be a style statement.

Design Q9623 incorporates some of the best details of the Southern-Style Farmhouse. Its wide covered porch extends around three sides of the design and is complemented by a beautiful deck with room for a spa to the rear. Three dormers appear at the second-story facade — the center one is a lovely Palladian-style. The characteristic protective, curved masonry piece caps the chimney which is just off center of the house. The floor plan is open and airy and contains a great room with cathedral ceiling for entertaining in high style.

Other plans in this section represent the gracious expression of Southern style. Together they provide a grand collection of homes for commodious living.

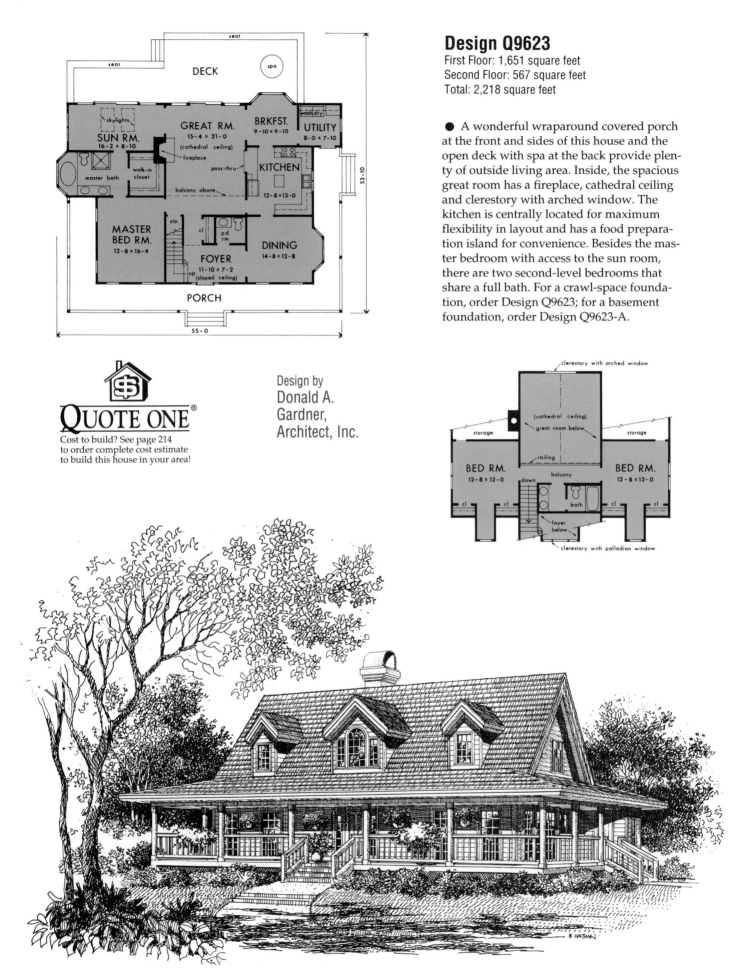

Design Q9623

First Floor: 1,651 square feet
Second Floor: 567 square feet
Total: 2,218 square feet

● A wonderful wraparound covered porch at the front and sides of this house and the open deck with spa at the back provide plenty of outside living area. Inside, the spacious great room has a fireplace, cathedral ceiling and clerestory with arched window. The kitchen is centrally located for maximum flexibility in layout and has a food preparation island for convenience. Besides the master bedroom with access to the sun room, there are two second-level bedrooms that share a full bath. For a crawl-space foundation, order Design Q9623; for a basement foundation, order Design Q9623-A.

QUOTE ONE®

Cost to build? See page 214 to order complete cost estimate to build this house in your area!

Design by
Donald A.
Gardner,
Architect, Inc.

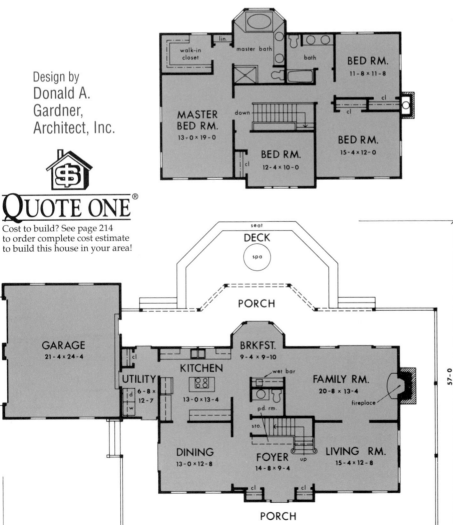

Design by
Donald A.
Gardner,
Architect, Inc.

QUOTE ONE®

Cost to build? See page 214
to order complete cost estimate
to build this house in your area!

Design Q9667

First Floor: 1,357 square feet
Second Floor: 1,204 square feet
Total: 2,561 square feet

● This grand four-bedroom farmhouse with wraparound porch has eye-catching features: a double-gabled roof, Palladian window at the upper level, arched window on the lower level and intricately detailed brick chimney. Entry to the home reveals a generous foyer with direct access to all areas. The living room opens to the foyer and provides a formal entertaining area. The exceptionally large family room allows for more casual living. Look for a fireplace, wet bar and direct access to a porch and deck here. The lavish kitchen boasts a cooking island and serves the dining room, breakfast and deck areas. The master suite on the second level has a large walk-in closet and master bath with a whirlpool tub, shower and double-bowl vanity. Three additional bedrooms share a full bath.

Design Q9632

First Floor: 1,756 square feet
Second Floor: 565 square feet
Total: 2,321 square feet

Design by
Donald A.
Gardner,
Architect, Inc.

● A wraparound covered porch at the front and sides of this house and an open deck at the back provide plenty of outside living area. The spacious great room features a fireplace, cathedral ceiling, and clerestory with an arched window. The first-floor master bedroom contains a generous closet and a master bath with garden tub, double-bowl vanity, and shower. The second floor sports two bedrooms and a full bath with double-bowl vanity. This plan includes a crawl-space foundation.

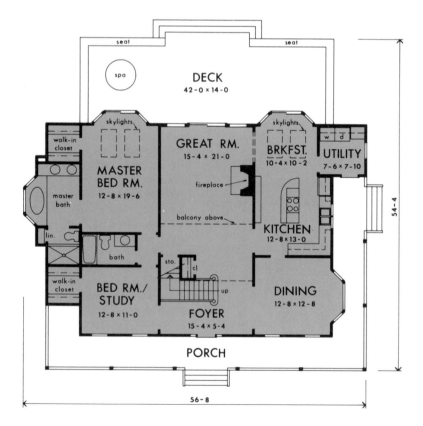

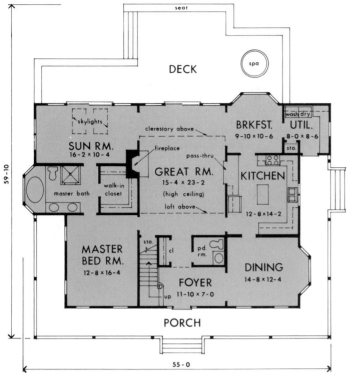

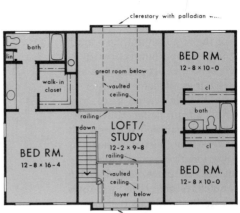

Design Q9616

First Floor: 1,734 square feet
Second Floor: 958 square feet
Total: 2,692 square feet

● A wraparound covered porch at the front and sides of this home and the open deck with spa and seating provide plenty of outside living area. A central great room features a vaulted ceiling, fireplace and clerestory windows above. The loft/study on the second floor overlooks this gathering area. Besides a formal dining room, kitchen, breakfast room and sun room on the first floor, there is also a generous master suite with garden tub. Three second-floor bedrooms complete sleeping accommodations. The plan includes a crawl-space foundation.

Design by
Donald A.
Gardner,
Architect, Inc.

FRONT

REAR

Design Q9621

First Floor: 1,325 square feet
Second Floor: 453 square feet
Total: 1,778 square feet

● For the economy-minded family desiring a wraparound covered porch, this compact design has all the amenities available in larger plans with little wasted space. In addition, a front Palladian window, dormer and rear arched windows provide exciting visual elements to the exterior. The spacious great room has a fireplace, cathedral ceiling and clerestory arched windows. A second-level balcony overlooks this gathering area. The kitchen is centrally located for maximum flexibility in layout and features a pass-through to the great room. Besides the generous master suite with well-appointed full bath, there are two family bedrooms located on the second level sharing a full bath with double vanity. Note the ample attic storage space. For a crawl-space foundation, order Design Q9621; for a basement foundation, order Design Q9621-A.

FRONT

REAR

Design by
Donald A.
Gardner,
Architect, Inc.

Quote One®

Cost to build? See page 214 to order complete cost estimate to build this house in your area!

Design Q9668
First Floor: 1,254 square feet
Second Floor: 1,060 square feet
Total: 2,314 square feet

Design by
Donald A.
Gardner,
Architect, Inc.

● This stylish country farmhouse shows off its good looks both front and rear. A wraparound porch allows sheltered access to all first-level areas along with a covered breezeway to the garage. On the first floor, the spacious, open layout has all the latest features. The master bedroom on the second level has a fireplace, large walk-in closet and a master bath with shower, whirlpool tub and double-bowl vanity. Three additional bedrooms share a full bath with double-bowl vanity.

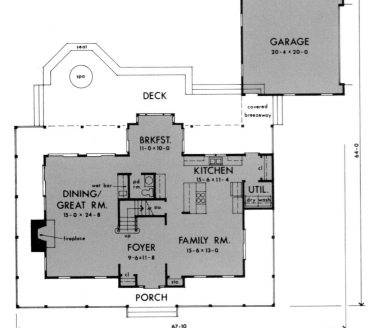

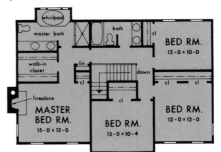

Quote One®

Cost to build? See page 214
to order complete cost estimate
to build this house in your area!

Design Q3510

First Floor: 1,120 square feet
Second Floor: 1,083 square feet
Third Floor: 597 square feet
Total: 2,800 square feet

● From the front and back covered porches to the open foyer with dining and living rooms on each side, this Colonial home offers a glimpse of the Old South. The large kitchen features an island cooktop, a breakfast nook and a convenient planning desk. The master bedroom exudes Southern flair with a spacious bathroom and a separate make-up table. An additional third-floor bonus room is also available. Fireplaces in the dining room, the living room and the family room complete the warmth and vitality of this fine home. All in all, it will serve your family well for generations to come.

Design by
Home Planners,
Inc.

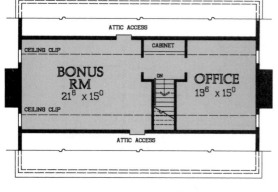

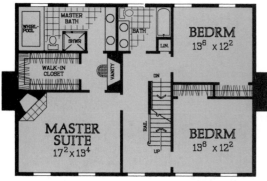

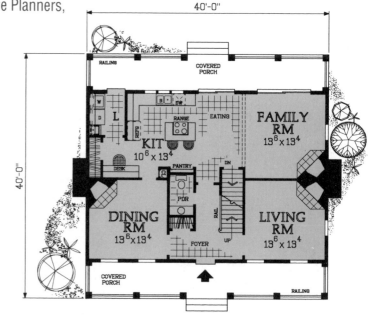

Design by
Home Planners,
Inc.

QUOTE ONE™

Cost to build? See page 214
to order complete cost estimate
to build this house in your area!

Design Q3570

First Floor: 1,578 square feet
Second Floor: 1,546 square feet
Total: 3,124 square feet
Bonus Room: 380 square feet

L **D**

● The unique design of this Colonial will satisfy the most refined tastes. Well-designed traffic patterns define family and formal areas. But that doesn't mean all the amenities are left for company. For example, the family room and its fireplace create a warm atmosphere for playing a board game with the kids or just relaxing. The kitchen features an island cooktop and a view onto the back porch. The roomy first-floor laundry includes space for drip drying. If it's not laundry day then take in the good weather from the second-floor balcony or slip into the master bath's whirlpool. With an additional three bedrooms and two bathrooms as well as a large bonus room above the garage, your family will have plenty of room to grow.

Design Q2981

First Floor: 2,104 square feet
Second Floor: 2,015 square feet
Total: 4,119 square feet

L

Design by
Home Planners, Inc.

● This formal two-story recalls a Louisiana plantation house, Land's End, built in 1857. The Ionic columns of the front porch and the pediment gable
echo the Greek Revival style. Highlighting the interior is the bright and cheerful spaciousness of the
informal family room area. It features a wall of
glass stretching to the second story sloping ceiling.
Enhancing the drama of this area is the adjacent
glass area of the breakfast room. Note the
"His/Her" areas of the master bedroom.

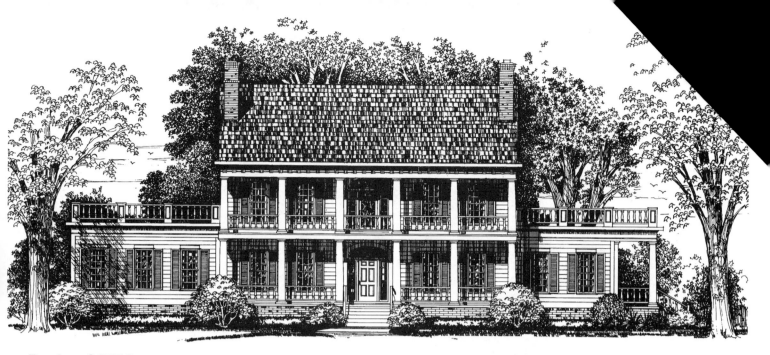

Design Q3508 First Floor: 2,098 square feet
Second Floor: 1,735 square feet; Total: 3,833 square feet

L

● Make history with this modern version of Louisiana's "Rosedown House." Like its predecessor—built in the 1800s—the modern adaptation exhibits splendid Southern styling, but with today's most sought-after amenities. The formal zone of the house is introduced by a foyer with a graceful, curving staircase. The dining and living rooms flank the foyer—each is highlighted by a fireplace. Off the living room, a library or music room offers comfort with a corner fireplace and a covered porch. This room also accesses the family room where more informal living takes off with a nearby breakfast room, expansive kitchen and rear covered porch. Upstairs, three bedrooms (one with its own bath) and a study (which may convert to an additional bedroom, if desired) include a gracious master suite. It opens with double doors and furthers this romantic feeling with a fireplace. A large dressing room with walk-in closets leads to the luxury bath. Two covered balconies complete the superb livability found in this plan.

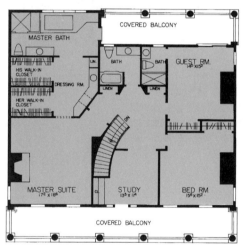

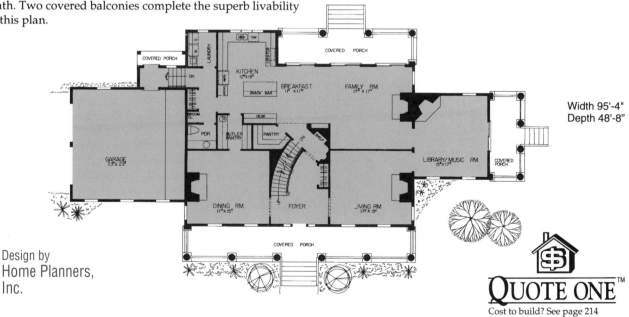

Width 95'-4"
Depth 48'-8"

Design by
Home Planners,
Inc.

Quote One™
Cost to build? See page 214
to order complete cost estimate
to build this house in your area!

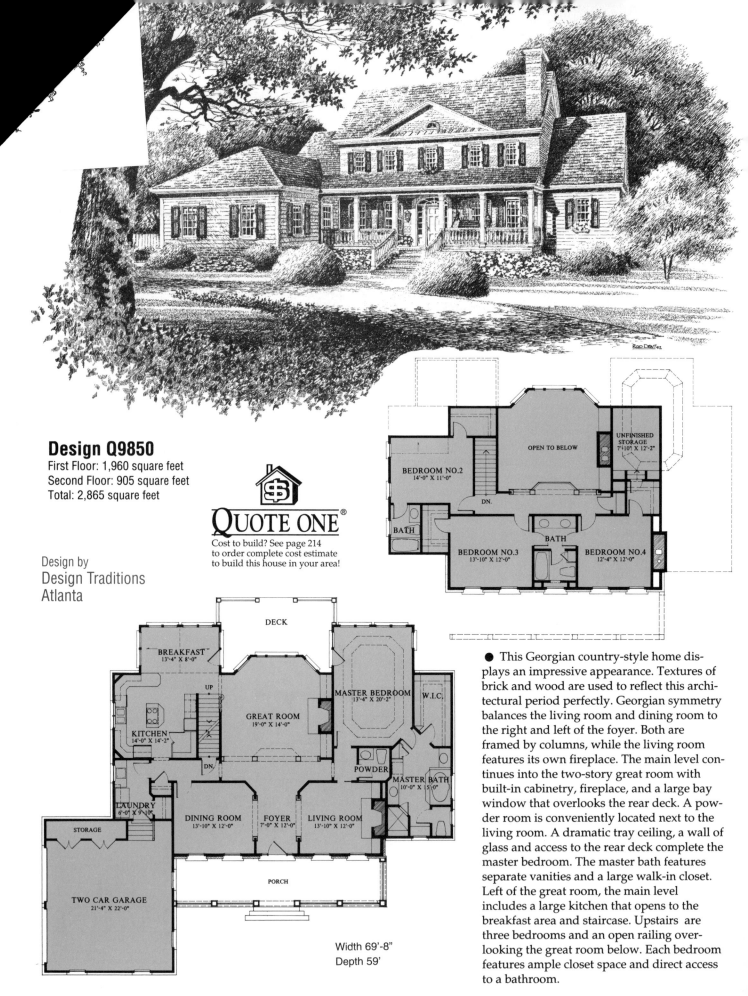

Design Q9850

First Floor: 1,960 square feet
Second Floor: 905 square feet
Total: 2,865 square feet

QUOTE ONE®
Cost to build? See page 214
to order complete cost estimate
to build this house in your area!

Design by
**Design Traditions
Atlanta**

● This Georgian country-style home displays an impressive appearance. Textures of brick and wood are used to reflect this architectural period perfectly. Georgian symmetry balances the living room and dining room to the right and left of the foyer. Both are framed by columns, while the living room features its own fireplace. The main level continues into the two-story great room with built-in cabinetry, fireplace, and a large bay window that overlooks the rear deck. A powder room is conveniently located next to the living room. A dramatic tray ceiling, a wall of glass and access to the rear deck complete the master bedroom. The master bath features separate vanities and a large walk-in closet. Left of the great room, the main level includes a large kitchen that opens to the breakfast area and staircase. Upstairs are three bedrooms and an open railing overlooking the great room below. Each bedroom features ample closet space and direct access to a bathroom.

Width 69'-8"
Depth 59'

Copyright 1992 Stephen S. Fuller, Inc.

Design Q9851

First Floor: 2,210 square feet
Second Floor: 1,070 square feet
Total: 3,280 square feet

● A generous front porch enhances the living area of this home with its sheltering welcome and Americana detailing. The classic style is also echoed in the use of wood siding, shuttered windows and stone finish work on two chimneys. The main level begins with a two-story foyer with tray ceiling.

Double doors open into the study with an exposed beam ceiling and fireplace. Left of the foyer lies the dining room drenched in natural sunlight. Across the hall, the great room with fireplace, wet bar and two sets of French doors provides a great gathering place. A hall powder room is to the right rear of the foyer. The master suite is located at the end of the main hallway. It features a tray ceiling and a complete master bath with separate shower, walk-in closet and dual vanities. The two-car garage is at the rear of the home, with convenient access from the expansive kitchen and breakfast area. Staircases from the family room and foyer lead to the upper level. Two additional bedrooms, each having walk-in closets and vanities, share the tub area. A third bedroom has a generous walk-in closet and private bath.

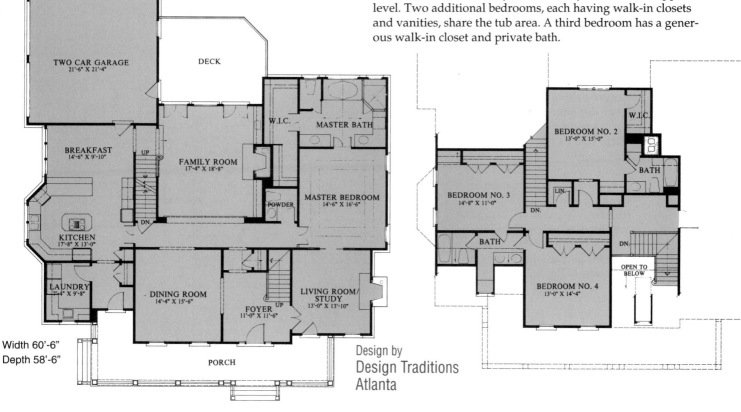

Width 60'-6"
Depth 58'-6"

Design by
Design Traditions
Atlanta

Design Q9669

First Floor: 1,759 square feet
Second Floor: 888 square feet
Total: 2,647 square feet

● This complete four-bedroom country farmhouse ignites a passion for both indoor and outdoor living with the well-organized open layout and the continuous flowing porch and deck encircling the house. Front and rear Palladian window dormers allow natural light to penetrate the foyer and family room below as well as adding exciting visual elements to the exterior. The dramatic family room with sloped ceiling envelopes a curved balcony. The master suite includes a large walk-in closet, a special sitting area, and a master bath with whirlpool tub, shower and double bowl vanity. A bonus room over the garage adds to the completeness of this house.

Design by
Donald A.
Gardner,
Architect, Inc.

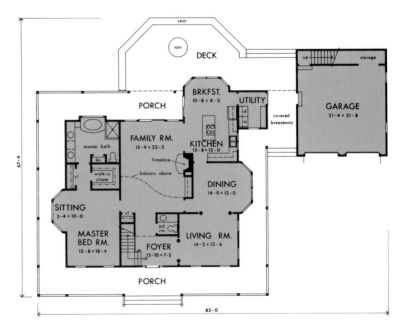

Design by
**Larry W.
Garnett &
Associates, Inc.**

Design Q9087
First Floor: 2,263 square feet
Second Floor: 787 square feet
Total: 3,050 square feet

● Excellent outdoor living is yours with this 1½-story home. The wrapping covered front porch gives way to a center hall entry with flanking living and dining rooms. The living room features a media center, two-way fireplace and columned entry. The attached garden room has French doors to the front porch and French doors to a smaller covered porch that is also accessed through the master bedroom suite. The family room is complemented by a fireplace, built-in bookshelves and another covered porch. An angled island counter separates it from the kitchen. Upstairs are three bedrooms and two full baths. Bedroom 4 has a beautiful bumped out window while Bedrooms 2 and 3 have dormer windows.

Bedroom 4 13' x 14'-8"
Bath 2
Balcony
Bath 3
Bedroom 2 11'-4" x 12'
Bedroom 3 11'-4" x 12'

Porch
Breakfast 9'-4" x 10'
Util.
Bath
Linen
Master Bedroom 19'-4" x 17'
French Door
Porch
French Door
Books
French Door
Family Room 13'-4" x 13'-4"
Kitchen 12' x 12'
1/2 Bath
Media Center
French Door
Living Room 14'-8" x 20'
Garden Room 12'-4" x 13'
Dining 15'-4" x 11'-4"
Foyer
2-Way Fireplace
French Door
Porch

Living Room

Width 68'-10"
Depth 52'-4"

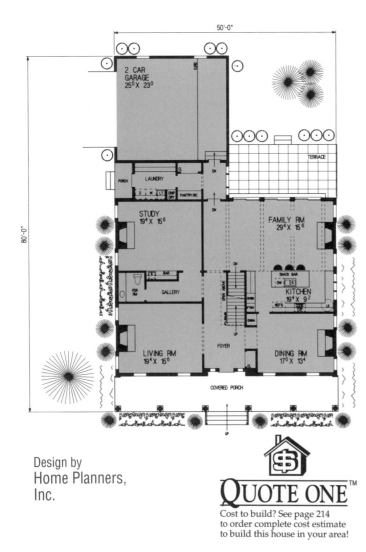

Design Q2996

First Floor: 2,191 square feet
Second Floor: 1,928 square feet
Total: 4,119 square feet

L **D**

● Covered porches upstairs and down are a charming addition to the well appointed two-story. Four chimney stacks herald four hearths inside: living room, dining room, family room and study. The second floor holds four bedrooms including a master suite with its own fireplace and a huge walk-in closet.

Design by
Home Planners,
Inc.

QUOTE ONE™

Cost to build? See page 214
to order complete cost estimate
to build this house in your area!

Design Q3567

First Floor: 1,778 square feet
Second Floor: 1,663 square feet
Bonus Room: 442 square feet
Total: 3,883 square feet

L **D**

● Spring breezes and summer nights will be a joy to take in on the verandas and balcony of this gorgeous Southern Colonial. Or, if you prefer, sit back and enjoy a good book in the library, or invite an old friend over for a chat in the conversation room. The first floor also includes formal dining and living rooms, a service entry with laundry and a three-car garage. You'll find a bonus room over the garage; you may decide to turn it into a media room or an exercise room. The master bedroom sports a fireplace, two walk-in closets, a double-bowl vanity, a shower and a whirlpool tub. Three other bedrooms occupy the second floor; one has its own full bath. Of course, the balcony is just a step away.

QUOTE ONE™

Cost to build? See page 214 to order complete cost estimate to build this house in your area!

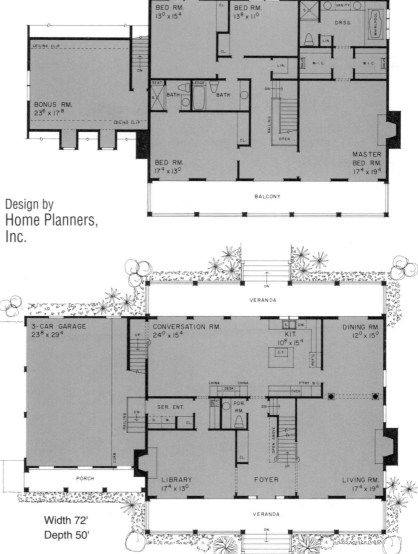

Design by
Home Planners, Inc.

Width 72'
Depth 50'

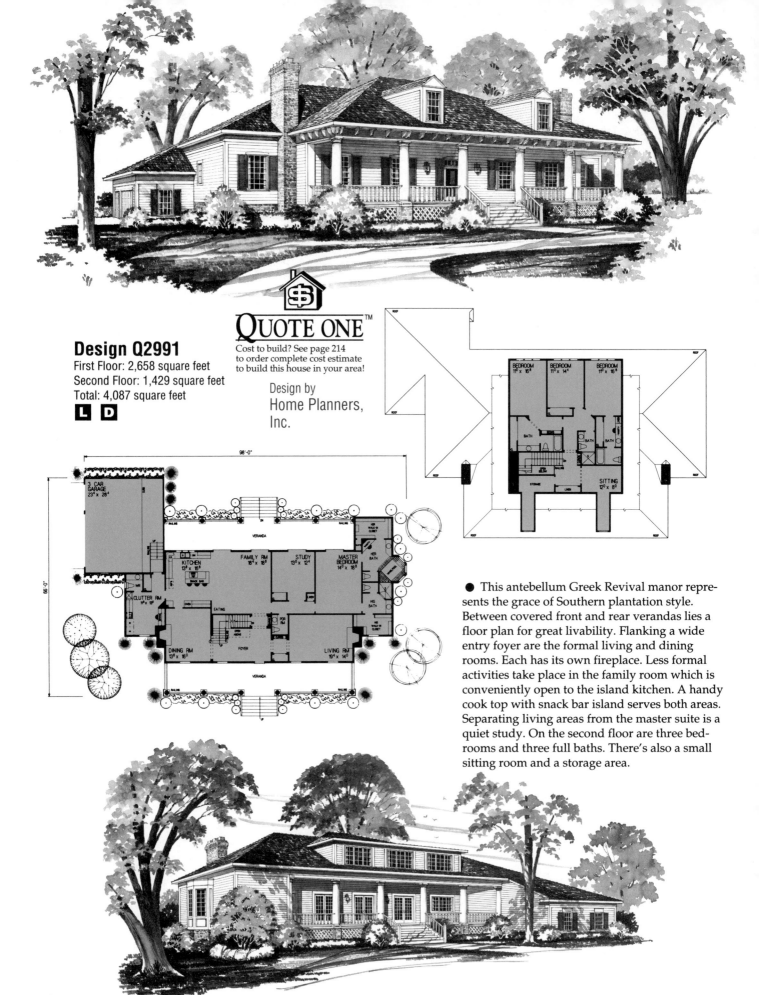

Design Q2991

First Floor: 2,658 square feet
Second Floor: 1,429 square feet
Total: 4,087 square feet

L D

Quote One™

Cost to build? See page 214
to order complete cost estimate
to build this house in your area!

Design by
Home Planners,
Inc.

● This antebellum Greek Revival manor represents the grace of Southern plantation style. Between covered front and rear verandas lies a floor plan for great livability. Flanking a wide entry foyer are the formal living and dining rooms. Each has its own fireplace. Less formal activities take place in the family room which is conveniently open to the island kitchen. A handy cook top with snack bar island serves both areas. Separating living areas from the master suite is a quiet study. On the second floor are three bedrooms and three full baths. There's also a small sitting room and a storage area.

VICTORIAN-INFLUENCED FARMHOUSES

In a time defined by freedom of expression, the Romantic ideals of architecture helped bring about Victorian style. For 70 years, from 1840 to 1910, people embraced the style and developed its various shapes and forms. So popular were the features of Victoriana that many of its more prominent, ornate characteristics began appearing on otherwise plain facades. Simple, unadorned farmhouses were seen sporting Queen-Anne-Style porch rails and posts, decorative corner brackets, spindlework friezes and other "gingerbread" details. This was possible (and practical) because of the availability of pre-cut Victorian trim pieces obtained through local lumber yards. The long-lasting appeal of Victorian detailing is evident, as the features appear on myriads of homes built throughout the country.

The Victorian Farmhouse today presents many of the same properties as the Classic Farmhouse — tall, upright proportions with wood siding and covered porches. However, the Victorian era influenced these rural residences by enhancing the plainness of Farmhouse style with detailing. Special features that became part of this newly integrated design include round or square double porch columns, spindled railings and friezes, spiderweb decoration at gables, shingle scallops, and cornice and dentil ornamentation.

Structural modifications were also accomplished to the basic Farmhouse design that make these simpler homes much more appealing. Plain, symmetrical windows became metal-clad, French-style bays or dormer windows. Even circle-head and fan-type windows were added. Wings and appendages were attached and took the shape of hexagons or octagons. Shingles took the place of horizontal wood siding in many instances.

In the following collection of Victorian Farmhouses, two designs are able representatives of the style: Design Q9015 and Design Q2970. Though obviously descended from stolid farmhouse roots, Design Q9015 is a model of exquisite detailing. Turned posts and delicate spindles adorn the covered front porch; eave brackets and lacy cornice trim grace the exterior. Of special note is the metal-clad roof over the porch and the decorative work on the pediments at the dormer windows. Design Q2970 presents many of the same details and also adds shingle scallops and a hexagonal bump-out that holds the dining room on the first floor and a sitting room on the second floor.

Displayed in both one- and two-story versions, the Victorian Farmhouses in this section are filled with the charm and delight that has always made Victorian styling so popular.

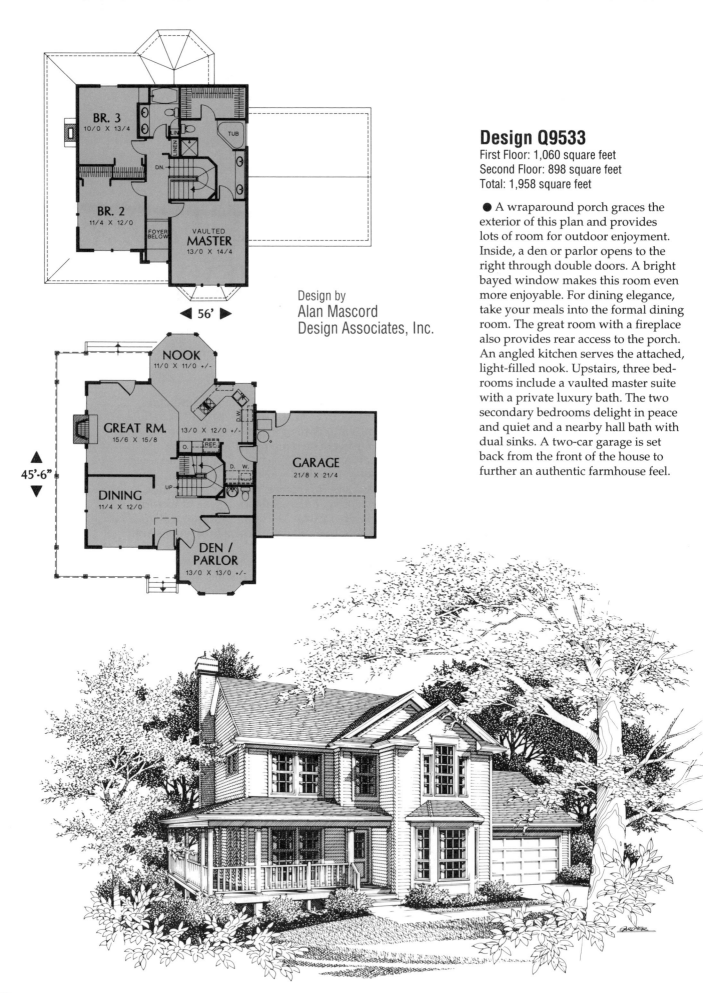

BR. 3
10/0 X 13/4

BR. 2
11/4 X 12/0

FOYER BELOW

DN.

LINEN

TUB

VAULTED
MASTER
13/0 X 14/4

◀ 56' ▶

Design by
**Alan Mascord
Design Associates, Inc.**

NOOK
11/0 X 11/0 +/-

GREAT RM.
15/6 X 15/8

45'-6"

DINING
11/4 X 12/0

UP

D. W.

REF.

GARAGE
21/8 X 21/4

DEN /
PARLOR
13/0 X 13/0 +/-

Design Q9533

First Floor: 1,060 square feet
Second Floor: 898 square feet
Total: 1,958 square feet

● A wraparound porch graces the exterior of this plan and provides lots of room for outdoor enjoyment. Inside, a den or parlor opens to the right through double doors. A bright bayed window makes this room even more enjoyable. For dining elegance, take your meals into the formal dining room. The great room with a fireplace also provides rear access to the porch. An angled kitchen serves the attached, light-filled nook. Upstairs, three bedrooms include a vaulted master suite with a private luxury bath. The two secondary bedrooms delight in peace and quiet and a nearby hall bath with dual sinks. A two-car garage is set back from the front of the house to further an authentic farmhouse feel.

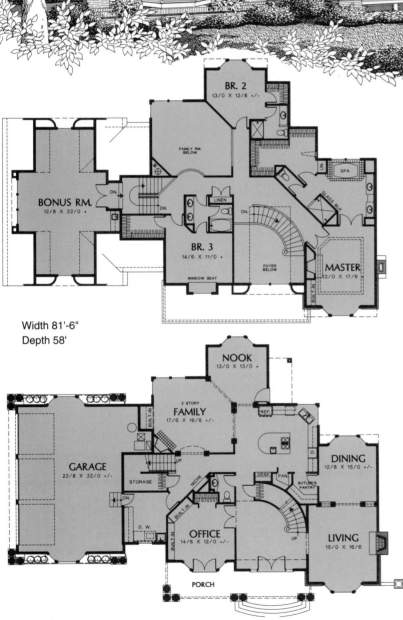

BR. 2
13/0 X 12/8 +/-

FAMILY RM.
BELOW

SPA

LIN.

BONUS RM.
12/8 X 32/0 +

DN.

DN.

LINEN

DN.

GLASS BLK.

BR. 3
14/6 X 11/0 +/-

FOYER
BELOW

MASTER
13/0 X 17/6

WINDOW SEAT

BUILT-IN

Width 81'-6"
Depth 58'

NOOK
13/0 X 13/0 +

FAMILY
17/6 X 16/6 +

2 STORY

REF.

BUILT-IN

DINING
12/8 X 15/0 +/-

GARAGE
22/8 X 32/0 +/-

UP

STORAGE

NICHE

DESK

PAN.

BUTLER'S
PANTRY

DN.

BUILT-IN

BUILT-IN

D. W.

OFFICE
14/6 X 12/0 +/-

UP

LIVING
15/0 X 16/6

PORCH

Design Q9544

First Floor: 2,197 square feet
Second Floor: 1,540 square feet
Total: 3,737 square feet
Bonus Room: 577 square feet

● This delightful home offers livability at its best. As you enter the foyer from the columned front porch you will find an office to the left that, with its built-ins, storage space, french doors to the porch and nearby bathroom, could easily double as a comfortable guest room. Beyond the foyer and the dramatically curved staircase is the spacious kitchen with its unique island cooktop. It is easily accessible from the family room with its corner fireplace, the bumped out breakfast nook or from the bay windowed dining room via the butlers pantry. A large laundry room with access to the three-car garage and plenty of storage space complete the first floor. Each of the upstairs bedrooms include walk-in closets, special window treatments and individual baths. The master bedroom also features a tray ceiling and a spa tub. Additional bonus room is available over the garage for future growth.

Design by
Alan Mascord
Design Associates, Inc.

71

Design Q7220

First Floor: 905 square feet
Second Floor: 863 square feet
Total: 1,768 square feet

● A covered porch and Victorian accents create a classical elevation. Double doors to the entry open to a spacious great room and an elegant dining room. In the gourmet kitchen, features include an island snack bar and a large pantry. French doors lead to the breakfast area which also enjoys access to a covered porch. Cathedral ceilings in the master bedroom and dressing area add an exquisite touch. His and Hers walk-in closets, a large dressing area with dual lavs and a whirlpool complement the master bedroom. A vaulted ceiling in Bedroom 2 accents a window seat and an arched transom window.

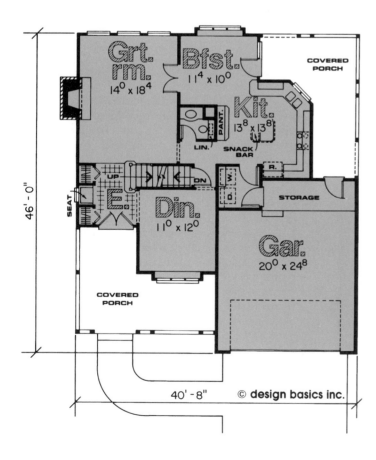

Grt. rm. 14⁰ x 18⁴

Bfst. 11⁴ x 10⁰

Kit. 13⁸ x 13⁸

PANT.

LIN.

SNACK BAR

Din. 11⁰ x 12⁰

Gar. 20⁰ x 24⁸

STORAGE

COVERED PORCH

COVERED PORCH

SEAT

UP · DN

R.

D. W.

46' - 0"

40' - 8"

© design basics inc.

Design by
Design
Basics,
Inc.

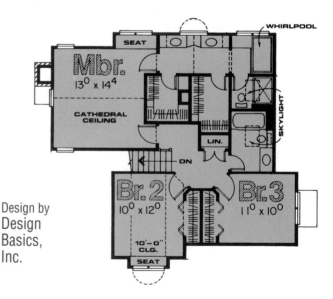

Mbr. 13⁰ x 14⁴

CATHEDRAL CEILING

SEAT

WHIRLPOOL

SKYLIGHT

LIN.

DN

Br. 2 10⁰ x 12⁰

Br. 3 11⁰ x 10⁰

10'-0" CLG.

SEAT

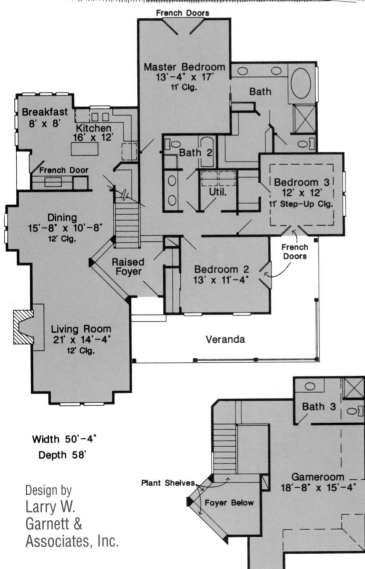

French Doors

Master Bedroom
13'-4" x 17'
11' Clg.

Bath

Breakfast
8' x 8'

Kitchen
16' x 12'

French Door

Bath 2

Util.

Bedroom 3
12' x 12'
11' Step-Up Clg.

Dining
15'-8" x 10'-8"
12' Clg.

Raised Foyer

French Doors

Bedroom 2
13' x 11'-4"

Living Room
21' x 14'-4"
12' Clg.

Veranda

Width 50'-4"
Depth 58'

Design by
Larry W.
Garnett &
Associates, Inc.

Plant Shelves

Foyer Below

Bath 3

Gameroom
18'-8" x 15'-4"

Design Q9030

First Floor: 1,837 square feet
Second Floor: 445 square feet
Total: 2,282 square feet

● A seven-foot wide veranda with ornate fretwork, porch railing and intricate post brackets, along with a copper-topped box window provide this home with old-fashioned charm and romance. Inside, the raised foyer opens into living and dining areas that are perfect for family activities or formal entertaining. Stairs lead to the second floor gameroom and bath. Bedrooms 2 and 3 each have French doors that open to the front veranda. The secluded master bedroom has an eleven-foot ceiling and French doors, while the spacious master bath features a garden tub with adjacent glass-enclosed shower, along with a large walk-in closet. The kitchen combines both form and function with ample cabinet space, a center work island, and a magnificent view through the breakfast area to the rear yard. Plans for a detached two-car garage are included with this design.

Design Q3384

First Floor: 1,399 square feet
Second Floor: 1,123 square feet; Total: 2,522 square feet

L **D**

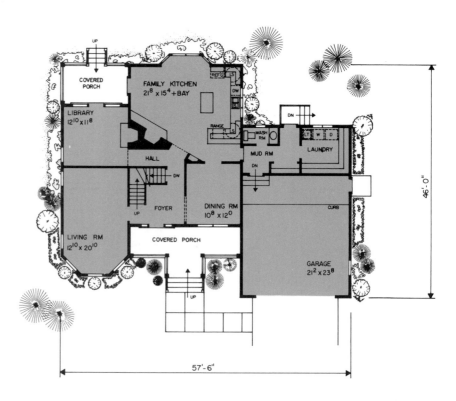

Quote One™

Cost to build? See page 214
to order complete cost estimate
to build this house in your area!

● Classic Victorian styling comes to the forefront in this Queen Anne two-story. Complementary fishscale-adorned pediments top the bayed tower to the left and garage to the right. Smaller versions are found at the dormer windows above a spindlework porch. The interior boasts comfortable living quarters for the entire family. On opposite sides of the wide foyer are the formal dining and living rooms. To the rear, is a country-style island kitchen with attached family room (don't miss the fireplace here). A small library shares a covered porch with this informal gathering area and also has its own fireplace. Three bedrooms on the second floor include a master suite with grand bath. The two family bedrooms share a full bath. Take special note of the service area conveniently attached to the two-car garage.

Design by
Home Planners, Inc.

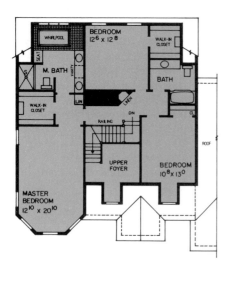

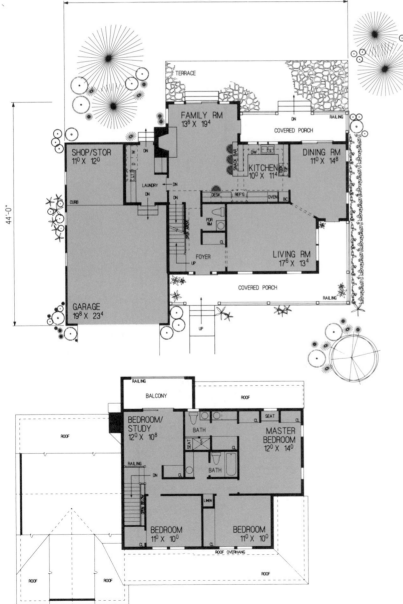

Design Q3385

First Floor: 1,096 square feet
Second Floor: 900 square feet
Total: 1,996 square feet

L **D**

● Covered porches front and rear are the first signal that this is a fine example of Folk Victorian styling. Complementing the exterior is a grand plan for family living. A formal living room and attached dining room provide space for entertaining guests. The large family room with fireplace is a gathering room for everyday. Both areas have access to outdoor spaces. Four bedrooms occupy the second floor. The master suite features two lavatories, a window seat and three closets. One of the family bedrooms has its own private balcony and could be used as a study. Note the open staircase and convenient linen storage.

Design by
Home Planners,
Inc.

Design Q3461

First Floor: 1,391 square feet
Second Floor: 611 square feet
Total: 2,002 square feet

L

● A Palladian window set in
a dormer provides a nice intro-
duction to this 1½-story country
home. The two-story foyer
draws on natural light and a
pair of columns to set a comfortable, yet elegant mood. The living room, to the left, presents a
grand space for entertaining.
From full-course dinners to family suppers, the dining room will
serve its purpose well. The
kitchen delights with an island
work station and openness to
the keeping room. Here, a
raised-hearth fireplace provides
added comfort. Sleeping accommodations are comprised of
four bedrooms, one a first-floor
master suite. With a luxurious
private bath, including dual
lavatories, this room will surely
be a favorite retreat. Upstairs,
three secondary bedrooms meet
the needs of the growing family.

Quote One™

Cost to build? See page 214
to order complete cost estimate
to build this house in your area!

Design by
**Home Planners,
Inc.**

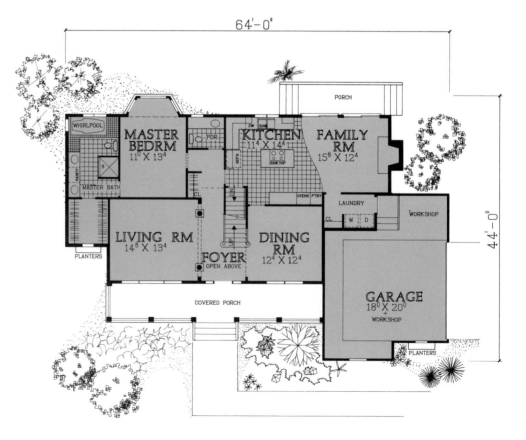

76

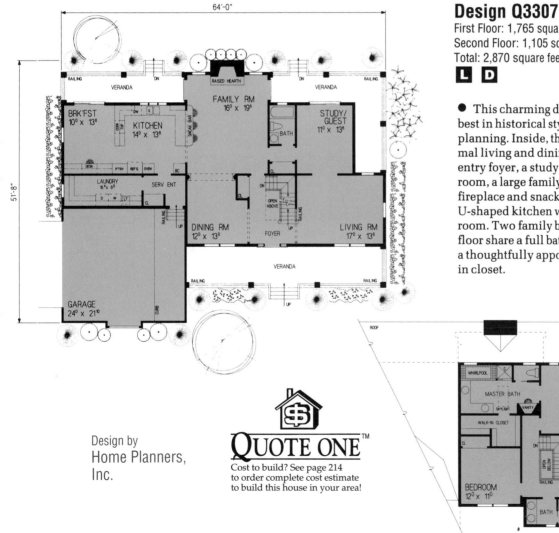

Design Q3307

First Floor: 1,765 square feet
Second Floor: 1,105 square feet
Total: 2,870 square feet

L **D**

● This charming design brings together the best in historical styling and modern floor planning. Inside, the first-floor plan boasts formal living and dining areas on either side of the entry foyer, a study that could double as a guest room, a large family room with raised-hearth fireplace and snack bar pass-through, and a U-shaped kitchen with attached breakfast room. Two family bedrooms on the second floor share a full bath; the master bedroom has a thoughtfully appointed bath and large walk-in closet.

Design by
Home Planners, Inc.

Quote One™

Cost to build? See page 214
to order complete cost estimate
to build this house in your area!

Design Q9854

Square Footage: 2,770

● This English cottage with cedar shake exterior displays the best qualities of a traditional design. With the bay window and recessed entry visitors feel warmly welcomed. The foyer opens to both the dining room with vaulted ceiling and great room with fireplace and built-in cabinetry. Surrounded by windows, the breakfast room opens to a gourmet kitchen and laundry room conveniently located near the garage entrance. To the right of the foyer is a hall powder room. Two bedrooms with large closets are joined by a full bath with individual vanities and window seat. Through double doors at the end of a short hall, the master suite awaits with tray ceiling and adjoining sunlit sitting room. The master bath has His and Hers closets, separate vanities, individual shower and a garden tub with bay window.

Design by
**Design Traditions
Atlanta**

Width 73'-6"
Depth 78'

Copyright 1992 Stephen S. Fuller, Inc.

Quote One®

Cost to build? See page 214
to order complete cost estimate
to build this house in your area!

PORCH

BREAKFAST
13'-4" X 9'-0"

BEDROOM/
OFFICE
10'-4" X 11'-0"

KITCHEN
13'-4" X 10'-6"

GREAT ROOM
17'-0" X 17'-8"

BATH

LAUNDRY

DN.

MASTER
BATH

MASTER BEDRDOOM
16'-4" X 13'-6"

BEDROOM NO. 2
10'-4" X 12'-0"

BATH

DINING ROOM
11'-4" X 12'-10"

FOYER
5'-4" X
12'-10"

BEDROOM/
STUDY
11'-2" X 12'-0"

TWO CAR GARAGE
20'-6" X 19'-6"

PORCH

WIDTH 61'
DEPTH 72'-6"

Design by
Design Traditions

Design Q9853
Square Footage: 2,090

● This traditional home features board and batten and cedar shingles in an attractively proportioned exterior. Finishing touches include a covered entrance and porch with column detailing and arched transom, flower boxes and shuttered windows. The foyer opens to both the dining room and great room beyond with French doors opening onto the porch. Through the double doors to the right of the foyer is the combination bedroom/study. A short hallway leads to a full bath and a secondary bedroom with ample closet space. The master bedroom is spacious, with walk-in closets on both sides of the entrance to the master bath. With separate vanities, shower and toilet, the master bath is of symmetrical design, and forms a private retreat at the rear of the home. Convenient to both the great room and dining room, the kitchen opens to an attractive breakfast area featuring a bay window. An additional room is remotely located off the kitchen, providing a retreat for today's at-home office or guest.

Design Q9852

First Floor: 1,840 square feet
Second Floor: 950 square feet
Total: 2,790 square feet

Design by
Design Traditions
Atlanta

● The appearance of this early American home brings the past to mind with its wraparound porch, wood siding and flower-box detailing. The uniquely shaped foyer leads to the dining room accented by columns, vaulted ceiling and bay window. Columns frame the great room as well, while a ribbon of windows creates a wall of glass at the back of the house from the great room to the breakfast area. The asymmetrical theme continues through the kitchen as it leads back to the hallway, accessing the laundry and two-car garage. Left of the foyer lies the living room with a warming fireplace. The master suite begins with double doors that open to a space with octagonal tray ceiling and bay window. The spacious master bath and walk-in closet complete the suite. Stairs to the second level lead from the breakfast area to an open landing overlooking the great room. Three additional bedrooms with large walk-in closets and a variety of bath arrangements complete this level.

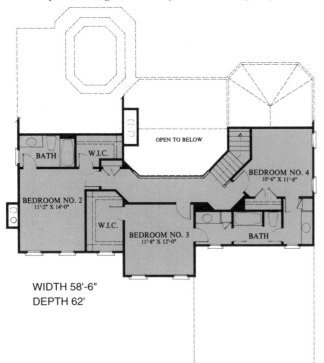

WIDTH 58'-6"
DEPTH 62'

Design Q9868
First Floor: 1,725 square feet
Second Floor: 650 square feet
Total: 2,375 square feet

● This example of Classic American architecture features a columned front porch and wood framing. Bay window detailing and an arched dormer above the porch complete the picture. The foyer includes a closet and an open staircase to the upper level. Straight ahead, the great room is largely glass, and opens to the vaulted breakfast area which leads outdoors to the patio. The octagonal kitchen is designed for ease of movement and to promote the flow of family traffic. The dining room and living room share a hearth and an open design with bay window treatments for interest and natural light. The

master bedroom at the right rear of the home features a tray ceiling and large bay window. The master bath with dual vanities, individual shower and walk-in closets completes the master suite. The upper level is comprised of a gallery and loft open to the great room and foyer below, which is warmed by the natural light from the dormer windows. Beyond the loft are two bedrooms that share a bath and an unfinished bonus room. Upper level attic storage is spacious and convenient with an entrance just at the top of the stairs.

Design Q9232

First Floor: 1,551 square feet
Second Floor: 725 square feet
Total: 2,276 square feet

● This narrow-lot plan features a wraparound porch at the two-story entry, which opens to the formal dining room with beautiful bay windows. The great room features a handsome fireplace and a ten-and-a-half foot ceiling. A well-equipped island kitchen with pantry and built-in desk is available for the serious cook. The large master bedroom has a vaulted ceiling and a luxury master bath with two-person whirlpool, skylight and large walk-in closet. Three secondary bedrooms with ample closet space share a compartmented bath including double vanity and a large linen closet.

Design by
**Design
Basics,
Inc.**

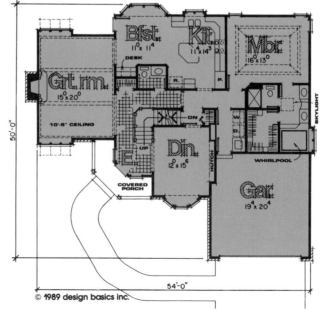

Design Q9252

First Floor: 1,113 square feet
Second Floor: 965 square feet
Total: 2,078 square feet

● Elegant detail, a charming veranda and a tall brick chimney make a pleasing facade on this four-bedroom, two-story Victorian home. Yesterday's simpler lifestyle is reflected throughout this plan. From the large bayed parlor with sloped ceiling to the sunken gathering room with fireplace, there's plenty to appreciate about the floor plan. The formal dining room opens to the parlor for convenient entertaining. An L-shaped kitchen with attached breakfast room is nearby. Upstairs quarters include a master suite with private dressing area and whirlpool, and three family bedrooms.

DECK

Breakfast
9⁸ × 12⁰

Kitchen
10⁰ × 10⁰

DESK

Gathering
Room
17³ × 15⁰

8'- 8" Ceiling

STORAGE

Dining
Room
12⁰ × 12⁰

DN.

DN.

Garage
19⁴ × 22⁰

41'- 5"

UP

ENTRANCE
HALL

Parlor
12⁰ × 16⁴

12'- 0"
Ceiling

COVERED
VERANDA

W.

D.

46'- 0"

© 1990 design basics inc.

SKYLIGHT

SKYLIGHT

W/P

Sleeping
Quarters
11⁰ × 10⁰

9'- 0" Ceiling

Master
Sleeping
Quarters
12⁰ × 17⁰

DN.

L

Sleeping
Quarters
10⁰ × 11⁰

Sleeping
Quarters
11⁰ × 12⁸

11'- 6"
Ceiling

Design by
Design
Basics,
Inc.

QUOTE ONE®

Cost to build? See page 214 to order complete cost estimate to build this house in your area!

Design Q3606

First Floor: 1,969 square feet
Second Floor: 660 square feet
Total: 2,629 square feet
Bonus Room: 360 square feet

L **D**

● Entertaining and comfortable living are the by-words for this gracious home. As you greet your guest from the two-story foyer, you can lead them into the cozy living room with its bay window, or into the spacious family/great room with its volume ceiling, central fireplace, built-in media center, and access to the enclosed sun room. The U-shaped kitchen features a center island, a large pantry, a writing desk, a snack bar and convenience to the family room, the dining room, the morning room, and the entertainment veranda. An efficient laundry provides access to the garage via a decorative arbor. The master suite is found on the first floor and includes a pampering master bath with a whirlpool, a separate shower and a walk-in closet. Both the bedroom and the bathroom access the private master suite veranda. The home office can also double as a fourth bedroom due to a nearby full bath. Two additional bedrooms with lots of closet space and a full bath with dual sinks are found on the second floor. Additional space is available over the garage. For information on customizing this design, call 1-800-521-6797, ext. 800.

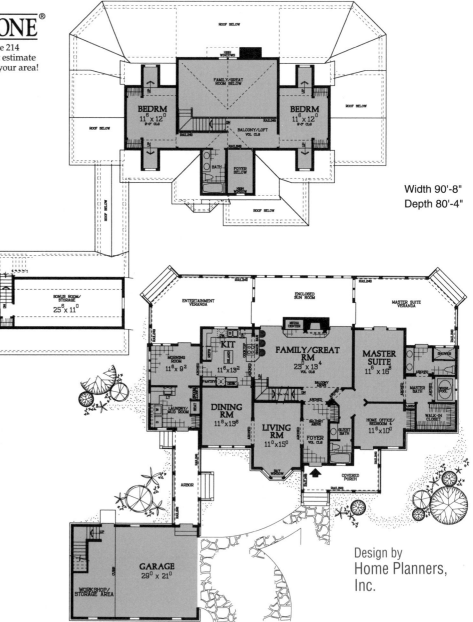

Width 90'-8"
Depth 80'-4"

Design by
Home Planners, Inc.

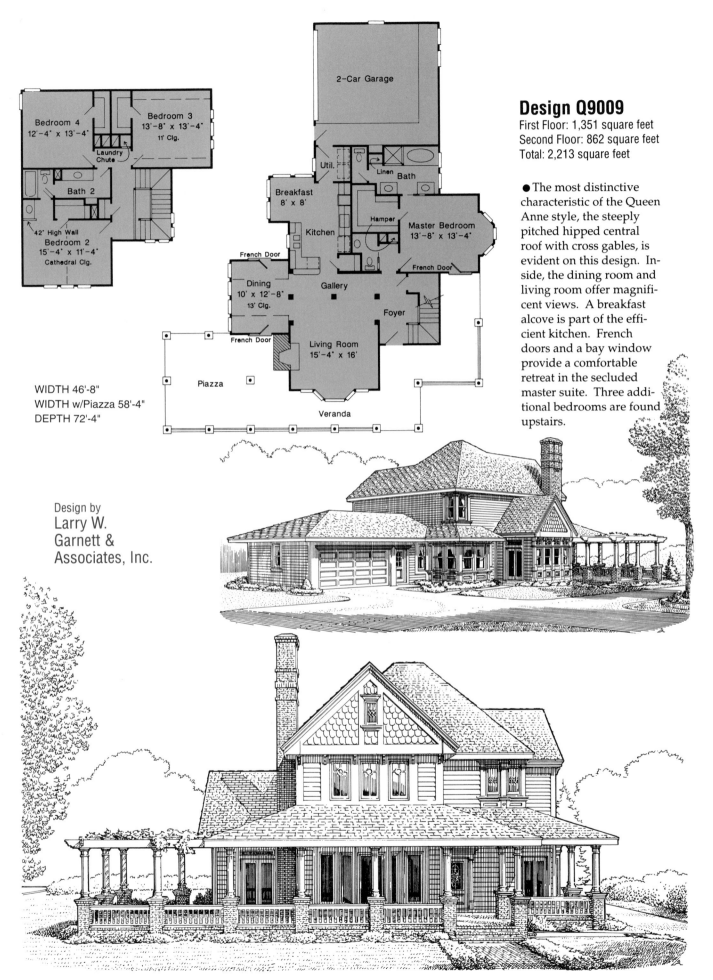

Floor plan labels:

2-Car Garage

Bedroom 4
12'-4" x 13'-4"

Bedroom 3
13'-8" x 13'-4"
11' Clg.

Laundry Chute

Bath 2

42" High Wall
Bedroom 2
15'-4" x 11'-4"
Cathedral Clg.

Util.

Linen

Bath

Breakfast
8' x 8'

Kitchen

Hamper

Master Bedroom
13'-8" x 13'-4"

French Door

French Door

Dining
10' x 12'-8"
13' Clg.

Gallery

Foyer

French Door

Piazza

French Door

Living Room
15'-4" x 16'

Veranda

WIDTH 46'-8"
WIDTH w/Piazza 58'-4"
DEPTH 72'-4"

Design by
Larry W.
Garnett &
Associates, Inc.

Design Q9009
First Floor: 1,351 square feet
Second Floor: 862 square feet
Total: 2,213 square feet

● The most distinctive characteristic of the Queen Anne style, the steeply pitched hipped central roof with cross gables, is evident on this design. Inside, the dining room and living room offer magnificent views. A breakfast alcove is part of the efficient kitchen. French doors and a bay window provide a comfortable retreat in the secluded master suite. Three additional bedrooms are found upstairs.

Design Q9053 First Floor: 811 square feet; Second Floor: 1,067 square feet; Total: 1,878 square feet

● Elaborate spindlework and ornate porch posts, along with detailed block-paneled trim at the symmetrical gables, give this Queen Anne Style two-story charm and elegance. The living room has a fireplace as its focal point, while at the same time providing a view of the built-in media center. The large kitchen opens to the dining area, and also has access to the garage and laundry room. The master bedroom is truly a luxurious private retreat. The sitting area has a built-in media center for audio and video equipment. The master bath contains a glass-enclosed shower and His and Hers lavatories. Two additional bedrooms, each with a walk-in closet, share a hall bath.

Width 45'
Depth 53'

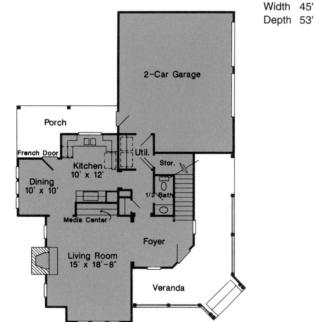

9' Clg. Throughout First and Second Floors

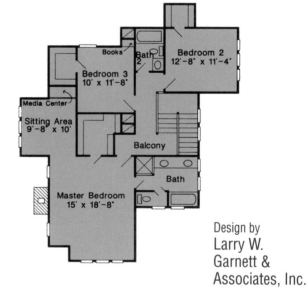

Design by
Larry W.
Garnett &
Associates, Inc.

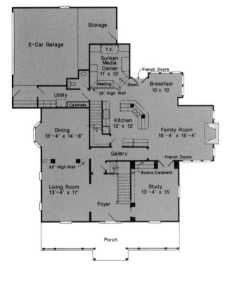

Width 59' - 4"
Depth 72' - 8"

Design by
Larry W.
Garnett &
Associates, Inc.

Design Q9015

First Floor: 1,948 square feet
Second Floor: 1,891 square feet
Total: 3,839 square feet

● As authentic as the exterior of this design is, the interior offers all the luxury and elegance that today's homeowners could desire. The formal living and dining rooms are separated by detailed wood columns. Built-in bookcases and cabinets highlight the block-paneled study. The centrally located kitchen becomes the focal point of a truly outstanding family living center which includes a sunken media area, breakfast alcove, and a family room with a fireplace. Adjacent to the kitchen is a large hobby room with a built-in desk, a space for a freezer, and generous cabinet storage. A rear staircase provides convenient access to the second floor. The secluded master suite is beyond compare, with such extras as a fireplace with flanking window seats and cabinets, an enormous walk-in closet, and a private deck. The luxurious bath features a dressing table, a whirlpool tub with a gazebo-shaped ceiling above, and an oversized shower. Finally, there is a private exercise room with a bay-window seat. Three additional bedrooms and a laundry room complete the second floor. A staircase leads to an optional third floor area.

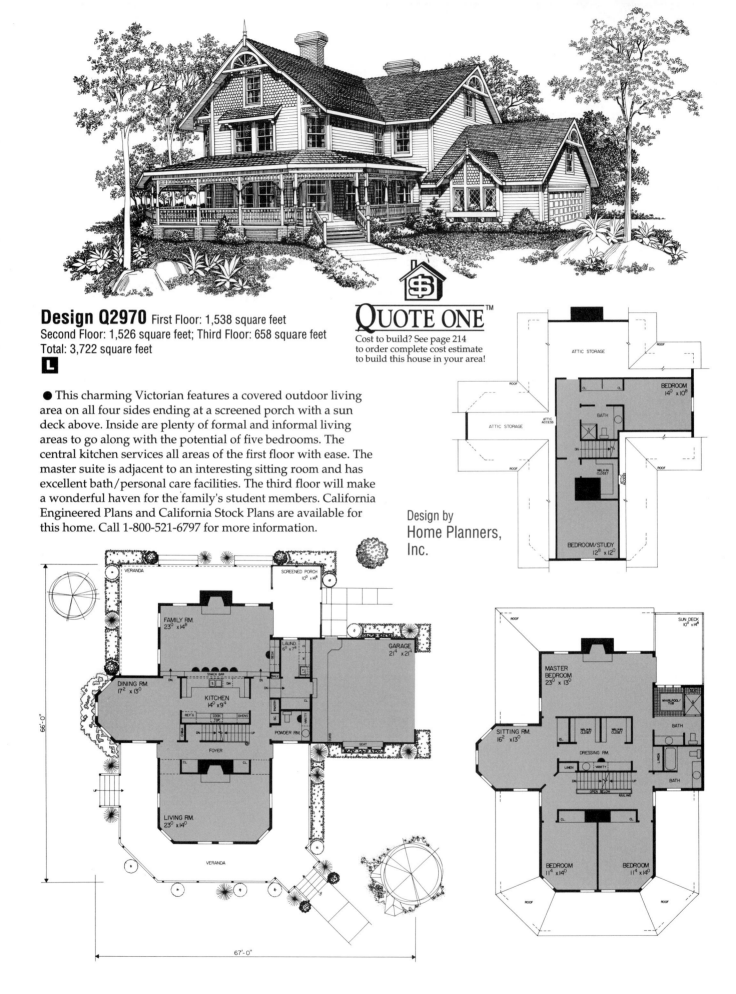

Design Q2970 First Floor: 1,538 square feet
Second Floor: 1,526 square feet; Third Floor: 658 square feet
Total: 3,722 square feet

L

QUOTE ONE™

Cost to build? See page 214
to order complete cost estimate
to build this house in your area!

● This charming Victorian features a covered outdoor living
area on all four sides ending at a screened porch with a sun
deck above. Inside are plenty of formal and informal living
areas to go along with the potential of five bedrooms. The
central kitchen services all areas of the first floor with ease. The
master suite is adjacent to an interesting sitting room and has
excellent bath/personal care facilities. The third floor will make
a wonderful haven for the family's student members. California
Engineered Plans and California Stock Plans are available for
this home. Call 1-800-521-6797 for more information.

Design by
Home Planners,
Inc.

Design Q2974 First Floor: 911 square feet
Second Floor: 861 square feet; Total: 1,772 square feet
Attic: 1,131 square feet

L

● Victorian homes are well known for their orientation on narrow building sites. This house is 38 feet wide, but the livability is tremendous. From the front covered porch, the foyer directs traffic all the way to the back of the house with its open living and dining rooms. The U-shaped kitchen conveniently services both the dining room and the front breakfast room. The rear living area is spacious and functions in an exciting manner with the outdoor areas. Bonus recreational, hobby and storage is offered by the basement and the attic. California Engineered Plans and California Stock Plans are available for this home. Call 1-800-521-6797 for more information.

Quote One™

Cost to build? See page 214 to order complete cost estimate to build this house in your area!

Design by
Home Planners, Inc.

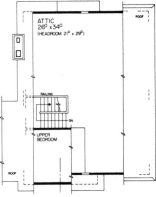

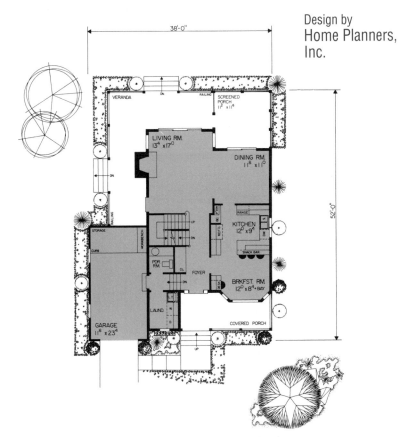

QUOTE ONE™
Cost to build? See page 214
to order complete cost estimate
to build this house in your area!

Design Q3394

First Floor: 1,531 square feet
Second Floor: 1,307 square feet
Third Floor: 664 square feet
Total: 3,502 square feet

L **D**

● The formal living areas of this Folk Victorian
home are set off by a family room which connects the
main house to the service areas. The laundry has
room for not only a washer and dryer but also a
freezer and sewing area. The second floor holds three
bedrooms and two full baths. A sitting area in the
master suite separates it from family bedrooms. On
the third floor is a guest bedroom with a gracious
bath and a large walk-in closet.

Design by
Home Planners,
Inc.

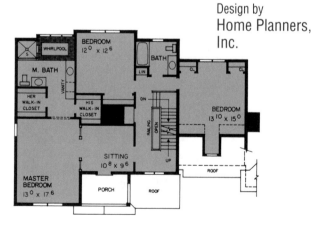

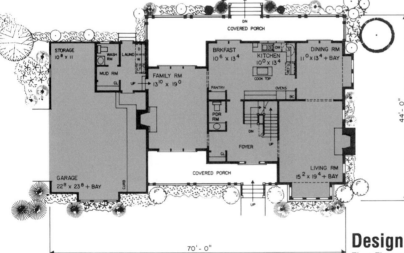

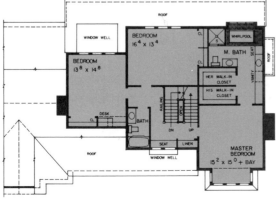

Design by
Home Planners,
Inc.

Quote One™

Cost to build? See page 214
to order complete cost estimate
to build this house in your area!

Design Q3388

First Floor: 1,517 square feet
Second Floor: 1,267 square feet
Third Floor: 480 square feet
Total: 3,264 square feet

L **D**

● A testament to real Folk Victorian styling, this
delightful home offers the best in thoughtful floor
planning. To the left of the foyer is the casual family
room with a fireplace and proximity to the laundry
area. To the right is the formal living room with a
bay window and a fireplace. From the connecting
formal dining room, the kitchen/breakfast room
combination features sliding glass doors to the rear
covered porch, an island cooktop and a large pantry.
Second-floor bedrooms include a well-planned master suite and two family bedrooms served by a full
bath. A guest room with its own bath dominates the
third floor.

Design Q9251

First Floor: 1,653 square feet
Second Floor: 700 square feet
Total: 2,353 square feet

● Beautiful arches and elaborate detail give the elevation of this four-bedroom, 1½-story home an unmistakable elegance. Inside the floor plan is equally appealing. Note the formal dining room with bay window, visible from the entrance hall. The large great room has a fireplace and a wall of windows out the back. A hearth room, with bookcase, adjoins the kitchen area with walk-in pantry. The master suite on the first floor features His and Hers wardrobes, a large whirlpool and double lavatories. Upstairs quarters share a full bath with compartmented sinks.

Quote One®

Cost to build? See page 214 to order complete cost estimate to build this house in your area!

Design by
Design Basics, Inc.

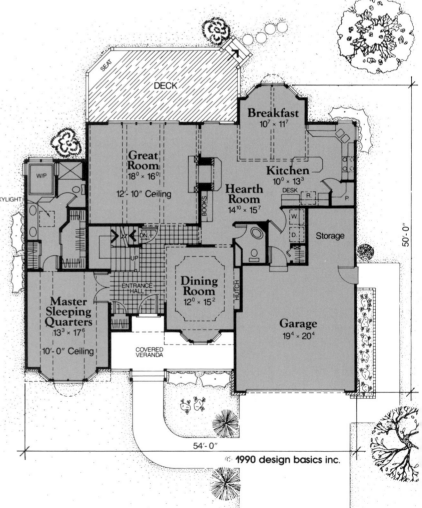

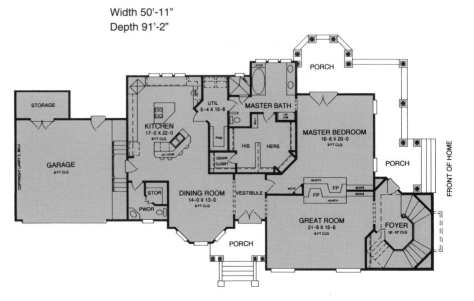

COPYRIGHT LARRY E. BELK

Design Q8095

First Floor: 2,194 square feet
Second Floor: 870 square feet
Total: 3,064 square feet
Bonus Room: 251 square feet

● With equally appealing front and side entrances, a charming Victorian facade beckons one to enter this stunning home. The foyer showcases the characteristic winding staircase and opens to the large great room with a masonry fireplace. An enormous kitchen features a cooktop island and a breakfast bar large enough to seat four. A lovely bay window distinguishes the nearby dining room. The master suite with a masonry fireplace is located on the first floor. The amenity-filled master bath features double vanities, a whirlpool tub, a separate shower and a gigantic His and Hers walk-in closet with an additional cedar closet. The second floor contains two bedrooms—one with access to the outdoor balcony on the side of the home. The third floor is completely expandable. This plan is available with either a crawlspace or slab foundation. Please specify when ordering.

Design by
Larry E. Belk
Designs

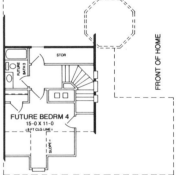

Width 50'-11"
Depth 91'-2"

Design Q9269

First Floor: 1,081 square feet; Second Floor: 1,136 square feet
Total: 2,217 square feet

● Victorian charm and detailing radiate from the elevation of this four-bedroom, two-story design. Inside, formal living spaces, visible from the entry, begin with a dining room with hutch space and a parlor highlighted by a bayed window and alluring angles. the T-shaped staircase allows quick access to the informal spaces at the rear, such as the comfortable gathering room with a fireplace, built-in bookcase and many windows. Casual traffic patterns flow through a sunny, open breakfast area and island kitchen. Upstairs, a compartmented bath is shared by the secondary sleeping quarters. Gracing the master sleeping quarters is an elegant vaulted ceiling and private dressing/bath area offering an oval whirlpool, angled vanity and walk-in wardrobe.

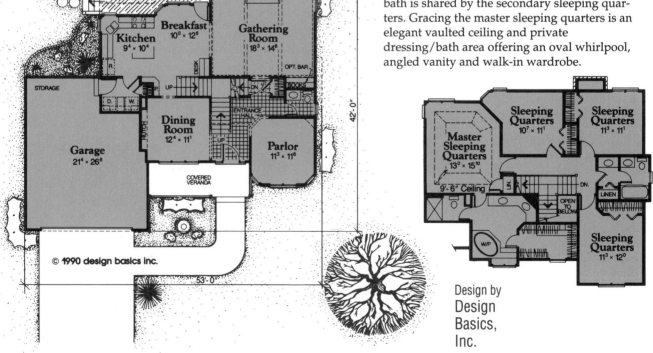

Design by
Design
Basics,
Inc.

CENTER-HALL COLONIAL FARMHOUSES

Colonial architecture is a reflection of a period of dedication to hard work, simple pleasures and solid virtues. As such, it brought together design characteristics that speak of symmetry and regularity of form. Straight lines and design details that were practical as well as ornamental took precedence over frivolous decoration. Floor plans featured square or rectangular rooms and stacked livability.

Popular today in the Northeastern region, particularly New England, the Center-Hall Colonial Farmhouse is an adaptation of the early homes built in the region and, as such, is a testament to symmetry and rigid adherence to traditional values. It is a classic, upright structure with a straight roof gable. The entry may be the only indication of ornamentation and can be detailed with a decorative frieze, pediment or portico over the front door. These details derive from Colonial and Georgian influences.

The characteristic central door opens to a center hall, from which all first-story rooms flow. This is usually where the stairwell to the second floor is found as well. These homes incorporate full two-story construction usually with all bedrooms found on the second floor.

Windows are regular, symmetrical and usually multi-paned and shuttered. Fireplace stacks are large, constructed of brick and may be placed centrally or to one end of the home. Horizontal wood siding is the most common exterior choice, but it is not unusual to see Center-Hall Colonials constructed in brick or part brick and part stone.

Garages and service areas tend to be appended to the main house with a service wing or entrance. In some cases, the connecting piece may be a family room or study.

Two fine examples of the Center-Hall Colonial Farmhouse are Design Q2188 and Design Q9299. Both have the symmetrical facade and straight-gabled roof that is common to Colonial architecture.

Design Q2188 features a strong center, brick chimney stack, a transommed double-door entry and a garage attached to the main house by a service entry. Added details include a weathervane at the end of the garage and symmetrical, shuttered windows.

Design Q9299 has the oval windows reminiscent of Country Colonial homes while the half-circle steps, entry columns, the acorn pediment over the front door and the front window headers add to the classic facade.

The fine grouping of Center-Hall Colonial Farmhouses offered in this section are apt reminders of America's architectural heritage. Large enough for virtually any family, they bring modern livability to a cherished historic style.

Design Q2654

First Floor: 1,152 square feet
Second Floor: 844 square feet
Total: 1,996 square feet

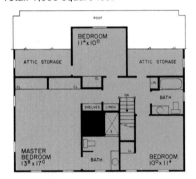

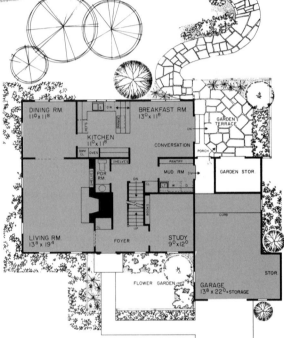

● This is certainly an authentic traditional salt-box. It features a symmetrical design with a center fireplace, a wide, paneled doorway and multi-paned, double-hung windows. Tucked behind the one-car garage is a garden shed which provides work and storage space. The breakfast room features French doors which open onto a flagstone terrace. The U-shaped kitchen has built-in counters which make efficient use of space. The upstairs plan houses three bedrooms.

Width 62'-4"

Design by Depth 42'

Home Planners,
Inc.

Design by
Home Planners,
Inc.

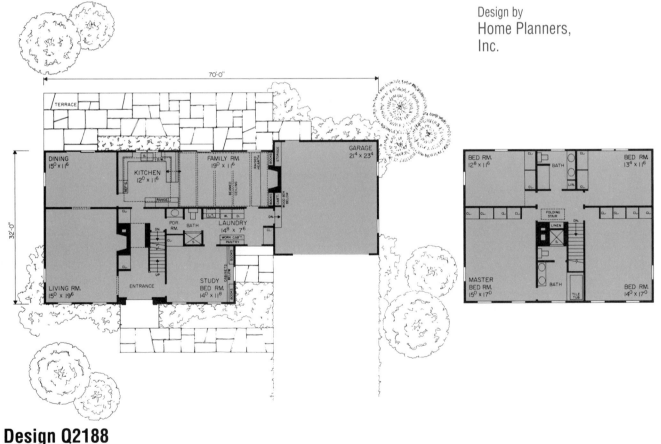

Design Q2188

First Floor: 1,440 square feet
Second Floor: 1,280 square feet
Total: 2,720 square feet

● This design is characteristic of early America and its presence will create an atmosphere of that time in our heritage. However, it will be right at home wherever located. Along with exterior charm, this design has outstanding livability to offer its occupants. Begin-ning with the first floor, there are for-mal and informal areas plus the work centers. Note the center bath which has direct access from three adjacent areas. Built-in book shelves are the feature of both the family room and the study/bedroom. Built-ins are also featured in the garage. Ascending up to the second floor, one will be in the private sleeping area. This area con-sists of the master suite, three bed-rooms and full bath. Folding stairs are in the upstairs hall for easy access to the attic.

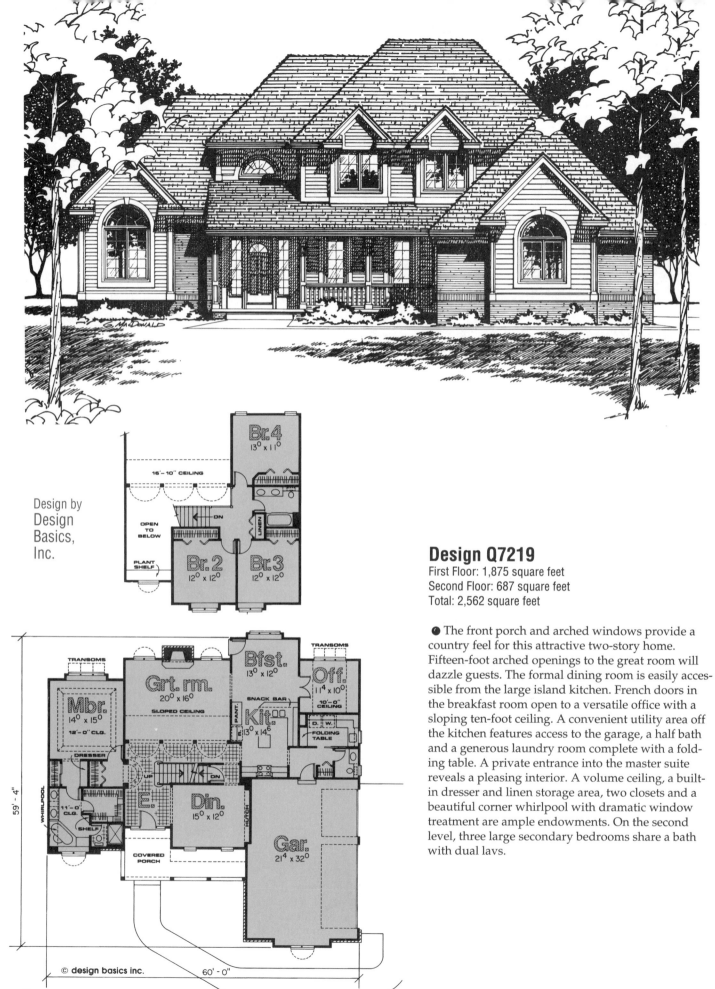

Design by
Design
Basics,
Inc.

Br. 4
13⁰ x 11⁰

16'-10" CEILING

OPEN
TO
BELOW

DN

LINEN

PLANT
SHELF

Br. 2
12⁰ x 12⁰

Br. 3
12⁰ x 12⁰

Design Q7219

First Floor: 1,875 square feet
Second Floor: 687 square feet
Total: 2,562 square feet

● The front porch and arched windows provide a
country feel for this attractive two-story home.
Fifteen-foot arched openings to the great room will
dazzle guests. The formal dining room is easily accessible from the large island kitchen. French doors in
the breakfast room open to a versatile office with a
sloping ten-foot ceiling. A convenient utility area off
the kitchen features access to the garage, a half bath
and a generous laundry room complete with a folding table. A private entrance into the master suite
reveals a pleasing interior. A volume ceiling, a built-
in dresser and linen storage area, two closets and a
beautiful corner whirlpool with dramatic window
treatment are ample endowments. On the second
level, three large secondary bedrooms share a bath
with dual lavs.

TRANSOMS

TRANSOMS

Grt. rm.
20⁰ x 16⁰

Bfst.
13⁰ x 12⁰

Off.
11⁴ x 10⁰

Mbr.
14⁰ x 15⁰

12'-0" CLG.

SLOPED CEILING

SNACK BAR

Kit.
13⁰ x 14⁶

PANT.

10'-0"
CEILING

D. W.

DRESSER

FOLDING
TABLE

WHIRLPOOL

11'-0"
CLG.

SHELF

UP

DN

Din.
15⁰ x 12⁰

HUTCH

Gar.
21⁴ x 32⁰

COVERED
PORCH

59'-4"

© design basics inc.

60'-0"

98

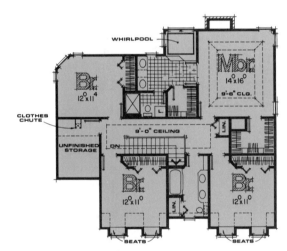

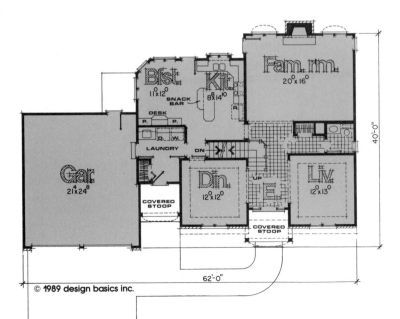

© 1989 design basics inc.

Design Q9301

First Floor: 1,279 square feet
Second Floor: 1,241 square feet
Total: 2,520 square feet

● Colonial flavor is evident on the elevation of this four-bedroom, two-story home. A separate service entry with a closet directly accesses the laundry/mud room. Entertaining will be enjoyable in the formal dining and living rooms. In the large family room, there is a beautiful segmented arched transom window and fireplace. Nearby is the island kitchen with snack bar, built-in desk, two generous pantries and sunny dinette. On the second level, two front secondary bedrooms feature window seats. Adjacent to a third secondary bedroom is an unfinished storage area. Two lavs grace the large hall bath. A vaulted master bedroom with His and Hers closets has double doors leading into a dressing room. This area contains a large whirlpool and two lavs. At 2,520 square feet, many family-style amenities are designed into this home.

Design by
Design
Basics,
Inc.

BED RM.
$11^0 \times 10^0$

VAN.

BATH

W.I.C.

WHIRLPOOL

S.

CL.

CL.

DN

LIN.

MASTER BED RM.
$11^4 \times 14^0$

BATH

STOR.

BED RM.
$10^4 \times 12^4$

CL.

CLG. CLIP

CLG. CLIP

QUOTE ONE™

Cost to build? See page 214
to order complete cost estimate
to build this house in your area!

Design Q3571

First Floor: 964 square feet
Second Floor: 783 square feet
Total: 1,747 square feet

L **D**

● For those interested in both
traditional charm and modern
convenience, this Cape Cod
fits the bill. Enter the foyer
and find a quiet study to the
left, a living room with a fireplace to the right. Straight
ahead: the kitchen and breakfast room with terrace access.
The island countertop affords
lots of room for meal preparation. A lazy Susan guarantees
easy storage and access of
kitchenware. The dining room
is conveniently located off the
breakfast room and enjoys formal space with the living
room. The service entry introduces a laundry and powder
room. Upstairs, the master
bedroom spoils with its
secluded bath—a whirlpool
tub is just one of the amenities
found here. Two additional
bedrooms complete the second floor. Each one partakes
in a full hall bath.

48'-0"

32'-0"

PDR. RM.

KIT.
$9^0 \times 11^8$

BRKFST. RM.
$8^0 \times 11^8$

DINING RM.
$10^0 \times 11^8$

S.

DW.

RANGE

CL.

SER. ENT.

D.

W.

P'TRY

REF'G.

DN

CL.

CURB

GARAGE
$13^8 \times 23^4$

STUDY
$11^4 \times 12^4$

FOYER

UP

LIVING RM.
$14^4 \times 15^0$

PORCH

Design by
Home Planners,
Inc.

Design Q1701 First Floor: 1,344 square feet
Second Floor: 948 square feet; Total: 2,292 square feet

D

● The garage wing of this Cape closely resembles the main dwelling: narrow clapboards, shutters and lintels over the multi-paned windows all match exactly. A narrow, shaded porch leads into the family room, which has twin bookcases framing the raised hearth as well as a rustic beamed ceiling. The study downstairs easily converts to a guest bedroom and is conveniently served by a bath that boasts its own shower. This bath opens to the back hall so that it can be reached easily from the back rooms in the house. Two of the upstairs bedrooms have both dressing rooms and walk-in closets. The secondary bedrooms can, like the master bedroom, be opened up into one commodious room by removing the wall in between them.

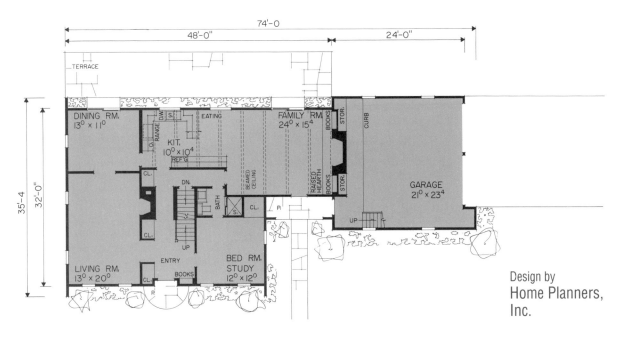

Design by
Home Planners,
Inc.

Design Q3505

First Floor: 2,899 square feet
Second Floor: 1,519 square feet
Total: 4,418 square feet
Bonus Room: 540 square feet

L

● A sweeping veranda with tapered columns supports the low-pitched roof and its delicately detailed cornice work. The wood railing effectively complements the lattice-work below. Horizontal siding and double-hung windows with muntins and shutters enhance the historic appeal of this 1½-story home. Inside, the spacious central foyer has a high ceiling and a dramatic, curving staircase to the second floor. Two formal areas flank the foyer and include the living room to the left and the dining room to the right. The U-shaped kitchen easily services the latter through a butler's pantry. A library and gathering room flank the kitchen and will delight the family. Sleeping accommodations excel with a spacious master suite. Here, a private bath and two closets—one a walk-in—guarantee satisfaction. At the top of the dramatic staircase to the second floor is a generous sitting area which looks down on the foyer. Three bedrooms are directly accessible from this area. A bonus room further enhances this fabulous family home.

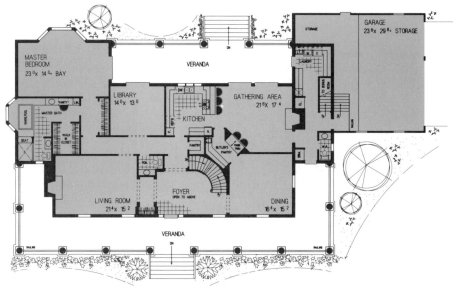

Width 108'-2"
Depth 62'-10"

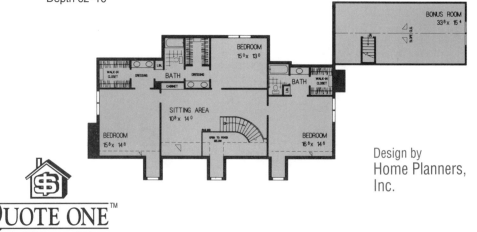

Design by
Home Planners,
Inc.

QUOTE ONE™

Cost to build? See page 214
to order complete cost estimate
to build this house in your area!

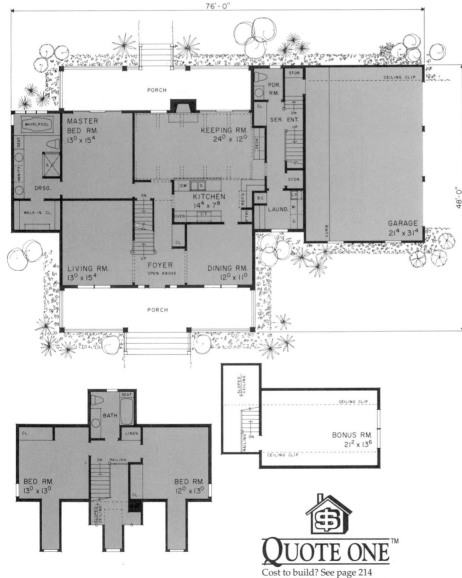

Design Q3566

First Floor: 1,635 square feet
Second Floor: 586 square feet
Total: 2,221 square feet
Bonus Room: 321 square feet

L **D**

● Don't be fooled by the humble appearance of this farmhouse. All the amenities abound. Covered porches are located to both the front and rear of the home. A grand front entrance opens into living and dining rooms. The family will surely enjoy the ambience of the keeping room with its fireplace and beamed ceiling. A service entry, with laundry nearby, separates the garage from the main house. An over-the-garage bonus room allows for room to grow or a nice study. Two quaint bedrooms and full bath make up the second floor. Each bedroom features a lovely dormer window.

Quote One™

Cost to build? See page 214 to order complete cost estimate to build this house in your area!

Design by
Home Planners, Inc.

Enhanced Plan

Design Q3702

First Floor: 850 square feet
Second Floor: 634 square feet
Total: 1,484 square feet

● An abundance of livability, together with ultimate affordability, is in this charming two-story, traditional home. The three bedrooms include a master bedroom with private bath. A full bath serves the two family bedrooms, while a powder room is located off the foyer. A formal dining room separates the kitchen and living room. A box bay window may be included in the dining room and a second bay window and fireplace are options in the living room. When the family room, porch and garage options are added to this great house, it takes on the appearance of a charming country estate.

   The highlighted areas of this floor plan are enhancements to the basic plan. The blueprints for this house show how to build both the basic, low-cost version, and the enhanced, upgraded version.

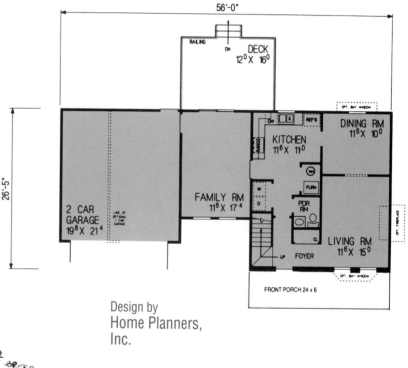

Design by
Home Planners,
Inc.

Basic Plan

Design Q1956 First Floor: 990 square feet
Second Floor: 728 square feet; Total: 1,718 square feet

D

Design by
Home Planners,
Inc.

QUOTE ONE™

Cost to build? See page 214
to order complete cost estimate
to build this house in your area!

● Simple, functional, and loaded with Colonial appeal, this versatile two-story plan features the finest in family floor plans. To the right of the entry foyer, a large formal living area connects to the dining room, allowing adequate space for entertaining in style. The U-shaped kitchen features a pass-through counter to the breakfast room. The sunken family room is enhanced by a beamed ceiling, raised-hearth fireplace and built-in bookshelves. Upstairs are four bedrooms (or choose the three-bedroom option included in the blueprint package). Other highlights of the plan include a full-length rear terrace and storage space galore. For information on customizing this design, call 1-800-521-6797, ext. 800.

Three-Bedroom Option

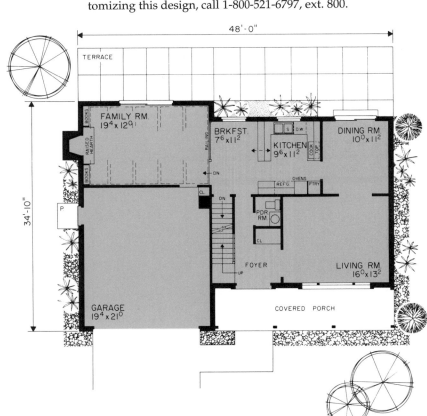

Design Q9239

First Floor: 998 square feet
Second Floor: 1,206 square feet
Total: 2,204 square feet

● The bright entry of this two-story home opens to formal living and dining space. To the back is the more informal family room with fireplace and built-in bookshelves. An island kitchen features a corner sink, pantry and convenient planning desk. Upstairs, the master bedroom has a vaulted ceiling and sumptuous master bath with skylit dressing area, whirlpool tub, and walk-in closet. Three family bedrooms and a full bath round out sleeping accommodations. Note the laundry area on the second floor as well.

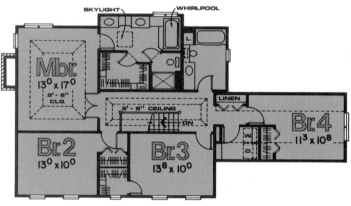

Design by
Design Basics, Inc.

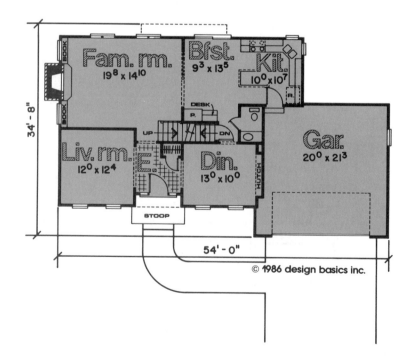

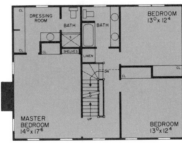
49'-8"

TERRACE

DINING RM
12⁰ x 9⁶+ BAY

BREAKFAST RM
11⁶ x 11⁶

KITCHEN
11⁶ x 11⁶

CURB

GARAGE
13⁴ x 21⁴

32'-0"

DESK

OVEN

MUD ROOM

WASH
RM

DN

LIVING RM.
14⁰ x 17⁶

FOYER

STUDY
10⁸ x 9⁸

CL

PORCH

Design Q2659 First Floor: 1,023 square feet
Second Floor: 1,008 square feet; Third Floor: 476 square feet Total: 2,507 square feet

L **D**

● The facade of this three-storied, pitch-roofed house has a symmetrical placement of windows and a restrained but elegant central entrance. The central hall, or foyer, expands midway through
the house to a family kitchen. Off the foyer are two rooms, a living room with fireplace and a study. The windowed third floor
attic can be used as a study and studio. Three bedrooms are
housed on the second floor.

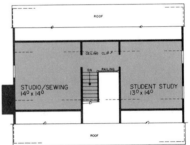

CL

DRESSING
ROOM

BATH

BATH

BEDROOM
13⁰ x 12⁴

CL

SHELVES

LINEN

CL

CL

DN

UP

MASTER
BEDROOM
14⁰ x 17⁶

BEDROOM
13⁰ x 12⁴

ROOF

CEILING CLG.

ON

RAILING

STUDIO/SEWING
14⁰ x 14⁰

STUDENT STUDY
13⁰ x 14⁰

ROOF

Design by
Home Planners,
Inc.

Design Q3600/Q3601

Square Footage: 2,258/2,424

L

● This unique one-story plan seems tailor-made for a small family or for empty-nesters. Formal areas are situated well for entertaining—living room to the right and formal dining room to the left. A large family room is found to the rear. It has access to a rear wood deck and is warmed in the cold months by a welcome hearth. The U-shaped kitchen features an attached morning room for casual meals. It is near the laundry and a washroom. Bedrooms are split. The master suite sits to the right of the plan and has a walk-in closet and a fine bath. A nearby study has a private porch. One family bedroom is on the other side of the home and also has a private bath. If needed the plan can also be built with a third bedroom sharing the bath. For information on customizing this design, call 1-800-521-6797, ext. 800.

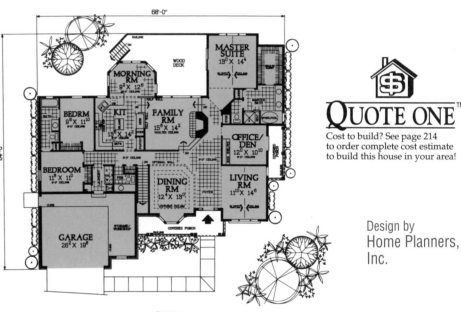

Q3601

Q3600

QUOTE ONE™

Cost to build? See page 214 to order complete cost estimate to build this house in your area!

Design by
Home Planners, Inc.

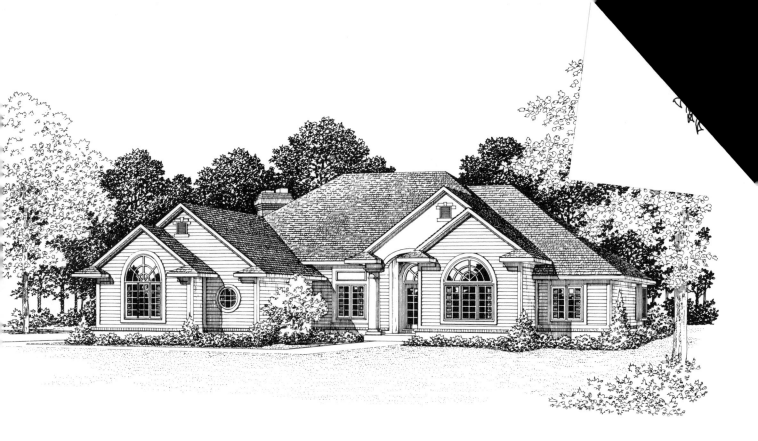

Design Q3327

Square Footage: 2,881

L **D**

● The high, massive hipped roof of this home creates an imposing facade while varying roof planes and projecting gables enhance appeal. A central, high-ceilinged foyer routes traffic efficiently to the sleeping, formal and informal zones of the house. Note the sliding glass doors that provide access to outdoor living facilities. A built-in china cabinet and planter unit are fine decor features. In the angular kitchen, a high ceiling and efficient work patterning set the pace. The conversation room may act as a multi-purpose room. For TV time, a media room caters to audio-visual activities. Sleeping quarters take off with the spacious master bedroom; here you'll find a tray ceiling and sliding doors to the rear yard. An abundance of wall space for effective and flexible furniture arrangement further characterizes the room. Two sizable bedrooms serve the children. For information on customizing this design, call 1-800-521-6797, ext. 800.

Width 77'-11"
Depth 73'-11"

Design by
Home Planners, Inc.

QUOTE ONE™
Cost to build? See page 214 to order complete cost estimate to build this house in your area!

Design Q9303

First Floor: 1,428 square feet
Second Floor: 1,304 square feet
Total: 2,732 square feet

● Nine-foot main level walls are a nice feature not readily apparent in the design of this popular Colonial home. Comfortable traffic patterns segregate formal and informal living spaces. To the left of the spacious two-story entry is a formal dining room with hutch space. Sunny windows bring light into the living room and throughout the whole home. The built-in bookcases in a generous family room can easily be converted to a wet bar. Highlights of the island kitchen/breakfast area are a wraparound counter, planning desk, walk-in pantry and a butler pantry. Upstairs, secondary bedrooms are served by a compartmented hall bath with double lavs. The large master suite sports a vaulted ceiling, His and Hers closets, corner whirlpool and double vanity with makeup counter.

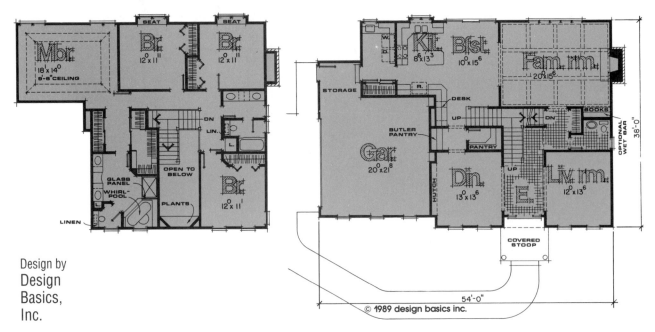

Design by
Design Basics, Inc.

© 1989 design basics inc.

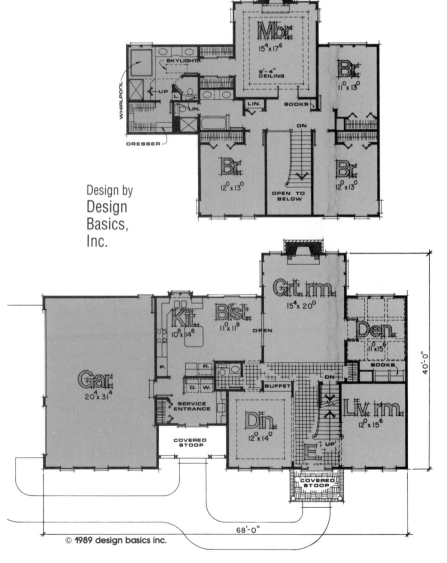

Design Q9302

First Floor: 1,536 square feet
Second Floor: 1,343 square feet
Total: 2,879 square feet

● A delightful elevation will be appreciated by anyone aspiring to live in Colonial comfort. Three arches encompass the covered porch at the service entry to mud/laundry room. Inside, bright windows shed sunlight into the formal dining room with serving buffet. To the right of the elegant two-story entry is the living room. Sparkling French doors access the private den with bookcases from the spacious great room. In the roomy island kitchen, cooks will enjoy the built-in pantry and breakfast area. Be sure to notice the fireplace in the spacious master suite with three closets and a built-in dresser. A sophisticated skylit master bath has a two-person whirlpool and plant shelf. The compartmented bath upstairs has a separate tub and shower for the secondary bedrooms.

Design by
Design
Basics,
Inc.

Design by
Home Planners,
Inc.

Design Q3317 First Floor: 1,507 square feet
Second Floor: 976 square feet; Total: 2,483 square feet

● Fine family living takes off in this traditional design. Step onto the portico and into the foyer where a graceful drawing room gains attention. It is set a few steps down from the foyer and features a central fireplace and access to a rear garden terrace, thus making elegant entertaining a cinch. In the family room, another terrace supports outdoor enjoyments. The efficient kitchen features a double sink and a Lazy Susan. Upstairs, three bedrooms include a master bedroom with its own bath. The two secondary bedrooms enjoy the use of a full bath with dual lavatories.

Design Q3472 First Floor: 1,532 square feet; Second Floor: 1,168 square feet; Total: 2,700 square feet

● This stately two-story home makes a grand first impression with its columned front entry and varying roof planes. Inside, the gracious foyer opens to a study on the left and a living room and dining room on the right. The spacious kitchen includes a work island and an open breakfast area. An expansive family room is just a step down from the kitchen and features a sloped ceiling and a raised hearth.

From here, a rear deck opens up to provide superb outdoor livability. Another deck opens off the breakfast nook, perfect for outdoor meals. Upstairs, four bedrooms include a master bedroom suite with a walk-in closet, a built-in vanity and a private whirlpool bath. All of the secondary bedrooms enjoy ample closet space. A full hall bath with dual lavatories is conveniently located to these bedrooms.

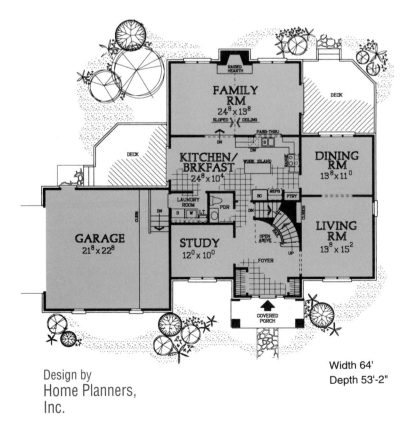

Design by
Home Planners,
Inc.

Width 64'
Depth 53'-2"

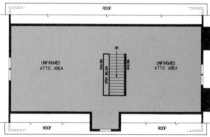

Design Q2998

First Floor: 2,243 square feet
Second Floor: 1,532 square feet
Total: 3,775 square feet

L **D**

● Symmetrical and simply lovely, this gambrel-roofed two-story is a fine example of historical homes. Its details will enchant the most particular enthusiast of early architecture. The floor plan is a classic as well. Note the formal dining and living rooms flanking the entry hall. The living room has a fireplace and the dining room a bay window. A media room/study also sports a fireplace and has access to a rear terrace. The family room connects to the kitchen via a through snack bar. There's also another fireplace here. On the second floor are three bedrooms and two full baths. The third floor contains unfinished space which acts as superb storage and can be developed later into more bedrooms if needed.

Design by
Home Planners,
Inc.

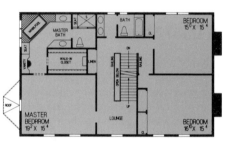

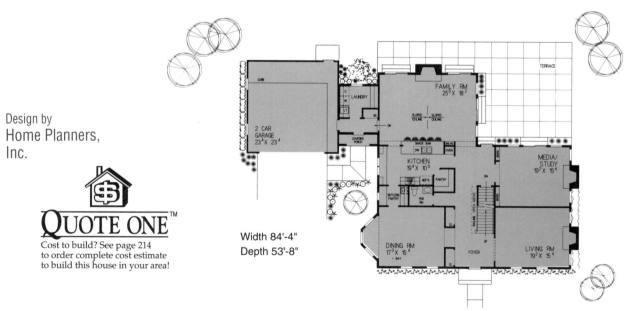

Width 84'-4"
Depth 53'-8"

Design Q2538

First Floor: 1,503 square feet
Second Floor: 1,095 square feet; Total: 2,598 square feet

L **D**

● This SaltBox is charming, indeed. The livability it has to offer to the large and growing family is great. The entry is spacious and is open to the second floor balcony. For living areas, there is the study in addition to the living and family rooms. The large kitchen has an island range and attached nook with sliding glass doors to the terrace. The master suite, on the second floor, has its own fireplace and a large walk-in closet in the dressing area. Three more bedrooms share a full bath.

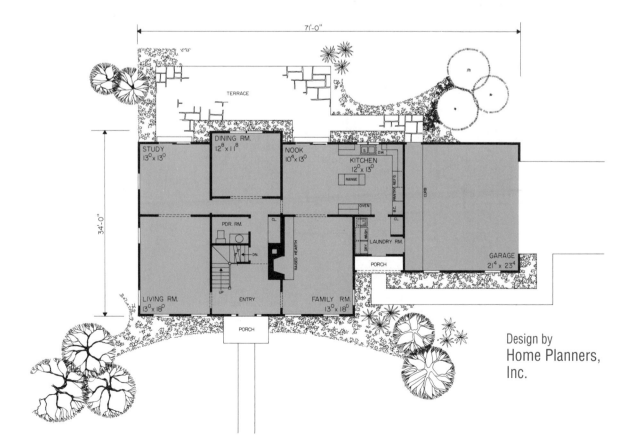

Design by
Home Planners,
Inc.

Design Q9299

First Floor: 2,063 square feet
Second Floor: 894 square feet
Total: 2,957 square feet

● An elegant brick elevation and rows of shuttered windows lend timeless beauty to this 1½-story Colonial design. The volume entry surveys formal dining and living rooms and the magnificent great room. Sparkling floor-to-ceiling windows flank the fireplace in the great room with a cathedral ceiling. French doors, bayed windows and a decorative ceiling, plus a wet bar highlight the private den. Special lifestyle amenities in the kitchen and bayed breakfast area include a built-in desk, wrapping counters and island. A boxed ceiling adds elegance to the master suite. In the master bath/dressing area, note the large walk-in closet, built-in dresser, His and Hers vanities, oval whirlpool and plant shelves. Each secondary bedroom upstairs has a roomy closet and private bath.

Quote One ®

Cost to build? See page 214
to order complete cost estimate
to build this house in your area!

EUROPEAN-INSPIRED FARMHOUSES

Centuries before coming to the New World, Europeans enjoyed farmhouse styles that were uniquely their own. Built originally of simple materials, these dwellings were functional, cozy and sturdy. They also reflected the distinct design bent of the country in which they were found, particularly with regard to rooflines. French country houses had the classic hipped roof so favored in that region; the Dutch maintained gambrel roofs; and the English added gabled roofs (often thatched) to their cottages. Each group incorporated design details that blended to charming result in the European-Inspired Farmhouse.

These homes are a development of European styles and influences imposed on basic American farmhouse structure. They represent an adaptation of those homes found in the countrysides of France, Germany, Holland and other Western European nations.

In general, the European Farmhouse has a classic, upright two-story stature. Like their historic equivalents, these homes may be characterized most easily by their roof types. While most are straight and gabled, they may vary to hipped versions in the French style or gambreled (or double-pitched) in the Flemish and Dutch tradition.

The windows, as well, echo European styling. Special details include metal-clad French bows and dormers, Dutch dormers protruding from the roof, Greek stone or brick arches over windows and doors, and the classic Palladian-style window grouping.

Siding on these homes is almost exclusively wood but may be accented with brick, stone or even stucco.

Among the European-Inspired Farmhouses in this section are some outstanding examples of the influences of various countries on the architectural details of the homes. Design Q9857, for instance, has many of the features of Country French homes: French bows with metal-clad roofs, a Palladian window and additional shuttered windows. Design Q9306 exudes more of a Modern French style with a strongly hipped roof and narrow, transommed windows. Dutch and Flemish design is apparent in Design Q2680 and Design Q9860. Both have gambrel roofs and twin chimney stacks, but Q9860 is sided almost entirely in stone while Q2680 sports only a stone fireplace.

All of the representative homes are alive with European country charm in conjunction with the best in up-to-date floor planning.

Copyright 1992 Stephen S. Fuller, Inc.

Design Q9870

First Floor: 2,155 square feet
Second Floor: 1,020 square feet
Total: 3,175 square feet

● To highlight the exterior of this home, wood siding and paneled shutters have been artfully combined with arched transoms, gables and a sweeping roof line to define the beautiful glass entry. The open foyer at once reveals the large living and dining rooms and a classic great room with coffered ceiling and hearth. Double doors open to the master bedroom with unique tray ceiling and fireplace. The master bath includes knee space with double vanities and shower, corner garden tub and His and Hers closets. The exercise room can be accessed from either the master bedroom or great room and opens onto the porch at the rear of the home. The generous corner breakfast area also opens to the porch. The large kitchen with a cook-top island, pantry and laundry room complete the main level. The gallery features built-in bookshelves and computer/study nook with easy access from all three bedrooms on the upper level. An unfinished bonus room with attic access offers room for expansion.

Design by
Design Traditions
Atlanta

WIDTH 62'
DEPTH 63'

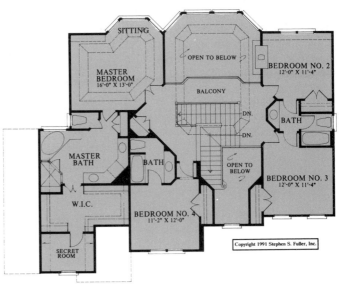

QUOTE ONE®
Cost to build? See page 214
to order complete cost estimate
to build this house in your area!

Design Q9869

First Floor: 1,475 square feet
Second Floor: 1,460 square feet
Total: 2,935 square feet

● This English country home of stucco and stone features elliptical keystone detailing and a covered entranceway. Through the columned entry, the two-story foyer opens to the living room with wet bar. The media room features a fireplace and is accessed from both the main hall and great room. A hall powder room and coat closet are located to the rear of the foyer. The two-story great room with fireplace is open to the breakfast area, kitchen and rear staircase, making entertaining a pleasure. The kitchen design is ideal with breakfast bar and preparation island and is conveniently located near the laundry room. The dining room with its elliptical window is ideal for formal entertaining. The upper level begins with the balcony landing overlooking the great room. The master bedroom features a bay-windowed sitting area and a tray ceiling. The master bath has dual vanities, a corner garden tub, separate shower, a large walk-in closet and an optional secret room. Across the balcony, Bedrooms 2 and 3 share a bath. Bedroom 4 in the front of the home has a private bath.

Design by
Design Traditions

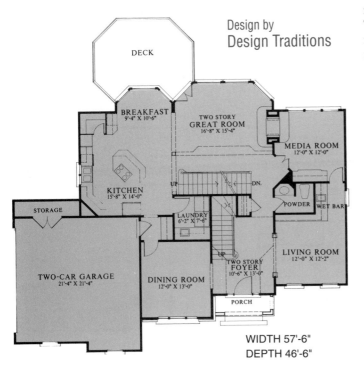

WIDTH 57'-6"
DEPTH 46'-6"

Design Q9855

Square Footage: 2,935

● A one-story plan for even a large family, this home provides all the necessities and many luxuries as well. For formal occasions, there's a grand dining room just off the entry foyer. It has a vaulted ceiling and is just across the hall from the gourmet kitchen. The great room has beautiful ceiling treatment and access to the rear deck. For more casual times, the breakfast nook and the adjoining keeping room with a fireplace fit the bill. The master suite is huge and contains every amenity. Its sitting room allows access to the rear deck. Note the gigantic walk-in closet here. Two family bedrooms share a full bath. Each of these bedrooms has its own lavatory. This home is designed with a basement foundation.

Design by
Design Traditions

Width 71'
Depth 66'

Design Q9963

First Floor: 1,407 square feet
Second Floor: 1,298 square feet
Total: 2,705 square feet

● Double doors provide entry into this fine traditional home. The living room with a bay window creates a delightful formal entertaining area. Through columns, the dining room remains open to this area for added possibilities. The kitchen satisfies with ample proportions and a nearby breakfast nook. In the family room, a warming hearth as well as a rear porch are sure to please. Three bedrooms reside upstairs with the master suite gaining a lot of attention. Spacious and elegant, it includes a sitting area and a roomy private bath. Also upstairs, a small alcove provides the perfect spot for reading. This home is designed with a basement foundation.

Design by
Design Traditions

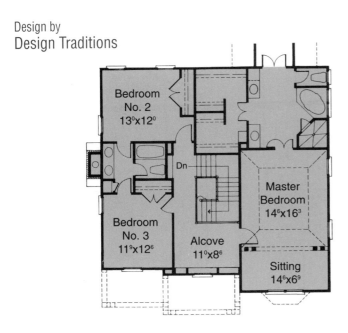

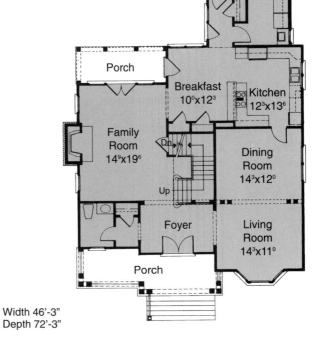

Width 46'-3"
Depth 72'-3"

Copyright 1992 Stephen S. Fuller, Inc.

Design Q9857

First Floor: 1,156 square feet
Second Floor: 1,239 square feet
Total: 2,395 square feet

● This Traditional home combines an attractive classic exterior with an open and sophisticated interior design. On approach, notice the use of brick and siding, Palladian and box bay windows, flower boxes and a covered entrance flanked by columns. The two-story foyer has a staircase to the left and a coat closet and powder room straight ahead. Proceeding right from the foyer are both the living and dining rooms with their individual window treatments. Entering the kitchen from the dining room is a corner butler pantry for added convenience while entertaining. The open design flows from the breakfast area to the family room with two large bay windows. The open foyer staircase leads to the upper level, beginning with the master suite. The bay window extends the eye beyond the attractive master bedroom. The master bath contains a luxurious tub, separate shower and dual vanities, as well as a large linen closet. A large walk-in master closet completes the suite. Bedroom 2 is inviting with its bay window and large closet. All three secondary bedrooms share a hall bath with separate vanity and bathing areas.

Design by
Design Traditions
Atlanta

Width 54'
Depth 39'-5"

Design Q9858 First Floor: 1,570 square feet
Second Floor: 1,630 square feet; Total: 3,200 square feet

● This classic Americana design employs wood siding, a variety of window styles, and a detailed front porch. Upon entry, the large two-story foyer flows into the formal dining room with arched window accents and the combination study and living room with a large bay window. A short passage with wet bar accesses the family room with a wall of windows, French doors and a fireplace. The large breakfast area and open kitchen with cooking island are spacious and airy as well as efficient. The walk-in pantry, laundry, and entry to the two-car garage complete this level. Upstairs, the master suite's sleeping and sitting room feature architectural details including columns, tray ceilings and a fireplace. The elegant master bath contains a raised oval tub, dual vanities and separate shower. Generous His and Hers closets are located beyond the bath. Additional bedrooms are complete with closets and a variety of bath combinations.

Design by
Design Traditions
Atlanta

40'-8"

59'-0"

COVERED
RETREAT
PATIO
SLOPED CLG

LIVING
RM
16⁸ x 14⁰
SLOPED CEILING

MASTER
SUITE
12⁶ x 14²
SLOPED CLG

TILE
HEARTH

KIT
10⁰ x 12²
9'-0" CLG

BREAKFAST
BAR

S   DW

REFG

BC

PANTRY

LOW WALL

DN

BATH

OPT.
DOOR

PLANT SHELF ABOVE

LINEN

LAUNDRY   W   D

WALK-IN
CLOSET

MASTER
BATH

WHIRLPOOL

SHELF

SHWR

DINING
RM
10⁰ x 11⁰
TRAY CLG

FOYER

MEDIA/
BEDRM
12⁶ x 11⁰
9'-0" CLG

PLANTER

COVERED
PORCH

SLPNG CLG

STEP

PLANTER

RAILING

RAILING

GARAGE
19⁸ x 21⁰

Design Q3442
Square Footage: 1,273

L D

● For those just starting out or the
empty-nester, this unique one-story
plan is sure to delight. A covered-
porch introduces a dining room with a
tray ceiling and views out two sides of
the house. The kitchen is just off this
room and is most efficient with a double sink, dishwasher and pantry. The
living room gains attention with a volume ceiling, fireplace and access to a
covered patio. The master bedroom
also features a volume ceiling while
enjoying the luxury of a private bath.
In it, a walk-in closet, washer/dryer,
double-bowl vanity, garden tub, separate shower and compartmented toilet
comprise the amenities. Not to be
overlooked, a second bedroom may
easily convert to a media room or
study–the choice is yours. For information on customizing this design,
call 1-800-521-6797, ext. 800.

Design by
Home Planners,
Inc.

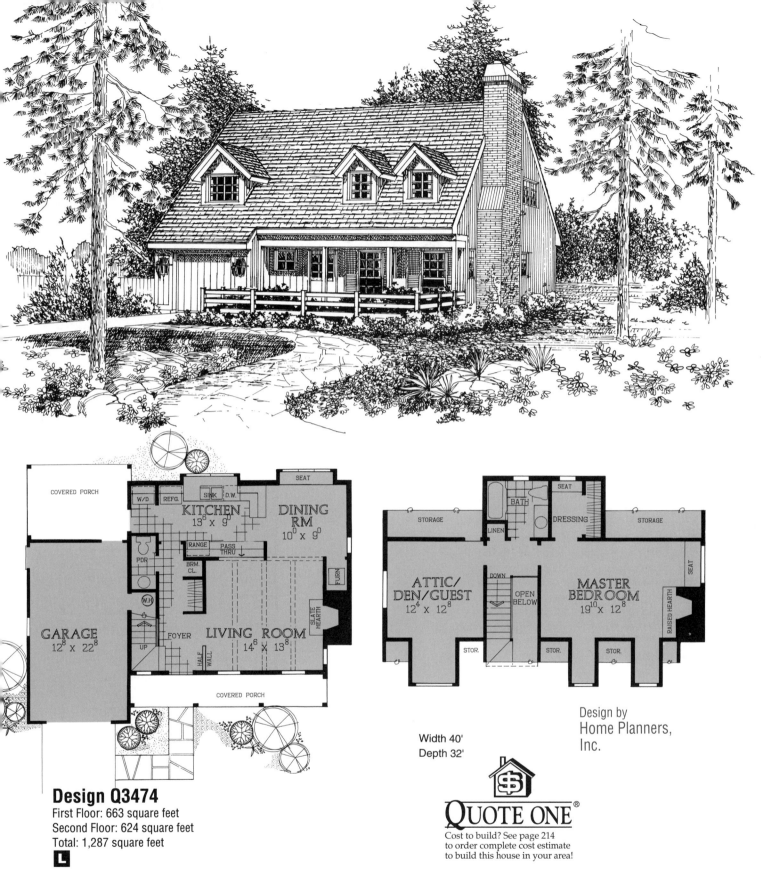

Design Q3474

First Floor: 663 square feet
Second Floor: 624 square feet
Total: 1,287 square feet

L

Width 40'
Depth 32'

Design by
Home Planners,
Inc.

QUOTE ONE®

Cost to build? See page 214
to order complete cost estimate
to build this house in your area!

● This rustic cabin is a delight. A spacious living room with a beam ceiling and warming fireplace greets you as you enter the foyer via the inviting covered porch. The adjoining dining room offers a picturesque window seat and convenience to the large kitchen with its window sink, pass-through to the living room and access to the powder room and rear covered porch. A roomy master bedroom featuring a fireplace and a walk-in closet with a seat and an attic den or guest room complete the second floor. Notice all the upstairs storage space available.

Design Q3481A

Square Footage: 1,091

L

● In just under 2,000 square feet, this pleasing one-story home bears all the livability of houses twice its size. A combined living and dining room offers elegance for entertaining; with two elevations to choose from, the living room can either support an octagonal bay or a bumped-out nook. The U-shaped kitchen finds easy access to the breakfast nook and rear family room; sliding glass doors lead from the family room to a back stoop. The master bedroom has a quaint potshelf and a private bath with a spa tub, a double-bowl vanity, a walk-in closet and a compartmented toilet. With two additional family bedrooms—one may serve as a den if desired—and a hall bath with dual lavatories, this plan offers the best in accommodations. Both elevations come with the blueprint package. For information on customizing this design, call 1-800-521-6797, ext. 800.

Quote One™

Cost to build? See page 214
to order complete cost estimate
to build this house in your area!

[Floor plan with rooms labeled: FAMILY RM VAULTED CLG 13² x 18⁴, MASTER BEDRM VAULTED CLG 13⁸ x 14⁸, MASTER BATH VAULT CLG, PLANT SELF ABOVE, LINEN, OVAL TUB, WALK-IN CLOSET, SNACK BAR, DW, BATH, BEDRM VAULTED CLG 13⁸ x 10⁰, KIT 13² x 12⁰, REF, LINEN, BEDRM/DEN VAULTED CLG 13⁸ x 11⁴, DINING, LAUNDRY, D W, F.A.U., LIVING RM VAULTED CLG 14⁶ x 27⁰, COFFERED CLG, ENTRY, COVERED PORCH, CURB, GARAGE 20⁰ x 21⁰]

Width 42'-4"
Depth 63'-10"

Design Q3481B

Square Footage: 1,908

L

Design by
**Home Planners,
Inc.**

126

Design Q3460

Square Footage: 1,389

L

● A double dose of charm, this special farmhouse plan offers two elevations in its blueprint package—one showcases a delightful wraparound porch. Though rooflines and porch options are different, the floor plan is basically the same and very livable. A formal living room has a warming fireplace and a delightful bay window. The kitchen separates this area from the more casual family room. In the kitchen, you'll find an efficient snack bar and a pantry for additional storage space. Three bedrooms include two family bedrooms served by a full bath and a lovely master suite with its own private bath. Notice the location of the washer and dryer—convenient to all of the bedrooms. For information on customizing this design, call 1-800-521-6797, ext. 800. California Engineered Plans and California Stock Plans are available for this home. Call 1-800-521-6797 for more information.

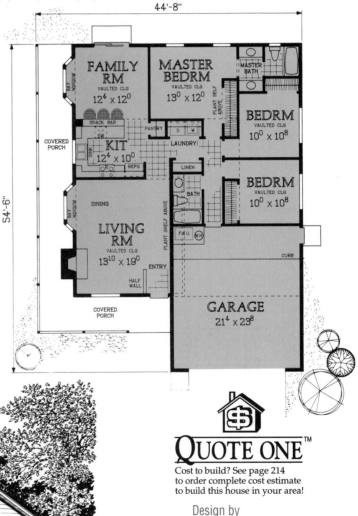

44'-8"

54'-6"

FAMILY RM
VAULTED CLG
12⁴ x 12⁰

MASTER BEDRM
VAULTED CLG
13⁰ x 12⁰

MASTER BATH

BEDRM
VAULTED CLG
10⁰ x 10⁸

SNACK BAR

PANTRY

KIT
12⁴ x 10⁰

LAUNDRY

COVERED PORCH

LINEN

BATH

BEDRM
VAULTED CLG
10⁰ x 10⁸

DINING

LIVING RM
VAULTED CLG
13¹⁰ x 19⁰

ENTRY

HALF WALL

CURB

GARAGE
21⁴ x 23⁸

COVERED PORCH

Quote One™

Cost to build? See page 214 to order complete cost estimate to build this house in your area!

Design by
Home Planners, Inc.

Design Q3507

First Floor: 1,360 square feet
Second Floor: 1,172 square feet
Total: 2,532 square feet

L

QUOTE ONE™

Cost to build? See page 214
to order complete cost estimate
to build this house in your area!

● After a brisk walk to the creek for some fly fishing or an invigorating day of raking leaves, enjoy some spiced hot apple cider by one of the four fireplaces highlighted in this delightful farmhouse. Leading inside is an elevated front entrance with a dual set of steps, an appealing patterned railing and a muntined door flanked by carriage lamps, all of which projects an engaging image of the raised cottage so popular in the South. To the left of the foyer is the formal living room with a corner fireplace. To the right is a formal dining room which also enjoys a fireplace. Open planning is the byword of the spacious family living area. An efficient kitchen possesses a cooking island, a snack bar, a planning desk and a breakfast area with access to the veranda. Twin pillars support an archway opening to the large family room which is enhanced by yet another fireplace. The expansive master bedroom is complemented by a sitting area and a warming fireplace. A luxurious master bath offers a vanity flanked by twin lavatories, a whirlpool bath, a shower and a large walk-in closet.

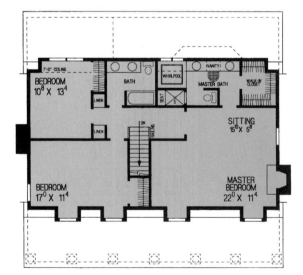

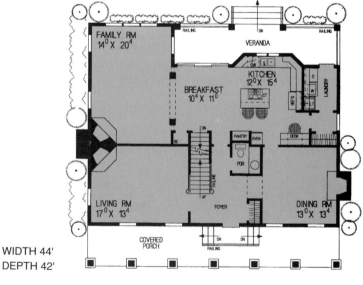

WIDTH 44'
DEPTH 42'

Design by
Home Planners,
Inc.

Design Q3495

First Floor: 1,457 square feet
Second Floor: 1,288 square feet
Total: 2,745 square feet

L **D**

● The very best in modern design comes into play with this extraordinary two-story home. Columns and half walls define the formal living and dining rooms—a curved niche adds appeal to the latter. Beyond the centrally located stair-case, the family room extends to its occupants a sloped ceiling, and an angled corner fireplace. At the other side of the house, the bright breakfast area—adjacent to the kitchen—enjoys the use of a patio. In the kitchen, an abundance of counter and storage space sets the stage for convenient food preparation. Notice, too, the powder room nestled between the kitchen and the laundry room. Two full bathrooms grace the upstairs: one in the master suite includes a soaking tub and separate shower; one in the hallway serves the three secondary bedrooms. For information on customizing this design, call 1-800-521-6797, ext. 800.

Design by
Home Planners,
Inc.

Width 42'
Depth 63'-4"

Cost to build? See page 214
to order complete cost estimate
to build this house in your area!

129

Design Q9305

Square Footage: 2,015

● Romantic appeal radiates from the elegant covered porch and gracious features of this ranch home. A formal dining room with bright windows is viewed from the entry. In the great room, featuring an entertainment center and bookcases, warmth emanates from the three-sided through-fireplace. Homeowners will enjoy the cozy retreat of the bay-windowed hearth room with 10-foot ceiling. Near the hearth is an open breakfast area and kitchen with snack bar, pantry and ample counter space. A window seat framed by closets highlights secondary Bedroom 2. The third bedroom easily converts to an optional den for quiet study. Designed for privacy, the master suite enjoys a boxed ceiling, skylit dressing area with His and Hers lavs, corner whirlpool and large walk-in closet. With many dramatic elements, this will be the home of your dreams!

Design by
**Design
Basics,
Inc.**

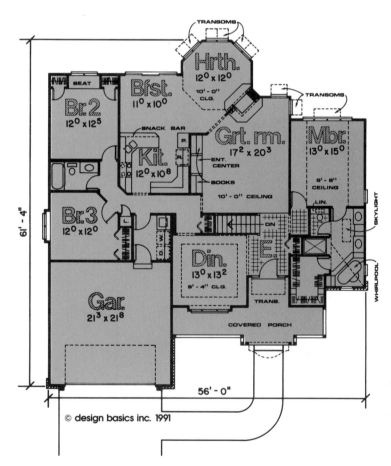

© design basics inc. 1991

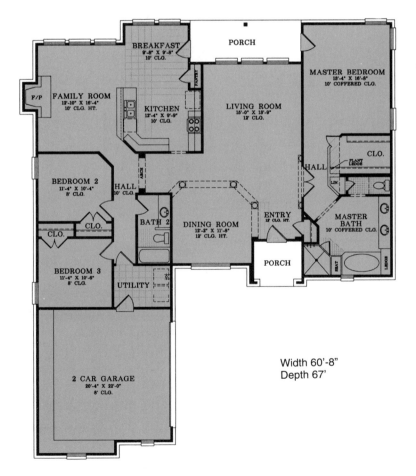

Width 60'-8"
Depth 67'

Design Q8113
Square Footage: 2,279

● Gracious living patterns characterize this one-story home. The front porch gives way to an entry that views the formal living and dining rooms. Columns define the dining room and a Palladian window illuminates it. For casual living, the kitchen and the breakfast room are open to the family room. A fireplace and three windows warm this room. Two secondary bedrooms include ample closet space and share a full hall bath. In the master bedroom, a large walk-in closet and a private bath are sure to please. Dual lavatories, a separate shower and a garden tub are set beneath a coffered ceiling. Please specify crawlspace or slab foundation when ordering.

Design by
Larry E. Belk
Designs

Design Q9306

First Floor: 1,268 square feet
Second Floor: 1,075 square feet
Total: 2,343 square feet

● Captivating! A covered front porch hints at the comfort within. An added perk is the large 3-car garage. Formal rooms are surveyed by the entry. To the right, a volume ceiling, elegant windows and through-fireplace lend atmosphere to the living room. A volume family room includes repeating arched windows, an entertainment center and bookcases. The sunny dinette area is served by a roomy kitchen with wrapping counters, snack bar and planning desk. Convenience was designed into the main floor utility/laundry room and large closet. Upstairs, comfortable secondary bedrooms are served by a walk-in linen closet and bath with dual lavs. French doors lead into the master suite with vaulted ceiling, whirlpool, dual vanities and a huge walk-in closet.

Design by
Design
Basics,
Inc.

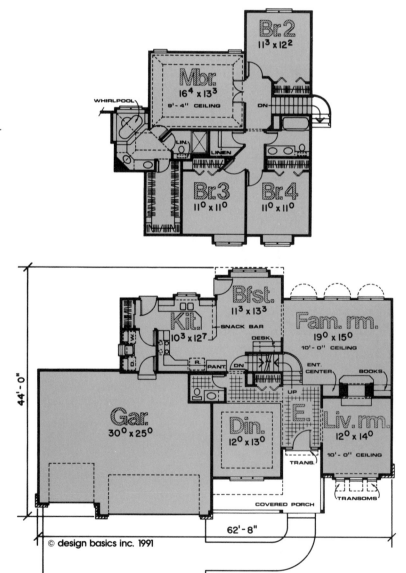

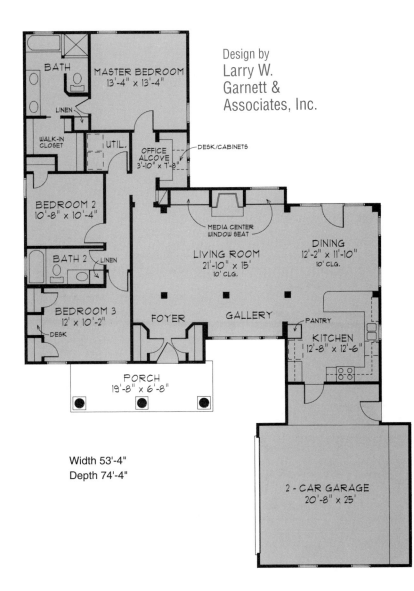

BATH

MASTER BEDROOM
13'-4" x 13'-4"

LINEN

WALK-IN CLOSET

UTIL.

OFFICE ALCOVE
3'-10" x 7'-8"

DESK/CABINETS

BEDROOM 2
10'-8" x 10'-4"

BATH 2

LINEN

MEDIA CENTER
WINDOW SEAT

DINING
12'-2" x 11'-10"
10' CLG.

LIVING ROOM
21'-10" x 15'
10' CLG.

BEDROOM 3
12' x 10'-2"

DESK

FOYER

GALLERY

PANTRY

KITCHEN
12'-8" x 12'-6"

PORCH
19'-8" x 6'-8"

2 - CAR GARAGE
20'-8" x 25'

Width 53'-4"
Depth 74'-4"

Design by
Larry W. Garnett & Associates, Inc.

Design Q9191
Square Footage: 1,672

● Amenities abound in this one-story home. The columned front porch makes it eye-catching while the combination living room and dining room and the efficient kitchen make it ideal for entertaining. The focal point in the living room is the central fireplace flanked by window seats with a media center above while the gallery opposite is a perfect place to show off family portraits. The U-shaped kitchen provides access to the garage and plenty of storage space. The master bedroom is located at the back of the house for privacy and features a full bath with dual lavs, a walk-in closet and an adjacent office alcove with a built-in desk and cabinet. Two other bedrooms share a full hall bath. Notice the convenient utility area.

Design Q3608

First Floor: 2,347 square feet
Second Floor: 1,087 square feet
Total: 3,434 square feet

L

● Dutch gable roof lines and a gabled wraparound porch with star-burst trim matching the star-burst clerestory window on the center dormer make this a farmhouse with style! The clerestory window sheds radiant light on the U-shaped stairway leading from the foyer to the upstairs family bedrooms and loft. Downstairs, the foyer opens to all areas of the home, from the study or guest bedroom on the left that leads to the master suite, to the formal dining room on the right and to the massive great room in the center of the home. A large fireplace in the great room provides a cozy centerpiece for gathering and entertaining. The kitchen is convenient to the great room, the breakfast nook and the dining room and features an island cooktop and an interesting snack bar and work area combination. The luxurious master suite includes access to the covered patio, a spacious walk-in closet and a master bath with a whirlpool tub, a separate shower, a compartmented toilet and a double-bowl vanity.

Design by
**Home Planners,
Inc.**

QUOTE ONE®

Cost to build? See page 214 to order complete cost estimate to build this house in your area!

Width 93'-6"
Depth 61'

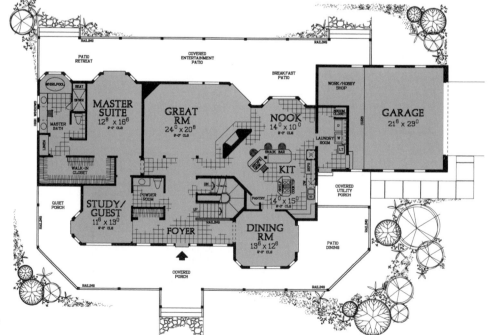

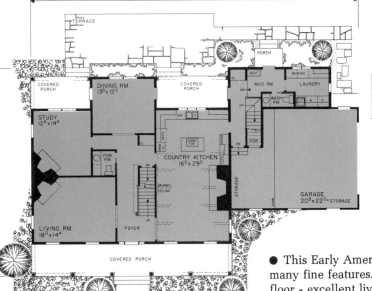

Design Q2680 First Floor: 1,707 square feet
Second Floor: 1,439 square feet; Total: 3,146 square feet

L D

● This Early American, Dutch Colonial not only has charm, but offers many fine features. The foyer allows easy access to all rooms on the first floor - excellent livability. Note the large country kitchen with beamed ceiling, fireplace and island cook top. A large, formal dining room and powder room are only a few steps away. A fireplace also will be found in the study and living room. The service area, mud room, wash room and laundry are tucked near the garage. Two bedrooms, full bath and master bedroom suite will be found on the second floor. A fourth bedroom and bath are accessible through the master bedroom or stairs in the service entrance.

Design by
Home Planners,
Inc.

Design Q9956

First Floor: 1,787 square feet
Second Floor: 851 square feet
Total: 2,638 square feet
Bonus Room: 189 square feet

● This beautiful brick design displays fine family livability in over 2,600 square feet. The wraparound porch welcomes family and friends to inside living areas. The great room sports an elegant ceiling, a fireplace and built-ins. The kitchen displays good traffic patterning. An island cooktop will please the house gourmet. The dining room features double doors that open out onto the porch. In the master bedroom, a pampering bath includes a whirlpool tub and separate vanities. A walk-in closet is located at the back of the bath. Two family bedrooms enjoy peace and quiet and a full hall bath with natural illumination. This home is designed with a basement foundation.

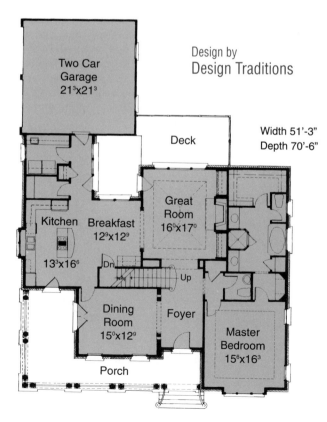

Design by
Design Traditions

Width 51'-3"
Depth 70'-6"

Two Car Garage 21³x21³
Deck
Kitchen 13³x16⁶
Breakfast 12⁹x12⁹
Great Room 16⁰x17⁰
Dn
Up
Dining Room 15⁰x12⁹
Foyer
Master Bedroom 15⁶x16³
Porch

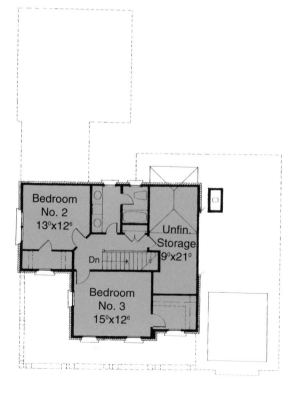

Bedroom No. 2 13⁰x12⁶
Unfin. Storage 9⁰x21⁰
Dn
Bedroom No. 3 15⁰x12⁶

Design Q9860

First Floor: 1,530 square feet
Second Floor: 1,515 square feet
Total: 3,045 square feet

Design by
Design Traditions
Atlanta

● The Country French charm of this home is irresistible; with gambrel roof, combined use of stone and wood, and segmented stone arch window detailing. The two-story foyer with staircase and tray ceiling gives a first impression of space and style. The large living and dining rooms are complemented by large window areas, a fireplace and detailed columns. The art of cooking is emphasized in the kitchen, with a work island and charming breakfast room that opens into a large family room with fireplace and wet bar. A second staircase from the family room allows easy access to the upper level. Touring the upper level, the hallway leads to additional bedrooms, both with large closets and a shared bath. A fourth bedroom has a walk-in closet and private bath. The master suite includes a large bay-windowed sitting area, a luxurious master bath and an extensive walk-in closet, as well as a perfectly located exercise room or hideaway.

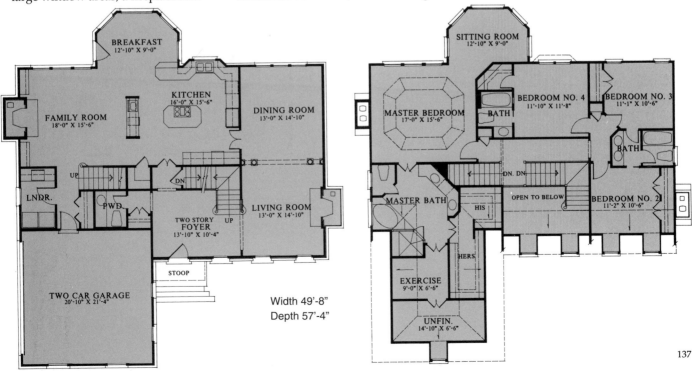

Width 49'-8"
Depth 57'-4"

BEDRM 15⁴ x 11⁸

BEDRM 11⁶ x 11⁰

BATH

LINEN

DN

COVERED PORCH

MASTER BEDRM 13⁴ x 18⁰

FAMILY ROOM 15⁴ x 11⁶

LINEN

MASTER BATH

BREAKFAST ROOM 15⁴ x 11⁸

DESK

KIT. 13⁰ x 11⁴

SINK DW

WET BAR

DINING RM 13⁴ x 11⁰

5' HIGH SHELVES

UP DW

OPEN ABOVE

LIVING RM 13⁴ x 11⁴

PDR

FOYER

COVERED PORCH

Width 35'-4"
Depth 66'

QUOTE ONE™

Cost to build? See page 214
to order complete cost estimate
to build this house in your area!

Design Q3497

First Floor: 1,581 square feet
Second Floor: 592 square feet
Total: 2,173 square feet

● For the best in traditional styling, this 1 ½-story bungalow design takes the cake. A shingled exterior complements raised roof lines and a front porch. Inside, the entry gives way to a living room with a fireplace and a dining room serviced by a U-shaped kitchen and a wet bar. An airy breakfast room is situated nearby. In the family room, a back porch acts as a pleasant enhancement. The first-floor master bedroom suite leaves room for a sitting area. Upstairs, two secondary bedrooms share a full bath with dual lavatories. No matter what your family's style, this home will provide all the desired livability.

Design by
Home Planners, Inc.

COUNTRY-STYLE CAPES & COTTAGES

Country Capes and Cottages are simple, economical homes with a New England Colonial heritage. They have roots in the down-to-earth shelters constructed by the early settlers which featured a basic, boxy design. These early models were small, square and simple, and, consequently, were easy to construct. They provided practical housing that could be expanded as needed. Today's Country Cape fits comfortably almost anywhere but works especially well situated on the smaller lots in lakeside and seaside settings.

The modern versions of this style are constructed in simple box-like fashion usually with classic horizontal siding and a steeply pitched gabled roof. They may be a full Cape with a center-hall floor plan or the entry may be off-center as in the half-Cape or the three-quarter Cape. Many are designed to "grow" by the addition of winged appendages that give these great starter houses an expandable nature.

Following classic traditional architecture for a facade, the Country Cape may be updated nicely with projecting dormers and sun rooms to the rear. They almost always feature symmetric, multi-paned shuttered windows and may include dormers on the second floor.

Decorative detailing may be very sparse or can include dove-cotes, cupolas, and arched garage doors or service entries. Some versions even have Victorian-style gingerbread details. Western examples of the Country Cape are more rustic and cabin-like and often include a front porch. It is common to see this style used for second homes or leisure living because of their time-honored design and low building costs.

Country Capes seem almost to be defined by their expandable nature. Consider, for example, Design Q2682 in this section which begins as a simple "half house" then adds double wings for a study and a garage. A large plan, Design Q2699, is a Full Telescoping Cape with multiple wings and true Cape Cod, 1½-story style.

Adapted versions include Design Q2995, a Modified Country Cape, and Design Q9007, a Victorian-Style Cape. Though both of these designs have elements of Cape Cod design, they have been altered with details borrowed from other styles to create a new look. Likewise, Designs Q2661 and Q9666 have taken on more dramatic country elements: shake roof, covered front porch, stone chimney stack.

Always a favorite, Cape Cods gain even more popularity when done in country accents. This section of Country-Style Capes and Cottages shows off the best components of this adapted design.

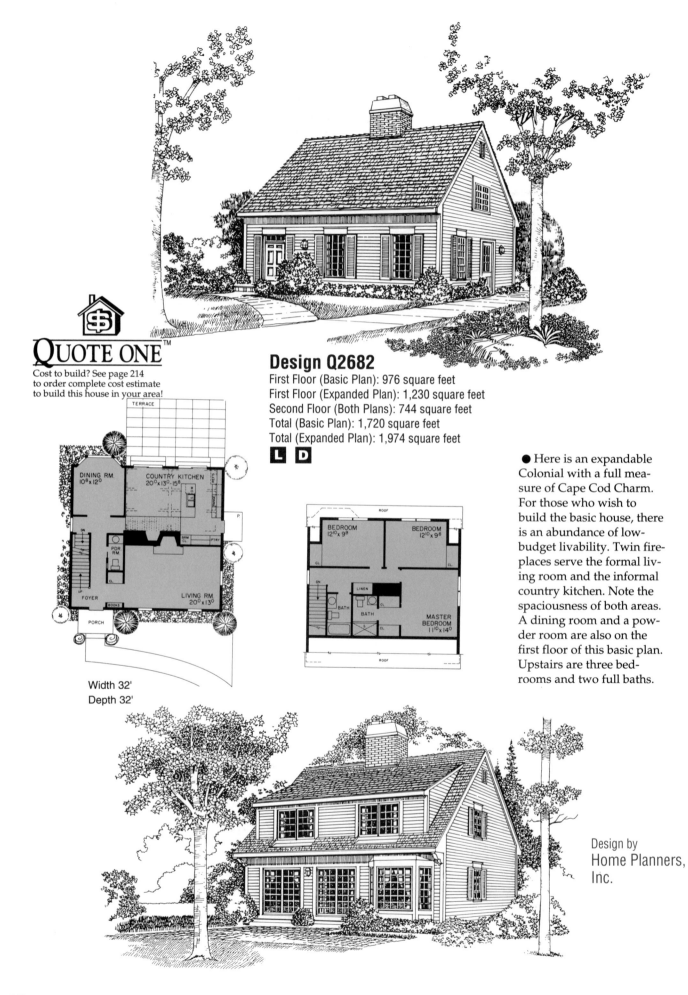

Quote One™

Cost to build? See page 214
to order complete cost estimate
to build this house in your area!

Design Q2682

First Floor (Basic Plan): 976 square feet
First Floor (Expanded Plan): 1,230 square feet
Second Floor (Both Plans): 744 square feet
Total (Basic Plan): 1,720 square feet
Total (Expanded Plan): 1,974 square feet

L **D**

● Here is an expandable
Colonial with a full mea-
sure of Cape Cod Charm.
For those who wish to
build the basic house, there
is an abundance of low-
budget livability. Twin fireplaces serve the formal living room and the informal
country kitchen. Note the
spaciousness of both areas.
A dining room and a pow-
der room are also on the
first floor of this basic plan.
Upstairs are three bed-
rooms and two full baths.

TERRACE

DINING RM.
10⁸ x 12⁰

COUNTRY KITCHEN
20⁰ x 13⁰-15⁸

PTRY

PDR
RM

LIVING RM
20⁰ x 13⁰

UP

FOYER

BOOKS

PORCH

Width 32'
Depth 32'

ROOF

BEDROOM
12¹⁰ x 9⁸

BEDROOM
12¹⁰ x 9⁸

CL

CL

DN

LINEN

BATH

BATH

CL

MASTER
BEDROOM
11¹⁰ x 14⁰

ROOF

Design by
Home Planners,
Inc.

140

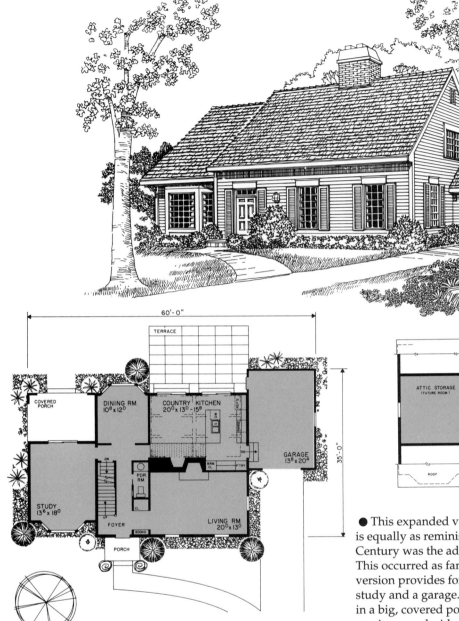

60'-0"

TERRACE

COVERED PORCH

DINING RM.
10⁸ x 12⁰

COUNTRY KITCHEN
20⁰ x 13⁰ - 15⁸

GARAGE
13⁸ x 20⁰

STUDY
13⁶ x 18⁰

PDR RM.

BRM CL

P'TRY

DN

UP

FOYER

BOOKS

CL

LIVING RM.
20⁰ x 13⁰

PORCH

35'-0"

ROOF

BEDROOM
12¹⁰ x 9⁸

BEDROOM
12¹⁰ x 9⁸

ATTIC STORAGE
(FUTURE ROOM)

DN

LINEN

BATH

BATH

CL

MASTER BEDROOM
11¹⁰ x 14⁰

ROOF

ROOF

ROOF

● This expanded version of the basic house on the opposite page is equally as reminiscent of Cape Cod. Common in the 17th Century was the addition of appendages to the main structure. This occurred as family size increased or finances improved. This version provides for the addition of wings to accommodate a large study and a garage. Utilizing the alcove behind the study results in a big, covered porch. Certainly a charming design whichever version you decide to build for your family. For information on customizing this design, call 1-800-521-6797, ext. 800.

Design Q2571

First Floor: 1,137 square feet
Second Floor: 795 square feet
Total: 1,932 square feet

L **D**

● This cozy Cape has an efficient plan that's long on affordable livability. Note the comfortable family room, which has both a fireplace and snack bar; separate dining room with gorgeous bay window; formal living room; and full bath down next to a study that could also be a fourth bedroom. Upstairs are three bedrooms, including a master suite, and two more full bathrooms.

Design by
Home Planners,
Inc.

Design Q3511

First Floor: 1,064 square feet
Second Floor: 582 square feet
Total: 1,646 square feet

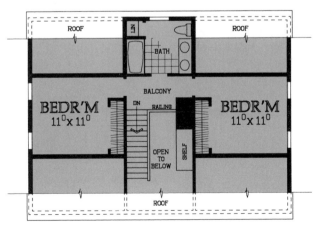

Quote One®

Cost to build? See page 214
to order complete cost estimate
to build this house in your area!

● This charming Cape Cod maximizes style and use of space. The living room features a corner fireplace and a built-in curio cabinet. Nearby, the dining room is high-lighted with a built-in china closet and access to the rear grounds. A warming fireplace shares space with the efficient kitchen and dining area. First-floor master suites are rarely found in Cape Cod-style homes, and this one is exceptional. The master bedroom combines with a master bath complete with a whirlpool tub, a separate shower, and a walk-in closet. The second floor is comprised of two family bedrooms sharing a full bath.

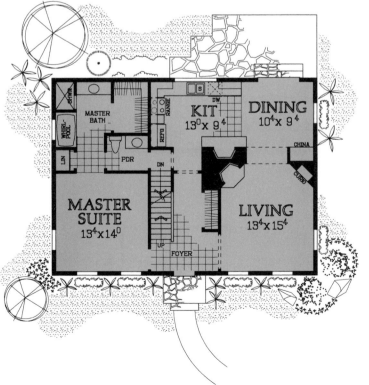

Width 38'
Depth 28'

Design by
Home Planners,
Inc.

Design Q3372

First Floor: 1,259 square feet
Second Floor: 942 square feet
Total: 2,201 square feet

L **D**

● Charm is the key word for this delightful plan's exterior, but don't miss the great floor plan inside. Formal living and dining rooms flank the entry foyer to the front; a family room and breakfast room with beamed ceilings are to the rear. The kitchen and service areas function well together and are near the garage and service entrance for convenience. Upstairs are the sleeping accommodations: two family bedrooms and a master suite of nice proportion.

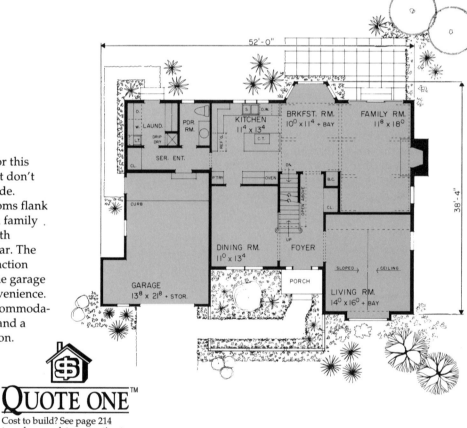

QUOTE ONE™
Cost to build? See page 214 to order complete cost estimate to build this house in your area!

Design by
Home Planners,
Inc.

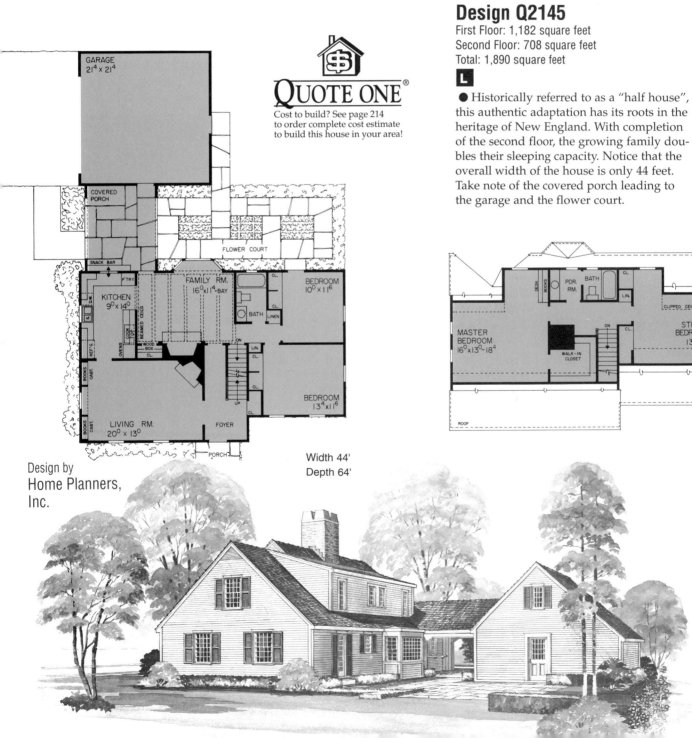

GARAGE
21⁴ x 21⁴

COVERED PORCH

FLOWER COURT

SNACK BAR

P'TRY

KITCHEN
9⁰ x 14⁰

FAMILY RM.
16⁰ x 11⁴·BAY

BATH

BEDROOM
10⁰ x 11⁶

LINEN

BEAMED CEIL'G

WOOD BOX

OVENS

BEDROOM
13⁴ x 11⁶

BOOKS CABT.

LIVING RM.
20⁰ x 13⁰

FOYER

PORCH

MASTER BEDROOM
16⁰ x 13⁰-18⁴

WALK-IN CLOSET

DESK BOOKS

PDR. RM.

BATH

LIN.

ROOF

CLIPPED CEIL'G

STUDY/ BEDROOM
13⁴ x 11⁴

ROOF

ROOF

QUOTE ONE®

Cost to build? See page 214
to order complete cost estimate
to build this house in your area!

Design by
**Home Planners,
Inc.**

Width 44'
Depth 64'

Design Q2145

First Floor: 1,182 square feet
Second Floor: 708 square feet
Total: 1,890 square feet

L

● Historically referred to as a "half house",
this authentic adaptation has its roots in the
heritage of New England. With completion
of the second floor, the growing family doubles their sleeping capacity. Notice that the
overall width of the house is only 44 feet.
Take note of the covered porch leading to
the garage and the flower court.

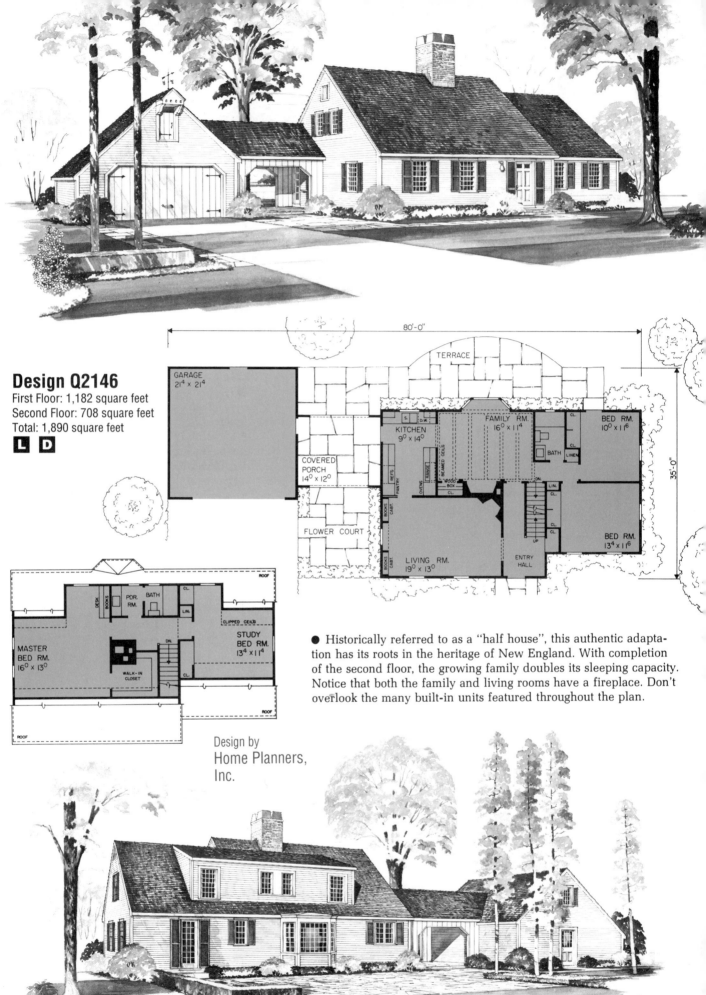

Design Q2146

First Floor: 1,182 square feet
Second Floor: 708 square feet
Total: 1,890 square feet

L D

Floor plan labels (first floor):

GARAGE 21⁴ x 21⁴

TERRACE

COVERED PORCH 14⁰ x 12⁰

FLOWER COURT

KITCHEN 9⁰ x 14⁰

FAMILY RM. 16⁰ x 11⁴

BED RM. 10⁰ x 11⁶

BATH

LINEN

CL.

BEAMED CEILG

S. D.W.

RANGE

OVENS

WOOD BOX

REF'G

PANTRY

BOOKS CABT.

BOOKS CABT.

LIVING RM. 19⁰ x 13⁰

ENTRY HALL

BED RM. 13⁴ x 11⁶

UP

DN.

LIN.

CL.

80'-0"

35'-0"

Floor plan labels (second floor):

DESK

BOOKS

PDR. RM.

BATH

CL.

LIN.

CLIPPED CEILG.

MASTER BED RM. 16⁰ x 13⁰

WALK-IN CLOSET

DN.

STUDY BED RM. 13⁴ x 11⁴

ROOF

CL.

Design by
Home Planners, Inc.

● Historically referred to as a "half house", this authentic adaptation has its roots in the heritage of New England. With completion of the second floor, the growing family doubles its sleeping capacity. Notice that both the family and living rooms have a fireplace. Don't overlook the many built-in units featured throughout the plan.

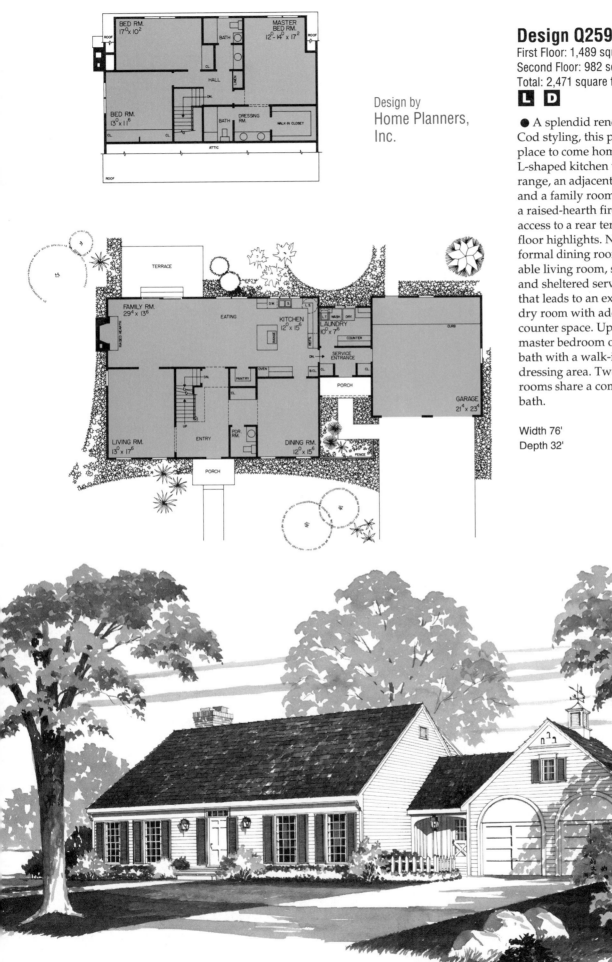

Design Q2596

First Floor: 1,489 square feet
Second Floor: 982 square feet
Total: 2,471 square feet

L **D**

● A splendid rendition of Cape Cod styling, this plan is a cozy place to come home to. An L-shaped kitchen with an island range, an adjacent eating area and a family room that features a raised-hearth fireplace and access to a rear terrace are first-floor highlights. Notice, too, the formal dining room, comfortable living room, spacious entry and sheltered service entrance that leads to an extra-large laundry room with additional counter space. Upstairs, the master bedroom offers a roomy bath with a walk-in closet and a dressing area. Two family bedrooms share a compartmented bath.

Width 76'
Depth 32'

Design by
Home Planners,
Inc.

147

KOIZUMI/BUTLER

ENTERTAINMENT TERRACE

DINING RM
12⁰ x 10⁸
SLOPED CLG

GATHERING RM
14⁴ x 18⁰

MASTER SUITE
12⁰ x 18⁰

WHIRLPOOL   SHWR

MASTER BATH

PLANT SHELF ABOVE

SHELF

PANTRY

KIT
14⁴ x 13⁰

BEDRM
10⁰ x 12⁴
9'-0" CLG

BATH   LAUNDRY

LINEN

DESK

WALK-IN CLOSET

LINEN

PLANT SHELF ABOVE

PDR

NICHE   NICHE

NICHE

BEDRM
11⁴ x 13⁴
9'-0" CLG

BEDRM
10¹⁰ x 13⁴
9'-0" CLG

FAMILY RM
11⁴ x 18²
SLOPED CLG

FOYER
SLOPED CLG

STORAGE

CURB

COVERED PORCH

RAILING   RAILING

GARAGE
23⁰ x 22⁶

Design Q3489
Square Footage: 2,415

L **D**

● This traditional design incorporates the perfect floor plan for a large family. Privacy is assured with three family bedrooms and a strategically placed laundry on the left side of the home, and a large master bedroom with a luxurious bath and spacious walk-in closet on the right side. A comfortable covered porch welcomes you to the living areas. The family room looks out to the covered porch and continues on to the efficient kitchen with a writing desk, a large pantry and access to the dining room. The kitchen also features a snack bar that provides a perfect opportunity to chat with folks in the large gathering room with its warming fireplace and access to the back-yard terrace. Sloped ceilings in the living areas and the master bedroom, and nine-foot ceilings in the other bedrooms, give this home a spacious, airy feel. For information on customizing this design, call 1-800-521-6797, ext. 800.

Quote One™

Cost to build? See page 214 to order complete cost estimate to build this house in your area!

Width 74'
Depth 54'

Design by
Home Planners, Inc.

148

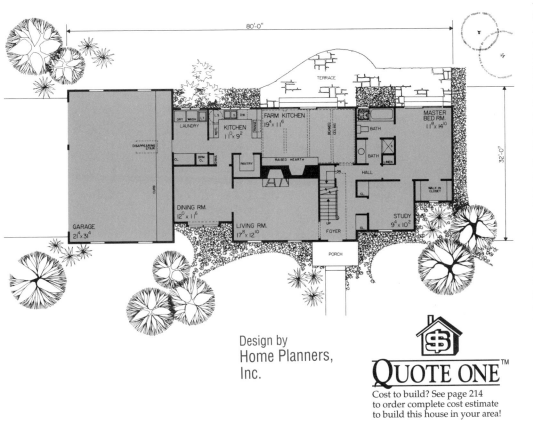

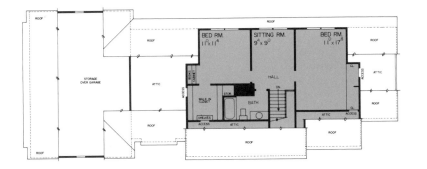

Design Q2563

First Floor: 1,500 square feet
Second Floor: 690 square feet
Total: 2,190 square feet

L **D**

● This charming Cape Cod will capture your heart with its warm appeal. This home offers you and your family a lot of livability. Upon entering this home, to your left, is a nice-sized living room with fireplace. Adjacent is a dining room. An efficient kitchen and a large, farm kitchen eating area with fireplace will be enjoyed by all. A unique feature on this floor is the master bedroom with a full bath and walk-in closet. Also take notice of the first-floor laundry, the pantry and a study for all of your favorite books. Note the sliding glass doors in the farm kitchen and master bedroom. Upstairs you'll find two bedrooms, one with a walk-in closet. Also here, a sitting room and a full bath are available. Lastly, this design accommodates a three car garage. For information on customizing this design, call 1-800-521-6797, ext. 800.

Design by
Home Planners,
Inc.

QUOTE ONE™

Cost to build? See page 214 to order complete cost estimate to build this house in your area!

Design Q9639
Square Footage: 1,541

● This traditional three-bedroom home projects the appearance of a much larger home. The great room features a cathedral ceiling, a fireplace and an arched window above the sliding glass doors to the expansive rear deck. The columned formal dining room leads to an efficient kitchen with a breakfast area and an adjoining utility room with access to the garage. The master suite contains a pampering master bath and a walk-in closet. Two other bedrooms share a full bath with a double-bowl vanity. Please specify crawlspace or basement foundation when ordering.

Design by
Donald A.
Gardner,
Architects, Inc.

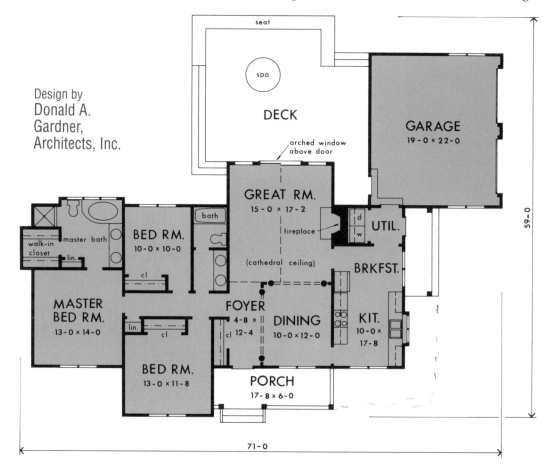

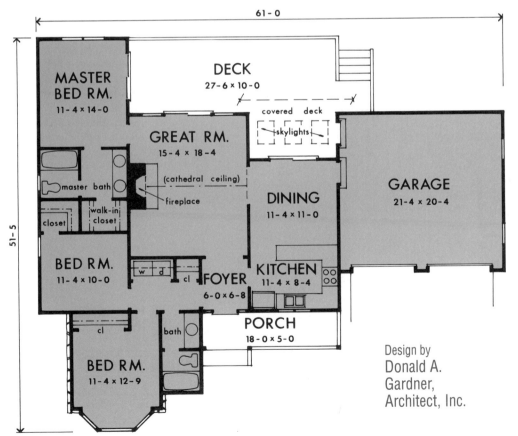

MASTER
BED RM.
11-4 × 14-0

DECK
27-6 × 10-0

covered deck

skylights

GREAT RM.
15-4 × 18-4

(cathedral ceiling)

fireplace

master bath

walk-in
closet

closet

GARAGE
21-4 × 20-4

DINING
11-4 × 11-0

BED RM.
11-4 × 10-0

w d cl

FOYER
6-0 × 6-8

KITCHEN
11-4 × 8-4

cl

bath

PORCH
18-0 × 5-0

BED RM.
11-4 × 12-9

61-0

51-5

Design by
Donald A.
Gardner,
Architect, Inc.

Design Q9620
Square Footage: 1,310

● A multi-paned bay window, dormers, a cupola, a covered porch and a variety of building materials dress up this one-story cottage. The entrance foyer leads to an impressive great room with cathedral ceiling and fireplace. The U-shaped kitchen, adjacent to the dining room, provides an ideal layout for food preparation. An expansive deck offers shelter while admitting cheery sunlight through skylights. A luxurious master bedroom located to the rear of the house takes advantage of the deck area and is assured privacy from two other bedrooms at the front of the house. These family bedrooms share a full bath.

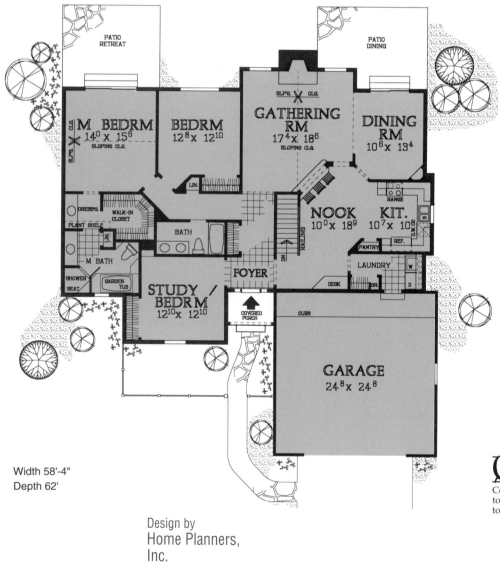

Design Q3490

Square Footage: 1,970

L **D**

● The focal point of this home is its open living area. It offers a large gathering room with a central fireplace which leads to a dining room with patio access and a built-in china cabinet and then on to the U-shaped kitchen and spacious breakfast nook. The sleeping zone is cozy and inviting. The master bedroom features a private bath, a walk-in closet, separate terrace access and an adjoining study that could double as a guest room. For information on customizing this design, call 1-800-521-6797, ext. 800.

Quote One ®

Cost to build? See page 214
to order complete cost estimate
to build this house in your area!

Width 58'-4"
Depth 62'

Design by
Home Planners,
Inc.

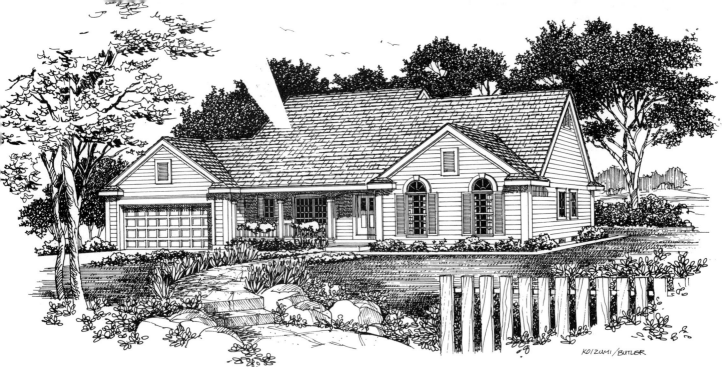

Design Q3487

Square Footage: 1,835

L

● Country living is the focus of this charming design. A cozy covered porch invites you into the foyer with the sleeping area on the right and the living area to the left and straight ahead. From the windowed front-facing breakfast room, enter the efficient kitchen with its corner laundry room, large pantry, snack-bar pass-through to the gathering room and entry to the dining area. The massive gathering room and dining room feature sloped ceilings, an impressive fireplace and access to the rear terrace. Terrace access is also available from the master bedroom with its sloped ceiling and a master bath that includes a whirlpool tub, a separate shower and a separate vanity area. A study at the front of the house can also be converted into a third bedroom.

Design by
Home Planners,
Inc.

Quote One™

Cost to build? See page 214 to order complete cost estimate to build this house in your area!

Width 71'
Depth 43'-5"

Design Q2699

First Floor: 2,188 square feet
Second Floor: 858 square feet
Total: 3,046 square feet

L

QUOTE ONE®

Cost to build? See page 214
to order complete cost estimate
to build this house in your area!

Design by
Home Planners,
Inc.

106'-8"

32'-0"

TERRACE

TERRACE

LIVING RM.
18⁴ x 15⁰

DINING RM.
12⁰ x 13⁰

GARAGE
21⁴ x 29⁴

MASTER
BEDROOM
15⁰ x 18⁰

WHIRLPOOL

BATH

EATING

COUNTRY
KITCHEN
15⁸ x 21⁰

COOK
TOP

MUD AREA

W.R

CL

LAUNDRY
11⁸ x 6⁰

WALK-IN CLOSET

LOUNGE
12⁰ x 8⁶

FOYER

BALCONY
ABOVE

LOUNGE ABOVE

PDR
RM

MEDIA RM.
12⁰ x 10⁰

PORCH

ROOF

BEDROOM
11⁰ x 15⁸

UPPER
LIVING RM.

BEDROOM
11⁰ x 12⁰

VANITY

BATH

LOUNGE

RAILING

BATH

CL

CL

CL

ACCESS
PANEL

ATTIC

BALCONY

LINEN

ROOF

ROOF

UPPER
FOYER

Enhanced Plan

68'-0"

RAILING

DECK
16⁰ x 12⁰

DN

STUDY-
BED RM.
11⁰ x 11²

BATH

DINING RM.
11⁰ x 10²

KITCHEN
11⁴ x 9⁴

DW S

LS

D

W

RANGE

REF'G

LT

SNACK BAR

30'-0"

CL CL LINEN

HALL

LAUNDRY RM
8⁰ x 11⁴

FURN

WH

CL

UP

OPT.
FIREPLACE

LIVING RM.
17⁰ x 13⁶

ENTRY

FAMILY RM.
12⁴ x 16⁸

2 CAR
GARAGE
19⁴ x 21⁴

COVERED PORCH

Design by
Home Planners,
Inc.

Design Q3715

First Floor: 1,312 square feet
Second Floor: 795 square feet
Total: 2,107 square feet

● The design of this 1½-story Cape Cod provides plenty of room for all your family's needs. The kitchen extends as one large room over the snack bar into an expansive family room. Both the family room and the living room open directly to the center hall, which also leads into the dining room at the back of the house. A study downstairs could be converted into yet another bedroom with an adjacent full bath. The house may be enhanced by the addition of a fireplace, a bay window, a two-car garage and laundry room and a rear deck.

The highlighted areas of this floor plan are enhancements to the basic plan. The blueprints for this house show how to build both the basic, low-cost version, and the enhanced, upgraded version.

Basic Plan

ROOF

CL

BATH

BED RM.
11⁸ x 10⁰

BATH

CL

CL

TWL.S

HALL

RAILING

DN

MASTER
BED RM.
14⁴ x 12⁰

WALK IN
CLOSET

BED RM.
12⁸ x 11⁰

ROOF

Design Q2995

First Floor: 2,465 square feet
Second Floor: 617 square feet
Total: 3,082 square feet

L **D**

● This New England Colonial delivers beautiful proportions and great livability on 1½ levels. The main area of the house, the first floor, holds a living room, library, family room, dining room and gourmet kitchen. The master bedroom, also on this floor, features a whirlpool tub and sloped ceiling. A long rear terrace stretches the full width of the house. Two bedrooms on the second floor share a full bath; each has a built-in deck. California Engineered Plans and California Stock Plans are available for this home. Call 1-800-521-6797 for more information.

Design by
Home Planners,
Inc.

Width 120'-11"
Depth 52'-6"

QUOTE ONE™
Cost to build? See page 214 to order complete cost estimate to build this house in your area!

Design Q3328

First Floor: 2,300 square feet
Second Floor: 812 square feet
Total: 3,112 square feet

● Dormered windows, a covered porch and symmetrical balustrades provide a warm country welcome. Formal living and dining rooms flank the foyer. To the left of the dining room is a spacious family room which contains a raised-hearth fireplace. It is conveniently located near the breakfast/kitchen area which features an island cook-top, a pantry and a planning desk. Just past the study, or optional guest room, is the master suite's sitting area which provides access to the covered patio and the master bedroom. A lavish master bath is complete with a whirlpool tub and separate His and Hers dressing areas. The second floor contains two family bedrooms and a full bath. For information on customizing this design, call 1-800-521-6797, ext. 800.

Design by
Home Planners,
Inc.

Quote One®

Cost to build? See page 214
to order complete cost estimate
to build this house in your area!

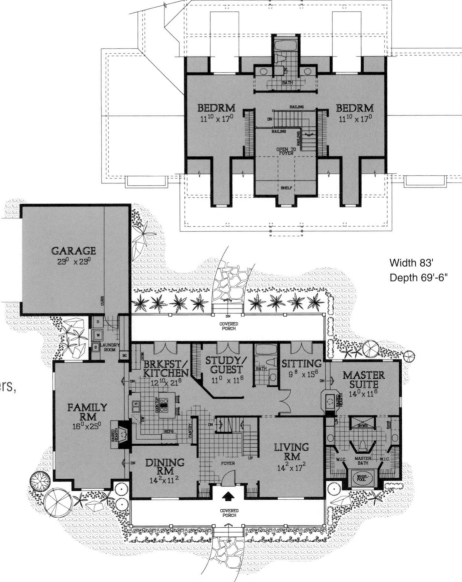

Width 83'
Depth 69'-6"

Design Q9307

Square Footage: 1,948

● Wood and brick details along with an elegant porch highlight the elevation of this special design. A 10-foot-high entry views the open dining room with tapered columns. Gourmet cooks will delight in the island kitchen with pantry and wrapping wet bar/servery. Outdoor access is available from the sunny bayed dinette. In the great room, a cozy fireplace is flanked by large windows with arched transoms above. Two secondary bedrooms share a Hollywood bath with a linen cabinet. At night, the lucky homeowners can retreat to the elegant master suite complete with vaulted ceilings and a pampering master bath. Special amenities include His and Hers vanities, linen closet, corner whirlpool, special shower and roomy walk-in closet. Truly, this home is delightful inside and out.

Design by
**Design
Basics,
Inc.**

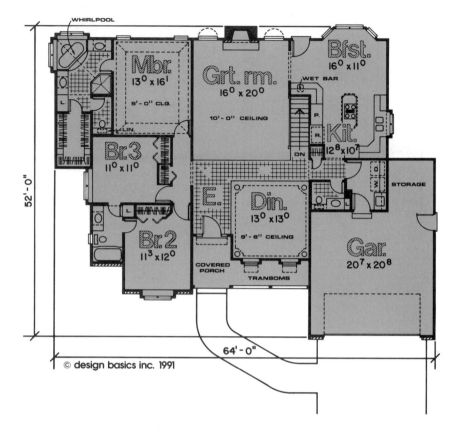

© design basics inc. 1991

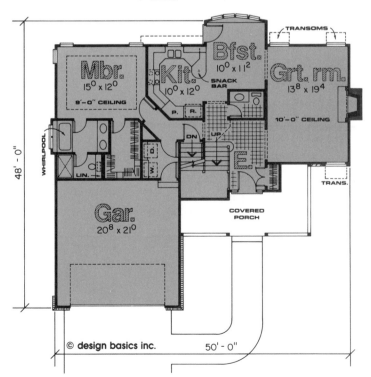

Design by
**Design
Basics,
Inc.**

Design Q7215

First Floor: 1,191 square feet
Second Floor: 405 square feet
Total: 1,596 square feet

● This charming country-style elevation features a wrapping porch and oval window accents. The spacious great room, directly accessible from the two-story entry and the bowed breakfast area, has a warming fireplace and transom windows. An angled wall adds drama to the peninsula kitchen and creates a private entry to the master suite. In the master suite, a boxed, nine-foot ceiling, a compartmented whirlpool bath and a spacious walk-in closet assure modern livability. The second-level balcony overlooks the U-stairs and entry. Twin linen closets just outside the upstairs bedrooms serve a compartmented bath with natural light.

Design Q9035

Square Footage: 1,341

● Great for narrow lots, this home delivers amazing livability within modest square footage. Notice the efficient U-shaped kitchen with attached dining room. Counter space is abundant for serving and eating. The large family room with fireplace and gambrel ceiling offers an open area that easily accommodates family gatherings and formal entertaining. The three-bedroom sleeping area includes a master suite with full bath and walk-in closet. Bedroom number 3 overlooks the welcoming covered front porch.

Design by
Larry W.
Garnett &
Associates, Inc.

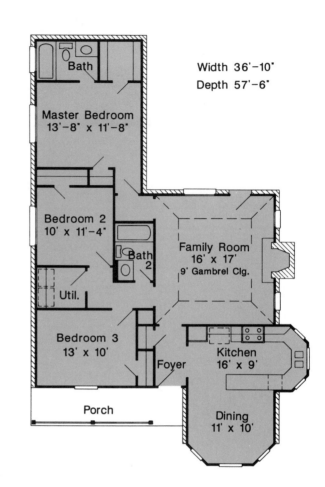

Width 36'-10"
Depth 57'-6"

Bath

Master Bedroom
13'-8" x 11'-8"

Bedroom 2
10' x 11'-4"

Bath
2

Util.

Family Room
16' x 17'
9' Gambrel Clg.

Bedroom 3
13' x 10'

Foyer

Kitchen
16' x 9'

Porch

Dining
11' x 10'

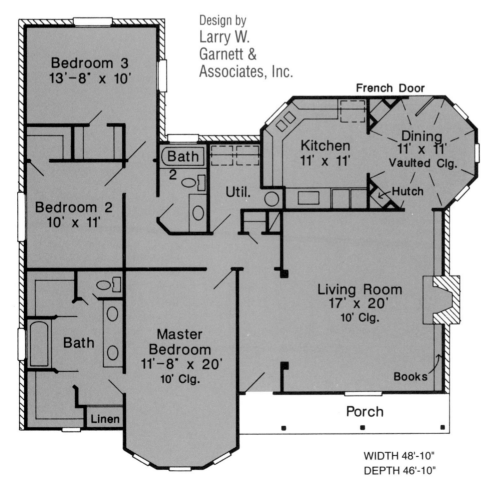

Design by
Larry W.
Garnett &
Associates, Inc.

Bedroom 3
13'-8" x 10'

Bedroom 2
10' x 11'

Bath
2

Util.

Kitchen
11' x 11'

French Door

Dining
11' x 11'
Vaulted Clg.

Hutch

Bath

Living Room
17' x 20'
10' Clg.

**Master
Bedroom**
11'-8" x 20'
10' Clg.

Linen

Books

Porch

WIDTH 48'-10"
DEPTH 46'-10"

Design Q9007
Square Footage: 1,669

● With an efficient floor plan and plenty of closet space, this farmhouse is rather economical to build. The simple roof design and well-proportioned bay window and front porch, which are far less costly than many farmhouse designs, allow extras: ten-foot ceilings in the master bedroom and the living room and a unique "gazebo" vaulted ceiling in the dining area. Optional bookcases are located on each side of the fireplace. The laundry room is conveniently located near the bedrooms. The sides and part of the rear of the home are brick veneer, providing for much less maintenance and painting. Plans for a two-car detached garage are included with this design.

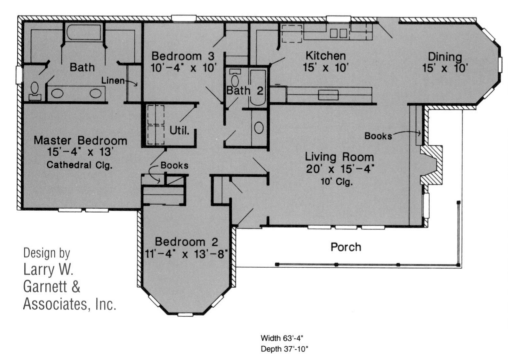

Bath

Linen

Bedroom 3
10'-4" x 10'

Kitchen
15' x 10'

Dining
15' x 10'

Bath 2

Master Bedroom
15'-4" x 13'
Cathedral Clg.

Util.

Books

Living Room
20' x 15'-4"
10' Clg.

Books

Bedroom 2
11'-4" x 13'-8"

Porch

Design by
Larry W.
Garnett &
Associates, Inc.

Width 63'-4"
Depth 37'-10"

Design Q9038
Square Footage: 1,659

● Here's a three-bedroom home
with style and comfort that meets
family living requirements with
less than 2,000 square feet!
Gathering areas are accommodat-
ed in the living room with built-
in bookshelves and fireplace, and
the well-planned kitchen/dining
area combination. Besides two
family bedrooms, there is a lovely
master with cathedral ceiling and
bath with double vanity. The bay
windows, covered front porch
and other special design details
make this a house to remember.

Design Q9039
Square Footage: 1,978

● In addition to the wrapping covered front porch of this farmhouse design, there is a second porch to the rear with French-door access to the eating area. Between the two, lies a great floor plan with features often found only in much larger homes: a ten-foot gambrel ceiling in the family room, a large dining room connecting directly to an efficiently planned kitchen, an octagonal breakfast room, and three bedrooms with walk-in closets. Little extras like the bay window in the master bedroom and the double vanity in the master bath make this home a true stand-out.

Design by
Larry W. Garnett & Associates, Inc.

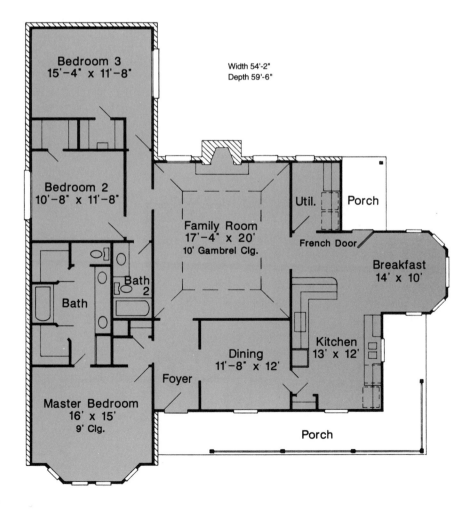

Bedroom 3
15'-4" x 11'-8"

Width 54'-2"
Depth 59'-6"

Bedroom 2
10'-8" x 11'-8"

Family Room
17'-4" x 20'
10' Gambrel Clg.

Util.

Porch

French Door

Breakfast
14' x 10'

Bath 2

Bath

Kitchen
13' x 12'

Dining
11'-8" x 12'

Foyer

Master Bedroom
16' x 15'
9' Clg.

Porch

Design Q9430

First Floor: 1,150 square feet
Second Floor: 543 square feet
Total: 1,693 square feet

● While fitting on some of the smallest lots imaginable, this great 1½-story still encompasses some dynamic features. Check out the dramatic, two-story hearth room that serves as the main living area in the home. Tall windows flank the fireplace and a glass door leads to the outdoor living area. A section of the upper hallway overlooks the hearth room integrating the upper floor with the lower floor. The master bedroom is conveniently located on the main floor overlooking the back yard, with direct access to the full bath serving the lower floor. Two large bedrooms and a bath round out the upper floor.

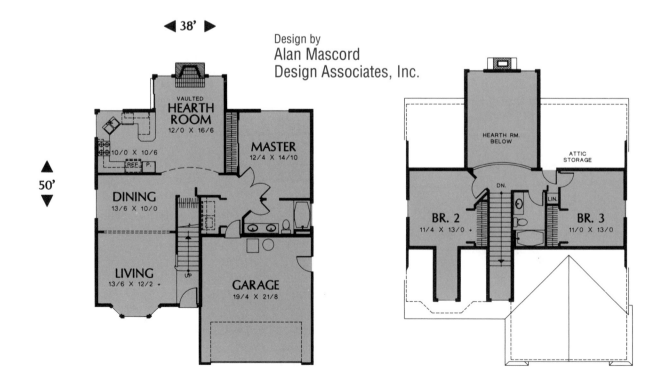

Design by
Alan Mascord
Design Associates, Inc.

Design Q9536

First Floor: 1,200 square feet
Second Floor: 1,339 square feet
Total: 2,539 square feet

● A covered front porch introduces this home's comfortable living pattern. The two-story foyer opens to a living room with a fireplace and lots of natural light. The formal dining room looks out over the living room. In the kitchen, an island cooktop, a pantry, a built-in planning desk and a nook with double doors to outside livability aims to please. A spacious family room with another fireplace will accommodate casual living. Upstairs, five bedrooms—or four and a den—make room for all family members and guests. The master bedroom suite exudes elegance with an elegant ceiling and a pampering spa bath. A full hall bath with a skylight and dual lavatories serves the secondary bedrooms.

Design by
Alan Mascord
Design Associates, Inc.

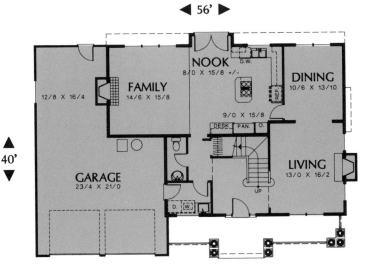

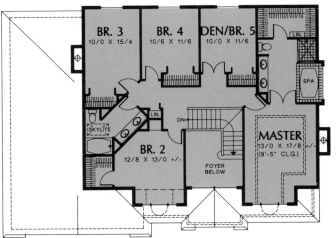

Design Q9006

Square Footage: 1,772

● Designed for casual living inside and out, this one-story farmhouse is an ideal family home. The family room features a ten-foot ceiling and a corner fireplace. An enormous dining area can handle even the largest family dinners. The large rear porch is perfect for outdoor entertaining. The laundry room is conveniently located near the three bedrooms. His and Hers walk-in closets and twin lavatories are part of the luxurious master bath. Plans for a 24' x 24' detached garage are included with this design.

Design by
Larry W.
Garnett &
Associates, Inc.

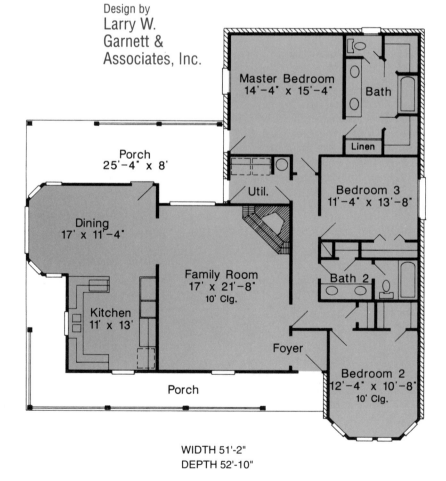

WIDTH 51'-2"
DEPTH 52'-10"

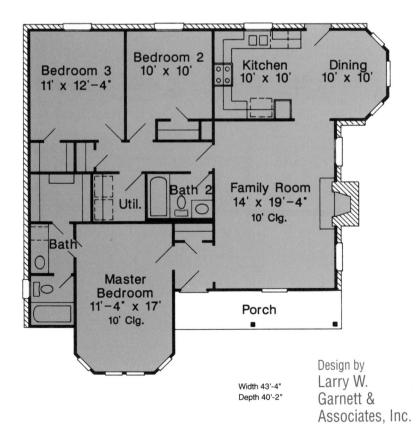

Bedroom 3
11' x 12'-4"

Bedroom 2
10' x 10'

Kitchen
10' x 10'

Dining
10' x 10'

Util.

Bath 2

Family Room
14' x 19'-4"
10' Clg.

Bath

Master
Bedroom
11'-4" x 17'
10' Clg.

Porch

Width 43'-4"
Depth 40'-2"

Design Q9032
Square Footage: 1,358

● This cozy little farmhouse presents all those special traits that makes it the perfect place to call home. From the covered front porch to the efficient floor plan, this is one that is sure to catch your eye. Living areas to the right of the front entry include a large family room with fireplace, octagonal dining area and U-shaped kitchen with rear yard access. The master bedroom is cleverly separated from two family bedrooms and has its own full bath and a walk-in closet. Note the location of the laundry room—near the bedrooms, the source of dirty clothes.

Design by
Larry W.
Garnett &
Associates, Inc.

Design Q9608

First Floor: 1,228 square feet
Second Floor: 492 square feet
Total: 1,720 square feet

● An open and spacious interior with the best in up-to-date floor planning offers new excitement in this delightful compact country-style home. Besides the oversized great room with fireplace, there is a wonderful country kitchen incorporating dining space and having access to the sun room for alternate dining and entertaining. The generous master bedroom has its own fireplace and also access to the sun room. A walk-in closet assures plenty of storage space. Upstairs, in addition to two bedrooms sharing a full bath, there is a charming balcony and ample attic storage. A covered porch and a deck — front and rear — add to outdoor lifestyles.

Design by
Donald A.
Gardner,
Architect, Inc.

FRONT

REAR

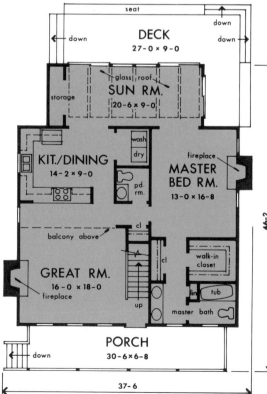

Design Q9666

First Floor: 1,027 square feet
Second Floor: 580 square feet;
Total: 1,607 square feet

● This economical, rustic three-bedroom plan sports a relaxing country image with both front and back covered porches. The openness of the expansive great room to kitchen/dining areas and loft/study areas is reinforced with a shared cathedral ceiling for impressive space. The first level allows for two bedrooms, a full bath and a utility area. The master suite on the second level has a walk-in closet and a master bath with whirlpool tub, shower and double-bowl vanity. The plan is available with a crawl-space foundation.

PORCH
34-4 × 8-0

KIT./DINING
18-0 × 11-8

bath

BED RM.
12-0 × 10-0

w
d

cl
cl

loft above

cl

GREAT RM.
17-4 × 16-4

fireplace

up

BED RM.
12-0 × 12-4

PORCH
34-4 × 8-0

44-8

37-4

LOFT/STUDY
11-4 × 13-8

STO.
3-4 × 6-4

walk-in closet

master bath

railing

down

MASTER BED RM.
12-0 × 14-0

great room below

Design by
Donald A. Gardner, Architect, Inc.

QUOTE ONE®

Cost to build? See page 214 to order complete cost estimate to build this house in your area!

Design Q2661

First Floor: 1,020 square feet
Second Floor: 777 square feet
Total: 1,797 square feet

● It would be difficult to find a starter or retirement home with more charm than this. Inside, it contains a very livable floor plan. An outstanding first floor centers around the huge country kitchen which includes a beam ceiling, raised-hearth fireplace, window seat and rear-yard access. The living room with warming corner fireplace and private study are to the front of the plan. Upstairs are three bedrooms and two full baths. Built-in shelves and a linen closet in the upstairs hallway provide excellent storage. For information on customizing this design, call 1-800-521-6797, ext. 800. California Engineered Plans and California Stock Plans are available for this home. Call 1-800-521-6797 for more information.

QUOTE ONE™

Cost to build? See page 214 to order complete cost estimate to build this house in your area!

Design by
Home Planners,
Inc.

BRICK OR STONE FARMHOUSES

Though not formally a *style* of Farmhouse, the brick or stone exterior is a popular choice for just about any variation. Because of their solid-looking appearance, brick and stone are used as a statement of permanence, antiquity and heritage. Either may be found as an exterior ingredient; one or both may serve as an accent or embellishment to other exterior sidings. These materials are easy to care for and retain their good looks and durability for many years.

Effective use of brick is accomplished in Design Q2614, where it is used as the primary exterior material. It is complemented by dove-cote detailing and siding over the garage as well as a covered front porch and three dormers. Also employing brick almost completely throughout the exterior is Design Q9247, a Traditional Farmhouse, borrowing design elements from winged Colonials and Center-Hall designs. Design Q9206, a Modern French-Style Brick, uses brick extensively but heightens the appeal with horizontal wood trim, wooden window trim and wooden trim at the pediment over the garage.

Stone takes on rustically defined proportions in Design Q3488, a one-story Ranch style with a Tudor flair, and Design Q3351, a Cape Cod Farmhouse, where it is employed in combination with wood siding and other wood design details. A Classic Pennsylvania Stone Farmhouse, Design Q2542, uses stone almost to the exclusion of any other material. Even the chimney stacks are constructed in stone. A French Country House, Design Q9862, presents a unique stone facade with horizontal wood accents at the wing extension. This home is further enhanced by stone chimney stacks and metal-clad roofs over the box window and dining porch.

All of the Farmhouse versions presented, from the basic one-story version to the elaborate two-story country estate, are representative of the sturdiness and long-lasting appeal of brick and stone.

COPYRIGHT LARRY E. BELK

Floor Plan Labels (First Floor)

- K.S.
- MASTER BATH 9 FT CLG
- FP
- GREAT ROOM 19-0 X 17-0 VOLUME CLG
- PORCH
- BRKFST ROOM 11-6 X 10-0 9 FT CLG
- LIN
- SEAT
- PWDR
- KITCHEN 16-6 X 15-4
- COATS
- MASTER BEDRM 13-0 X 15-6 9 FT CLG
- FOYER 9 FT CLG
- DINING ROOM 12-6 X 13-6 9 FT CLG
- 9 FT CLG
- PAN
- UTIL 9-6 X 5-8
- STORAGE
- PORCH
- GARAGE
- COPYRIGHT LARRY E. BELK

Floor Plan Labels (Second Floor)

- BEDROOM 2 14-0 X 13-8
- OPEN TO BELOW
- BATH 2
- ATTIC
- EXPANDABLE AREA 1 12-6 X 17-0
- LINEN
- BEDROOM 3 12-6 X 10-6
- EXPANDABLE AREA 2 12-0 X 25-0
- 4' KNEE WALL
- 8' CLG LINE
- 8' CLG LINE
- 4' KNEE WALL

Width 49'-6"
Depth 37'-9"

Design by
Larry E. Belk
Designs

Design Q8090

First Floor: 1,635 square feet
Second Floor: 624 square feet
Total: 2,259 square feet
Bonus Room: 550 square feet

● A large front porch provides a perfect retreat for those lazy summer evenings and adds charm to this traditional Southern facade. A compact floor plan awaits inside with the kitchen, breakfast room and great room conveniently grouped. The master suite is located downstairs and features His and Hers vanities with a seating area, a corner whirlpool tub and a separate shower with a seat. An oversized walk-in closet is also noteworthy. The second floor is comprised of two secondary bedrooms and a bath. The bonus area contains two expandable spaces: Area 1 is designed for Bedroom 4, Area 2 is great for use as a recreation room or office. This plan is available with either a crawlspace or slab foundation. Please specify when ordering.

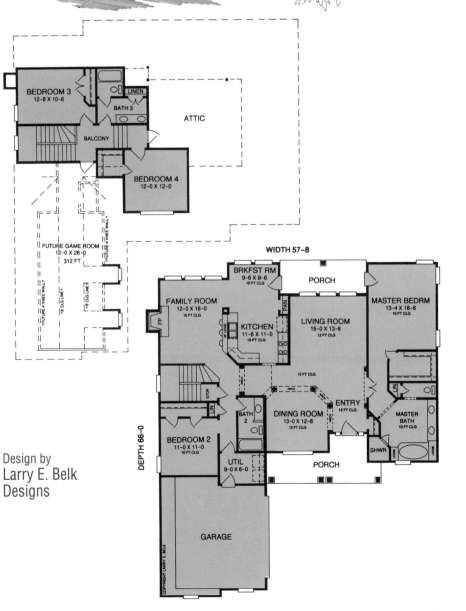

Design Q8091

First Floor: 2,087 square feet
Second Floor: 553 square feet
Total: 2,640 square feet
Bonus Room: 312 square feet

● A gable with a Palladian window and a large covered front porch make this home a charming classic. An angled entry opens up the living room and dining room and makes the home feel larger. The master suite is privately located on one side of the home. The kitchen, breakfast room and family room are combined and provide a great, open place for informal gatherings. Bedroom 2 and Bath 2 are nearby. A conveniently located stair originates in the family room. Two bedrooms and a bath are upstairs along with an expandable area to develop as you choose. This plan is available with either a crawlspace or slab foundation. Please specify when ordering.

Design by
Larry E. Belk
Designs

173

Design Q2805 Square Footage: 1,547

L **D**

● Compact but completely livable, this one-story home offers the best in country living. From its delightful stone exterior to rear covered porch the look is definitely distinctive. Inside, there's a large living room/dining room area with fireplace and sloped ceiling. It adjoins a breakfast room and U-shaped kitchen for convenient cooking and serving. The bedrooms are located to the front of the plan and include a master bedroom and two family bedrooms (or make one a study or TV room). The main part of the home connects to the two-car garage with a mud room. A huge storage area is found in the garage.

Width 58'-4"
Depth 51'-5"

OPTIONAL NON-BASEMENT

Design by
Home Planners,
Inc.

QUOTE ONE™
Cost to build? See page 214
to order complete cost estimate
to build this house in your area!

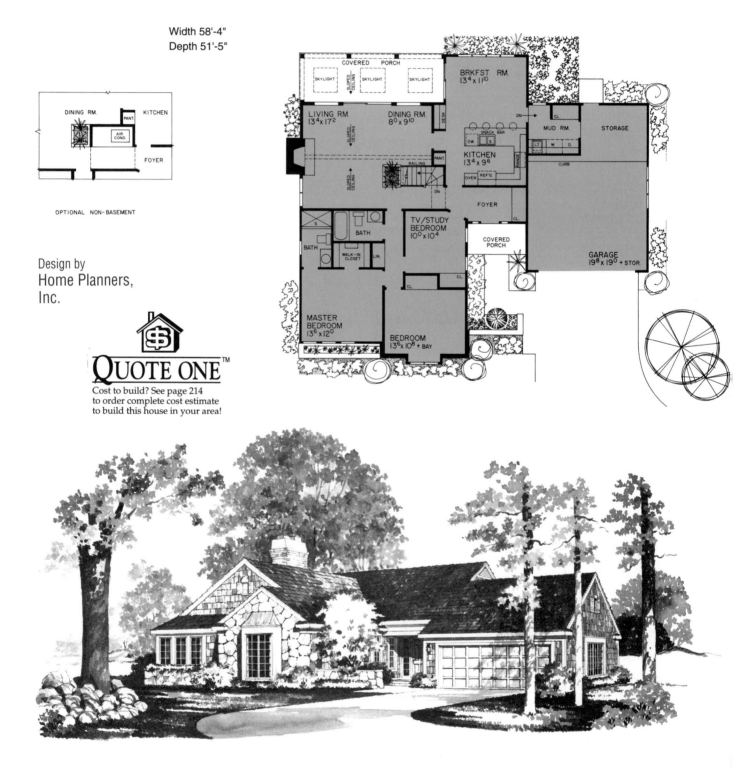

Design Q3488

Square Footage: 1,944

L **D**

● The tudor facade of this comfortable home is just the beginning to a truly unique design. As you enter the foyer via a quaint covered porch, you are greeted by the sleeping zone on the right and the living zone on the left, beginning with the breakfast area which faces the front. A large kitchen connects to this room and includes a desk, a walk-in pantry, a spacious counter area with a snack bar that connects to the gathering room and entry to the for-

mal dining room. The massive gathering room features a fireplace, a sloped ceiling and access to the back-yard terrace. The master bedroom also accesses the terrace and revels in a master bath with a whirlpool tub, a separate shower, dual lavs and an individual vanity. A study at the front of the home could be converted into an additional bedroom. For information on customizing this design, call 1-800-521-6797, ext. 800.

Quote One™

Cost to build? See page 214 to order complete cost estimate to build this house in your area!

Width 72'-8"
Depth 47'-4"

Design by
Home Planners, Inc.

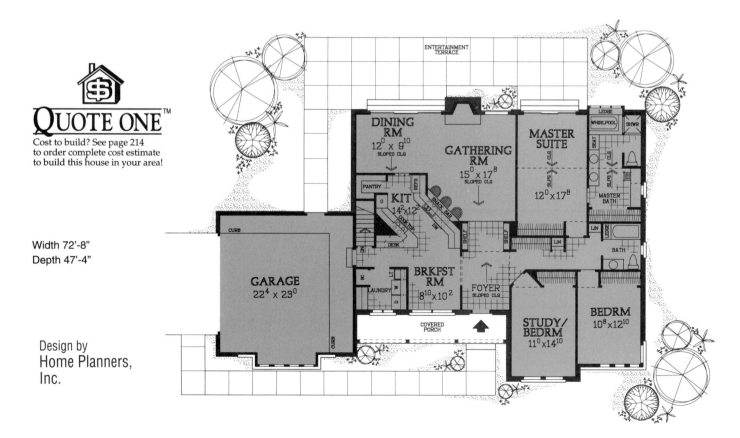

Design Q2174

First Floor: 1,506 square feet
Second Floor: 1,156 square feet
Total: 2,662 square feet

L **D**

● Your building budget could hardly buy more charm, or greater livability. The appeal of the exterior is wrapped up in a myriad of design features. They include: the interesting roof lines; the effective use of brick and horizontal siding; the delightful window treatment; the covered front porch; the chimney and dove-cote detailing. The livability of the interior is represented by a long list of convenient living features. There is a formal area consisting of a living room with fireplace and dining room. The family room has a raised hearth fireplace, wood box and beamed ceiling. Also on the first floor is a kitchen, laundry and bedroom with adjacent bath. Three bedrooms, lounge and two baths upstairs plus plenty of closets and bulk storage over garage. Don't overlook the sliding glass doors, the breakfast area and the basement. An excellent plan.

Design by
Home Planners,
Inc.

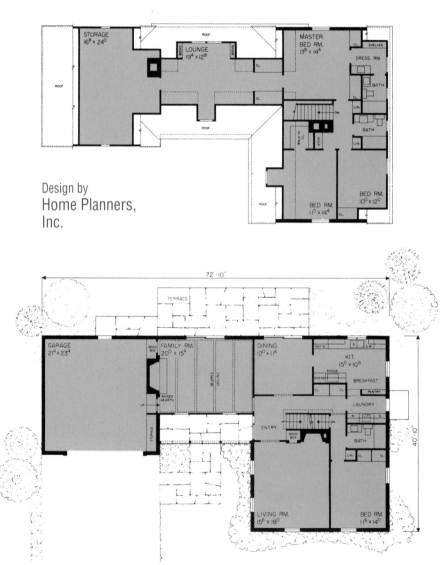

Design Q2614

First Floor: 1,701 square feet
Second Floor: 1,340 square feet
Total: 3,041 square feet

D

● Pleasing appearance, with an excellent floor plan. Notice how all the rooms are accessible from a hall. That's a plus for easy housekeeping. Some other extras: an exceptionally large family room which is more than 20' x 15', a gracious living room, formal dining room adjacent to the kitchen/nook area, four large bedrooms, a secluded guest suite plus a huge storage area.

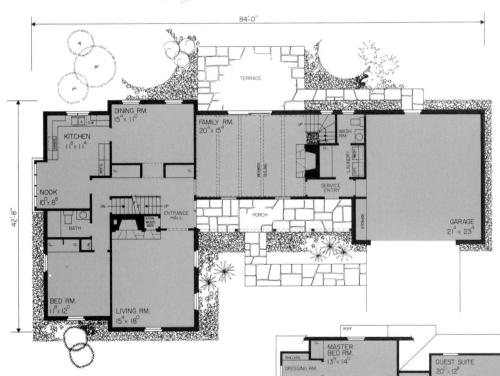

Note that the large guest suite, featuring a full bath, is only accessible by the back stairs in the family room. You could use it as a spacious library, play-room, or a hobby area. Two fireplaces (one with a built-in wood box), walk-in closets, covered front porch and rear terrace also highlight this home.

Design by
Home Planners,
Inc.

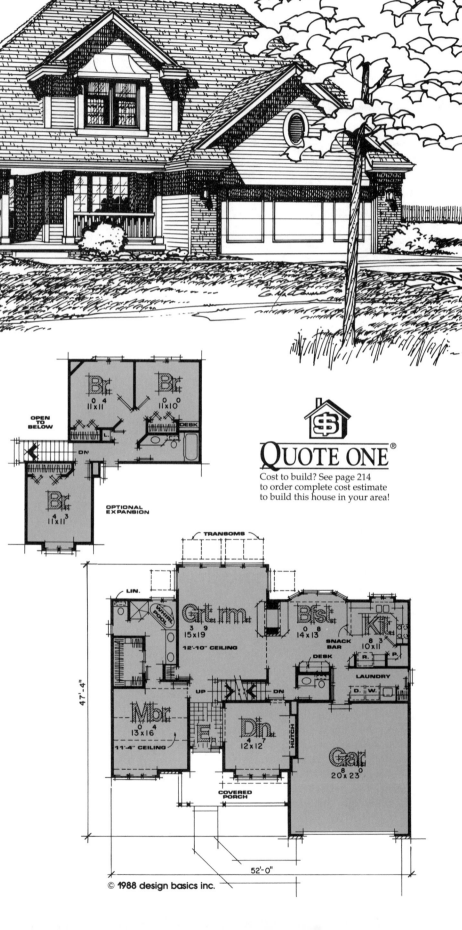

Design Q9206

First Floor: 1,421 square feet
Second Floor: 578 square feet
Total: 1,999 square feet

● Growing families will love this
unique plan which combines all the
essentials with an abundance of stylish
touches. Start with the living areas — a
spacious great room with high ceilings,
windows overlooking the back yard, a
through-fireplace to the kitchen and
access to the rear yard. A dining room
with hutch space accommodates formal
occasions. The hearth kitchen features a
well-planned work area and a bay-
windowed breakfast area. The master
suite with whirlpool and walk-in closet
is found downstairs while three family
bedrooms are upstairs.

Design by
Design
Basics,
Inc.

Quote One®

Cost to build? See page 214
to order complete cost estimate
to build this house in your area!

© 1988 design basics inc.

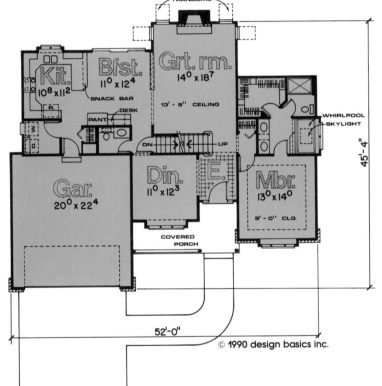

© 1990 design basics inc.

Design Q9247

First Floor: 1,297 square feet
Second Floor: 558 square feet
Total: 1,855 square feet

● Here's the perfect family plan with loads of livability. Go beyond the front covered porch and you'll find a thoughtful floor plan. A formal dining room with large boxed window is a complement to the great room with handsome fireplace and tall windows. A snack bar, pantry, two lazy Susans and planning desk grace the kitchen/breakfast room area. The master suite is conveniently located on the first floor and features a boxed window and well-appointed bath. Three family bedrooms upstairs share a full bath. Note the volume ceiling above the arched window in bedroom 4.

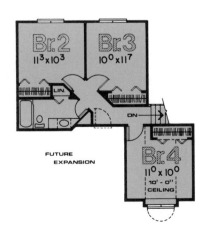

Design by
Design
Basics,
Inc.

Design Q9309

First Floor: 1,506 square feet
Second Floor: 633 square feet
Total: 2,139 square feet

● Graceful lines and arched windows create a delightful country flair for this 1½-story home. From the volume entry, there's a clear view of the stunning great room enhanced by the handsome fireplace and windows with a view. The adjacent dining room is perfect for entertaining. A dinette, open to the island kitchen, allows sunlight to brighten and warm this family-sized eating area. The covered patio is accessed from the dinette. In the gourmet kitchen, convenience is evident through features such as a snack bar, planning desk and walk-in pantry. The main-floor master suite sports a beautiful arched window, double doors and sloped ceiling. A two-person whirlpool, His and Hers vanities and a decorator plant ledge complement the master dressing area. Three secondary bedrooms upstairs share a hall bath.

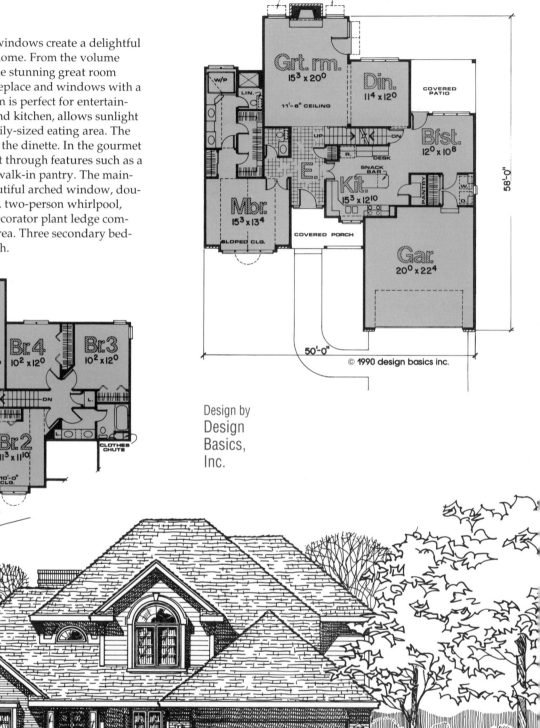

Design by
Design Basics, Inc.

© 1990 design basics inc.

Design Q9219

First Floor: 1,132 square feet
Second Floor: 1,087 square feet
Total: 2,219 square feet

● The detailed front porch, attractive chimney and overall pleasing exterior make this home a delight in any neighborhood. The interior features a floor plan for active families. The front dining room includes a formal, tiered ceiling and hutch space. The great room with fireplace and ten-foot ceiling provides multi-purpose living space. The ample kitchen includes a breakfast room with bay window. The highlight of the four-bedroom sleeping area is the master suite with elegant vaulted ceiling and skylit bath with whirlpool.

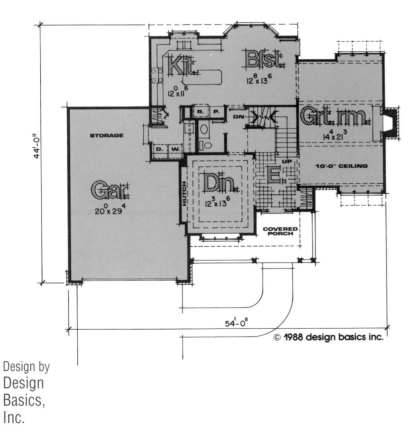

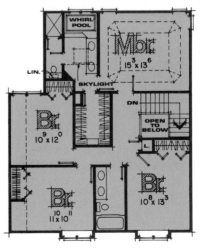

Design by
Design
Basics,
Inc.

© 1988 design basics inc.

Design Q3356

First Floor: 1,610 square feet
Second Floor: 1,200 square feet
Total: 2,810 square feet

L **D**

● Traditionally speaking, this home takes blue ribbons. Its family room has a raised-hearth fireplace and there's a covered porch reached through sliding glass doors for informal eating. The living room also has a fireplace and is near the boxed-windowed dining room. A large clutter room off the garage could be turned into a hobby or sewing room. Four bedrooms on the second floor include a master suite with His and Hers walk-in closets and three family bedrooms.

Design by
**Home Planners,
Inc.**

Quote One™

Cost to build? See page 214 to order complete cost estimate to build this house in your area!

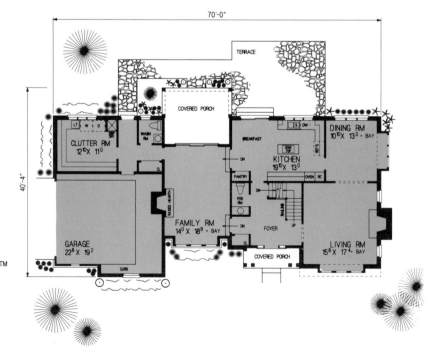

Design Q3351

First Floor: 1,794 square feet
Second Floor: 887 square feet
Total: 2,681 square feet
Attic: 720 square feet

L **D**

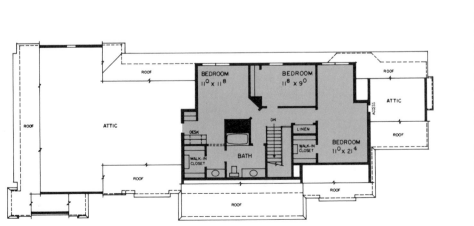

QUOTE ONE™

Cost to build? See page 214
to order complete cost estimate
to build this house in your area!

● Home-grown comfort is the key to
the appeal of this traditionally styled
home. From the kitchen with attached
family room to the living room with
fireplace and attached formal dining
room, this plan has it all. Notice the
first-floor master bedroom with
whirlpool tub and adjacent study. A
nearby powder room turns the study
into a convenient guest room. On the
second floor are three more bedrooms
with ample closet space and a full
bath. The two-car garage has a large
storage area.

Design by
Home Planners,
Inc.

Width 66'
Depth 68'-4"

Design by
Home Planners,
Inc.

Design Q3502

First Floor: 2,086 square feet
Second Floor: 2,040 square feet
Total: 4,126 square feet

L **D**

QUOTE ONE™

Cost to build? See page 214
to order complete cost estimate
to build this house in your area!

● This lovely stone farmhouse is reminiscent of the solid, comfortable homes once so prevalent on homesteads throughout America. The columned front porch leads to a formal foyer with living room on the left and library on the right. The formal dining room connects directly to the living room and indirectly to the island kitchen through a butler's pantry. The family room and breakfast room have beamed ceilings and are both open to the kitchen. A covered veranda is accessed from the breakfast room and leads to a side yard. On the second floor are three bedrooms and a guest room with private bath. The master bedroom has a fireplace and a fine bath with separate shower and whirlpool tub. Two walk-in closets grace the dressing area. The two secondary bedrooms share a full bath with double vanity.

Design Q2542 First Floor: 2,025 square feet
Second Floor: 1,726 square feet; Total: 3,751 square feet

L

Design by
**Home Planners,
Inc.**

● Here is a fieldstone Farmhouse that has its roots in the rolling countryside of Pennsylvania. In addition to its stone exterior, the charm of such a house is characterized by the various appendages. These additions, of course, came into being as the size of the family fortune increased. The living potential offered by this Farmhouse adaptation can hardly be topped. Imagine, five fireplaces! Study the outstanding livability offered in this house from the past. Surely its floor plan has been up-dated to serve today's contemporary family.

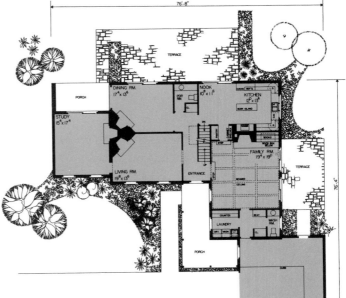

Copyright 1992 Stephen S. Fuller, Inc.

Design Q9862

Square Footage: 2,120

● This classic cottage features a stone and wooden exterior with an arch-detailed porch and box bay window. From the foyer, double doors open to the den with built-in bookcases and a fireplace. A full bath is situated next to the den, allowing for an optional guest room. The family room is centrally located, just beyond the foyer. Its hearth is framed by windows overlooking the porch at the rear of the home. The master bedroom opens onto the rear porch. The master bath, with large walk-in closet, double vanities, corner tub and separate shower completes this relaxing retreat. Left of the family room awaits a sun room with access to the covered porch. A breakfast area complements the attractive and efficiently-designed kitchen. A short hallway from the sun room leads to two bedrooms with large closets and shared full bath featuring double vanities.

Design by
Design Traditions

WIDTH 62'
DEPTH 62'-6"

Quote One®

Cost to build? See page 214 to order complete cost estimate to build this house in your area!

Copyright 1992 Stephen S. Fuller

Design Q9861

First Floor: 1,960 square feet
Second Floor: 965 square feet
Total: 2,925 square feet

● The facade of this charming home is Americana at its best with a rocking-chair porch, bay window and dormers above, finished in stone and wood siding and faithfully detailed. A convenient outdoor entrance to the two-car garage is located to the right of the front porch. The main level features an easy flow, beginning with the dining room to the right of the foyer. A hallway between the foyer and main staircase helps to promote a sense of openness. The great room features a large hearth and French doors to the patio, and leads directly to the breakfast area and kitchen. Storage closets and a counter-top desk area highlight the kitchen which, along with the laundry room, is conveniently located to the rear of the home. Left of the foyer is an attractive study with a large bay window. The master suite, featuring a bay-windowed sitting area, large master bath with double vanities and shower and ample closet space, completes the main level. On the upper level, bedroom two features a full bath and has three dormer windows overlooking the front lawn. The third and fourth bedrooms share another full bath.

Design by
Design Traditions
Atlanta

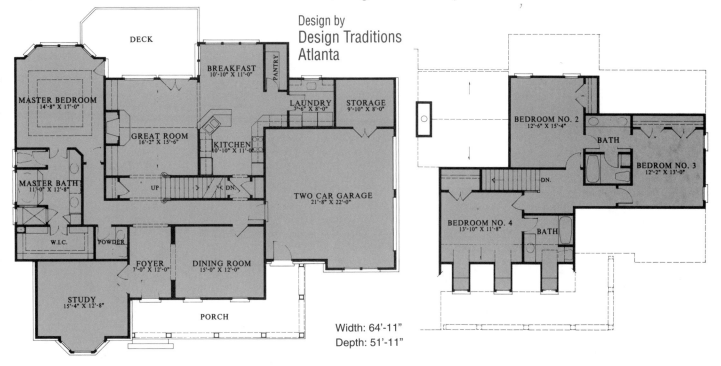

Width: 64'-11"
Depth: 51'-11"

Design Q2633

First Floor: 1,338 square feet
Second Floor: 1,200 square feet
Third Floor: 506 square feet
Total: 3,044 square feet

● This is certainly a pleasing Georgian. Its facade features a front porch with a roof supported by 12'' diameter wooden columns. The garage wing has a sheltered service entry and brick facing which complements the design. Sliding glass doors link the terrace and family room, providing an indoor/outdoor area for entertaining as pictured in the rear elevation. The floor plan has been designed to serve the family efficiently. The stairway in the foyer leads to four second-floor bedrooms. The third floor is windowed and can be used as a studio and study.

Design by
Home Planners,
Inc.

● This two-story farmhouse brings to mind the stone houses of Bucks County, Pa. The recessed center entrance opens to the foyer. To the left is the living room with its adjacent music alcove. The sunken study offers a guest retreat. The efficient, U-shaped kitchen functions

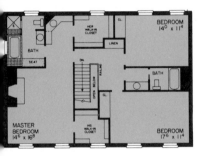

well with the large breakfast room and separate dining room with fireplace. The three bedroom upstairs features nice sized rooms and a fourth fireplace. Note the laundry.

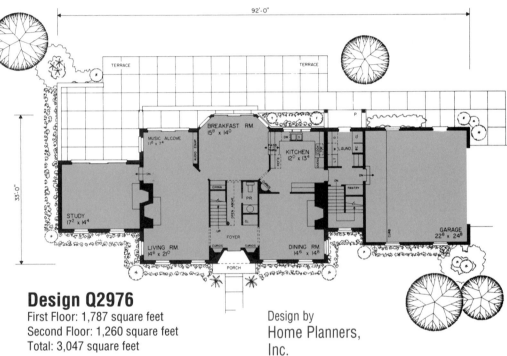

Design Q2976

First Floor: 1,787 square feet
Second Floor: 1,260 square feet
Total: 3,047 square feet

Design by
**Home Planners,
Inc.**

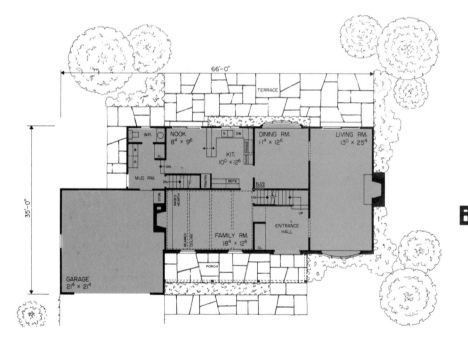

Design by
Home Planners,
Inc.

Design Q2223 First Floor: 1,266 square feet
Second Floor: 1,232 square feet; Total: 2,498 square feet

L **D**

● The appealing double front doors of this home open wide to fine livability for the large, growing family. The spacious entrance hall is flanked by the formal, end living room and the all-purpose, beamed ceiling family room. Both rooms have a commanding fire-

place. The U-shaped kitchen overlooks the rear yard and is but a step, or two, from the breakfast nook and the formal dining room. The mud room controls the flows of traffic during the inclement weather. Observe the laundry equipment and the washroom. Five

bedrooms, two full baths, and plenty of closets are what make the second floor truly outstanding. There are a number of other convenient living features that make this design distinctive. How many of these can you list?

CONTEMPORARY FARMHOUSES

Seemingly diverse, the notions of *contemporary* and *farmhouse* blend surprisingly well. In the Contemporary Farmhouse, design takes a classic 1½- or two-story farmhouse structure and modifies it with more rounded, open or vaulted forms.

The style may have begun in the West, particularly California and the Pacific Coast, and spread eastward to the Midwest, South and East — in direct opposition to traditional farmhouse evolution.

Wood, stone and glass are the major components of the style and afford it a contemporary look and ambience. The contemporary use of glass gives the style its characteristic open-air, light-filled properties. The open floor plans that are usually contained in these homes allow for easy traffic patterns and great indoor/outdoor livability.

Many fine examples of this divergent style are presented. Designs Q9310 and Q9311 represent the Modern Midwest Wood style and take their forms and feeling from traditional dwellings popular in the Midwest. Adding a more contemporary feel, however, are the arched details, half-round windows and the clean, simple lines. More reminiscent of the Pacific Northwest are designs such as Q9480 which stands tall and upright and features French-styled rooflines. The arched window in the foyer is repeated in the bonus room over the garage. In the best Southern tradition are two designs, Q9761 and Q9619, which feature contemporary additions such as the skylit sun rooms and the lovely rear decks. Maintaining traditional appeal, however, is the chimney cap on Design Q9619. Designs Q3404 and Q3438 are exquisite echoes of the Tin-Roof or Shed-Roof style but are often referred to as the California Farmhouse or California Contemporary Farmhouse. Each has the bold statement of contemporary design, yet keeps a rustic sense. Both floor plans are open and spacious in the best contemporary style. Blending the best elements of traditional and contemporary details, Design Q2931 can be classified as a Transitional home. Resembling a Cape Cod, with winged extensions and multi-paned windows, it also incorporates large patio areas and vertical wood siding, giving it a contemporary accent.

The Contemporary Farmhouses in this section represent an entirely new and exciting form for the standard country residence. Though perhaps not for the farmhouse purist, these evolved designs provide a wonderful option for those who love the fluidity of contemporary form and the grace of traditional style.

Design Q3466

Square Footage: 1,800

L D

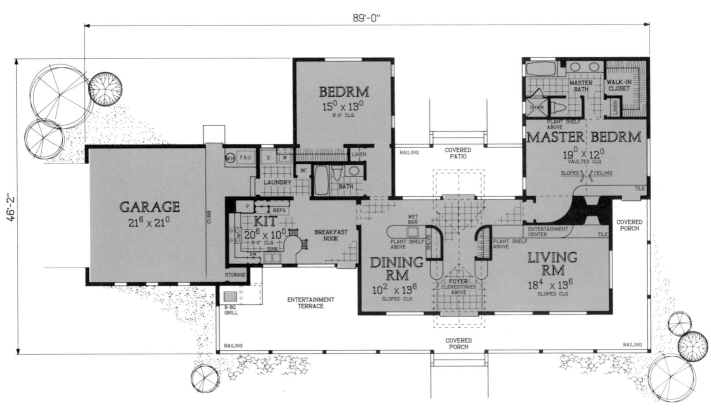

QUOTE ONE™

Cost to build? See page 214 to order complete cost estimate to build this house in your area!

● Small but inviting, this one-story ranch-style farmhouse is the perfect choice for a small family or empty-nesters. It's loaded with amenities even the most particular homeowner can appreciate. For example, the living room and dining room each have plant shelves, sloped ceilings and built-ins to enhance livability. The living room also sports a warming hearth. The master bedroom contains a well-appointed bath with dual vanity and walk-in closet. The additional bedroom has its own bath with linen storage. The kitchen is separated from the breakfast nook by a clever bar area. Access to the two-car garage is through a laundry area with washer/dryer hookup space. For information on customizing this design, call 1-800-521-6797, ext. 800.

Design by
Home Planners,
Inc.

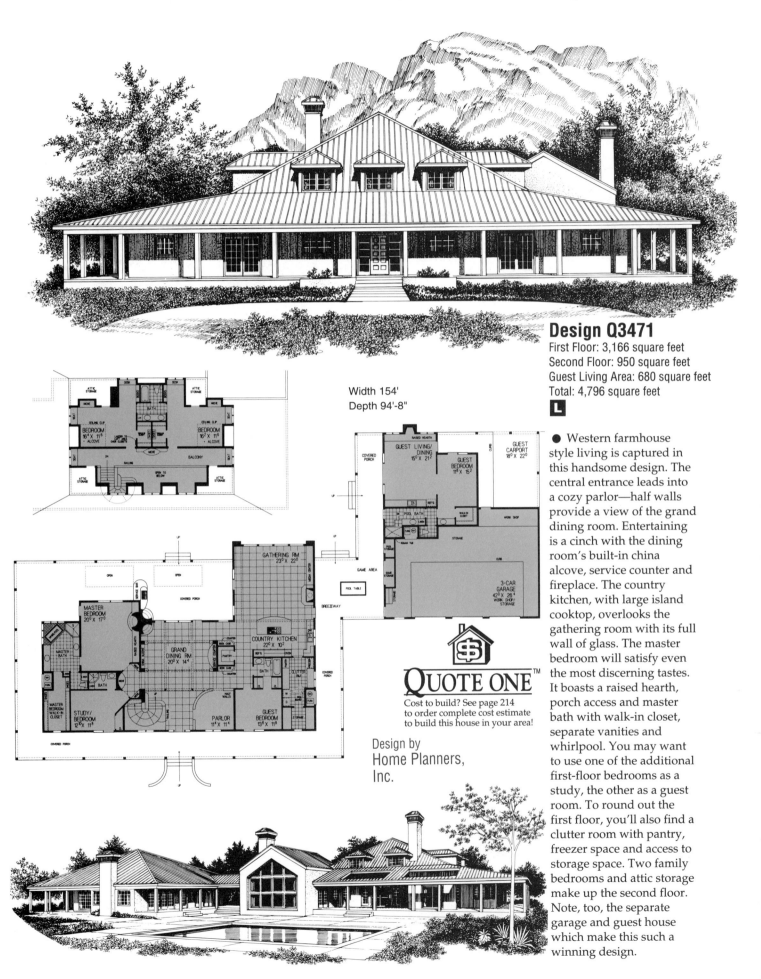

Design Q3471

First Floor: 3,166 square feet
Second Floor: 950 square feet
Guest Living Area: 680 square feet
Total: 4,796 square feet

Width 154'
Depth 94'-8"

Quote One™

Cost to build? See page 214
to order complete cost estimate
to build this house in your area!

Design by
Home Planners,
Inc.

● Western farmhouse style living is captured in this handsome design. The central entrance leads into a cozy parlor—half walls provide a view of the grand dining room. Entertaining is a cinch with the dining room's built-in china alcove, service counter and fireplace. The country kitchen, with large island cooktop, overlooks the gathering room with its full wall of glass. The master bedroom will satisfy even the most discerning tastes. It boasts a raised hearth, porch access and master bath with walk-in closet, separate vanities and whirlpool. You may want to use one of the additional first-floor bedrooms as a study, the other as a guest room. To round out the first floor, you'll also find a clutter room with pantry, freezer space and access to storage space. Two family bedrooms and attic storage make up the second floor. Note, too, the separate garage and guest house which make this such a winning design.

Design Q3438

First Floor: 1,489 square feet
Second Floor: 741 square feet
Total: 2,230 square feet

L

● A unique farmhouse plan which provides a grand floor plan, this home is comfortable in country or suburban settings. Formal entertaining areas share first-floor space with family gathering rooms and work and service areas. The master suite is also on this floor for convenience and privacy. Upstairs is a guest bedroom, private bath and loft area that makes a perfect studio. Special features make this a great place to come home to.

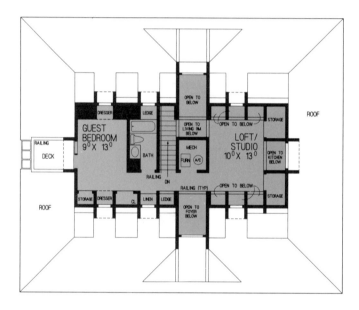

Design by
Home Planners,
Inc.

QUOTE ONE™
Cost to build? See page 214
to order complete cost estimate
to build this house in your area!

Design Q3443

First Floor: 1,211 square feet
Second Floor: 614 square feet
Total: 1,825 square feet

L **D**

QUOTE ONE™

Cost to build? See page 214
to order complete cost estimate
to build this house in your area!

Design by
Home Planners,
Inc.

● What a pampering retreat! The master suite in this house is on a level all its own. The 21-foot bedroom includes a sitting area. The master bath features a walk-in closet, dual vanities, separate tub and shower and a compartmented toilet. A second bedroom or optional den, with a full bath nearby, is located on the first floor. The formal living and dining room have sloped ceilings separated by a plant shelf and bay windows. The family room features a snack bar to the kitchen and patio access. Tiled floors throughout add a special touch. Note the hobby shop in the garage. For information on customizing this design, call 1-800-521-6797, ext. 800.

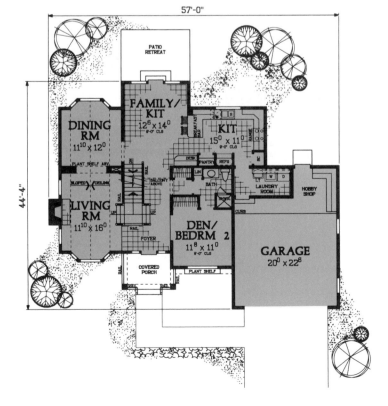

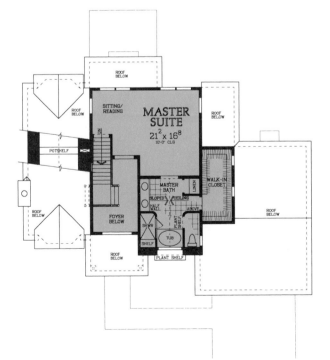

Design Q9312

First Floor: 1,150 square feet
Second Floor: 1,120 square feet
Total: 2,270 square feet

● Lap siding, special windows and a covered porch enhance the elevation of this popular style. The spacious two-story entry surveys the formal dining room with hutch space. An entertainment center, through-fireplace and bayed windows add appeal to the great room. Families will love the spacious kitchen, breakfast and hearth room. Enhancements to this casual living area include a through-fireplace, gazebo dinette, wrapping counters, an island kitchen and planning desk. An efficient U-shaped staircase routes traffic throughout. Comfortable secondary bedrooms and a sumptuous master suite feature privacy by design. Bedroom 3 is highlighted by a half round window, volume ceiling and double closets while Bedroom 4 features a built-in desk. The master suite has a vaulted ceiling, large walk-in closet, His and Hers vanities, compartmented stool/shower area and an oval whirlpool tub.

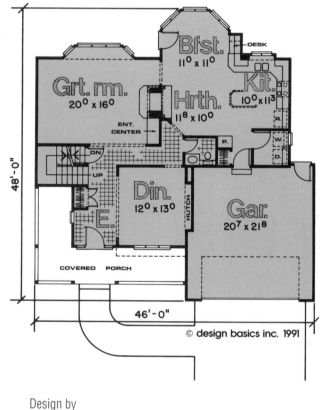

© design basics inc. 1991

Design by
Design
Basics,
Inc.

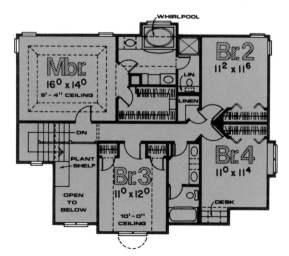

196

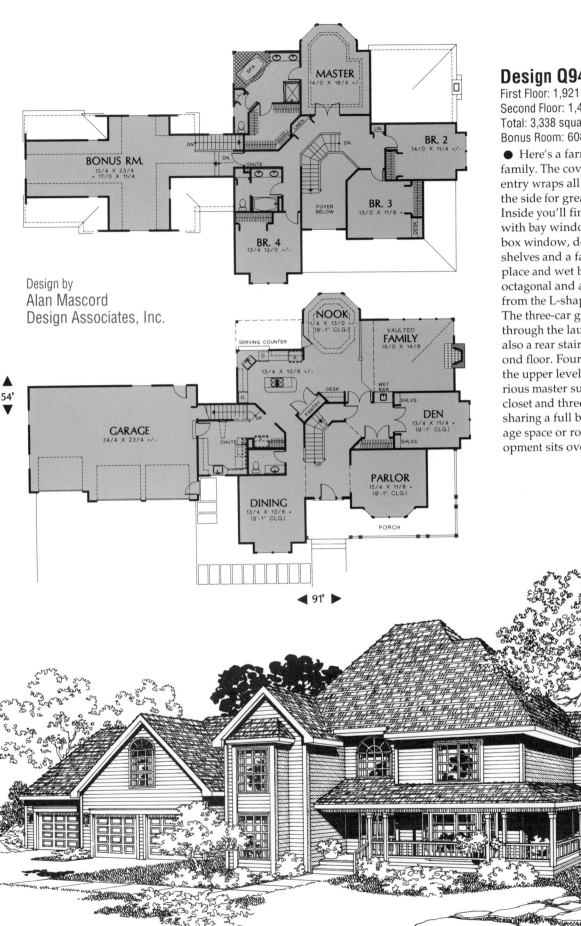

BONUS RM.
12/4 X 23/4
+ 17/0 X 11/4

MASTER
14/0 X 18/4 +/-

SPA

BR. 2
14/0 X 11/4 +/-

BR. 3
13/0 X 11/8

FOYER
BELOW

BR. 4
13/4 12/0 +/-

DN.

CHUTE

LINEN

LIN.

DESK

Design by
Alan Mascord
Design Associates, Inc.

NOOK
11/4 X 13/0 +/-
(9'-1" CLG.)

VAULTED
FAMILY
19/0 X 14/8

SERVING COUNTER

13/4 X 10/8 +/-

DESK

WET BAR

SHLVS.

DEN
13/4 X 11/4 +/-
(9'-1" CLG.)

PANTRY

SHLVS.

GARAGE
34/4 X 23/4 +/-

CHUTE

UP

UP

PARLOR
15/4 X 11/8 +/-
(9'-1" CLG.)

DINING
13/4 X 13/8
(9'-1" CLG.)

PORCH

54'

91'

Design Q9480

First Floor: 1,921 square feet
Second Floor: 1,417 square feet
Total: 3,338 square feet
Bonus Room: 608 square feet

● Here's a farmhouse for a large family. The covered porch at the entry wraps all the way around to the side for great outdoor living. Inside you'll find a formal parlor with bay window, dining room with box window, den with built-in shelves and a family room with fireplace and wet bar. The nook is octagonal and allows casual meals from the L-shaped island kitchen. The three-car garage is reached through the laundry area. There is also a rear staircase here to the second floor. Four bedrooms reside on the upper level. Included are a luxurious master suite with huge walk-in closet and three family bedrooms sharing a full bath. Additional storage space or room for future development sits over the garage.

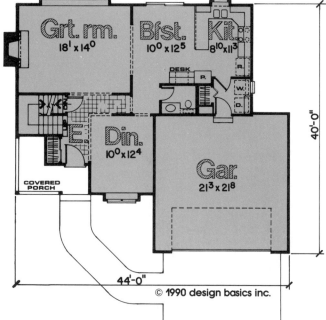

COVERED PORCH

Grt. rm.
18¹ x 14⁰

Bfst.
10⁰ x 12⁵

Kit.
8¹⁰ x 11³

DESK

Din.
10⁰ x 12⁴

Gar.
21³ x 21⁸

40'-0"

44'-0"

© 1990 design basics inc.

Design Q9260

First Floor: 891 square feet
Second Floor: 759 square feet
Total: 1,650 square feet

● A quaint covered porch leads to a volume entry with decorator plant ledge above the closet in this home. The formal dining room has a boxed window that can be seen from the entry. A fireplace in the large great room adds warmth and coziness to the attached breakfast room and well-planned kitchen. Notice the nearby powder room for guests. Upstairs are three bedrooms. Bedroom 3 has a beautiful arched window under a volume ceiling. The master bedroom has a walk-in closet and pampering dressing area with double vanity and a whirlpool under a window. The upstairs landing overlooks the entry below.

Design by
Design Basics, Inc.

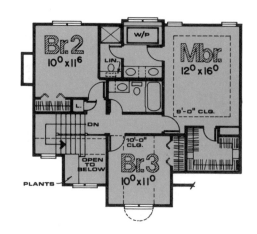

Br. 2
10⁰ x 11⁶

w/p

Mbr.
12⁰ x 16⁰

9'-0" CLG.

LIN.

DN

10'-0" CLG.

OPEN TO BELOW

Br. 3
10⁰ x 11⁰

PLANTS

Design Q9235

First Floor: 919 square feet
Second Floor: 927 square feet
Total: 1,846 square feet

● Wonderful country design begins with the wraparound porch of this plan. Explore further and find a two-story entry with a coat closet and plant shelf above and a strategically placed staircase alongside. The island kitchen with a boxed window over the sink is adjacent to a large bay-windowed dinette. The great room includes many windows and a fireplace. A powder bath and laundry room are both conveniently placed on the first floor. Upstairs, the large master suite contains His and Hers walk-in closets, corner windows and a bath area featuring a double vanity and whirlpool tub. Two pleasant secondary bedrooms have interesting angles and a third bedroom in the front features a volume ceiling and arched window.

Design by
Design Basics, Inc.

© 1989 design basics inc.

QUOTE ONE®

Cost to build? See page 214 to order complete cost estimate to build this house in your area!

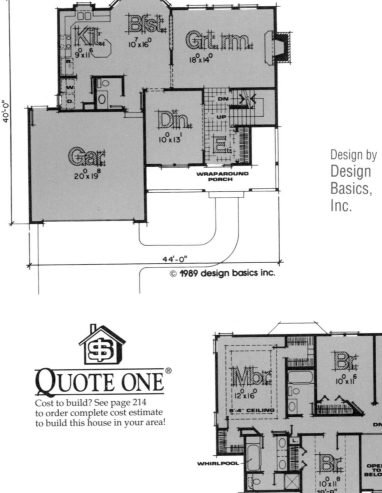

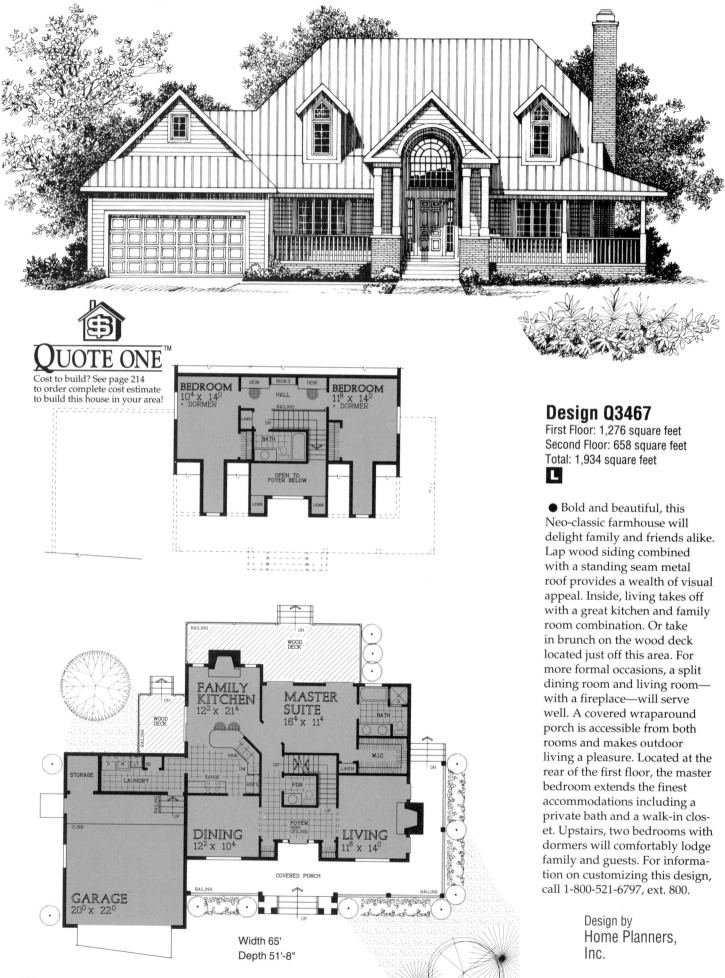

BEDROOM
10⁴ x 14⁰
+ DORMER

DESK   BOOKS   DESK
HALL

BEDROOM
11⁸ x 14⁰
+ DORMER

LINEN
DN
BATH
RAILING

OPEN TO
FOYER BELOW

LEDGE   LEDGE

Design Q3467

First Floor: 1,276 square feet
Second Floor: 658 square feet
Total: 1,934 square feet

L

● Bold and beautiful, this Neo-classic farmhouse will delight family and friends alike. Lap wood siding combined with a standing seam metal roof provides a wealth of visual appeal. Inside, living takes off with a great kitchen and family room combination. Or take in brunch on the wood deck located just off this area. For more formal occasions, a split dining room and living room—with a fireplace—will serve well. A covered wraparound porch is accessible from both rooms and makes outdoor living a pleasure. Located at the rear of the first floor, the master bedroom extends the finest accommodations including a private bath and a walk-in closet. Upstairs, two bedrooms with dormers will comfortably lodge family and guests. For information on customizing this design, call 1-800-521-6797, ext. 800.

RAILING

WOOD
DECK

DN

WOOD
DECK

DN

FAMILY
KITCHEN
12² x 21⁴

MASTER
SUITE
16⁴ x 11⁴

BATH

SINK

DW

W.I.C.

STORAGE

D   W   LT   BC

LAUNDRY

RANGE

REF'G

DN

LINEN

DN

CURB

RAILING

UP

PDR

UP

DINING
12² x 10⁴

FOYER
HIGH
CEILING

LIVING
11⁸ x 14⁰

GARAGE
20⁰ x 22⁰

COVERED PORCH

RAILING

RAILING

UP

Width 65'
Depth 51'-8"

Design by
Home Planners, Inc.

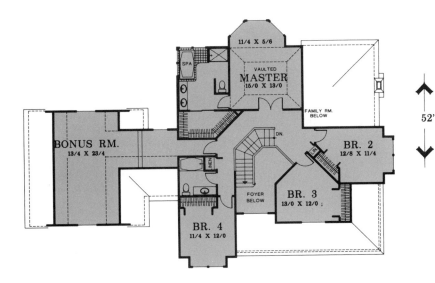

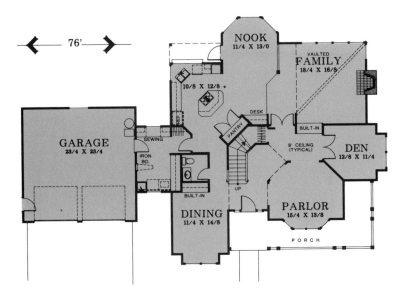

Design Q9458

First Floor: 1,730 square feet
Second Floor: 1,215 square feet
Total: 2,945 square feet
Bonus Room: 462 square feet

● Though its facade says country casual, this home has a floor plan that is as elegant and modern as any. The front porch wraps around a formal farmhouse parlor with bay window. This room is almost completely open to the foyer and sits right next to the more private den. The large family room features a vaulted ceiling and fireplace. It blends into the bay-windowed nook adjacent to the L-shaped island kitchen. A powder room separates the space between the kitchen and formal dining room with boxed window. Up an open staircase is the four-bedroom second floor. Three family bedrooms share a full bath. The master suite has a vaulted ceiling, large walk-in closet and bath with spa.

Design by
**Alan Mascord
Design Associates, Inc.**

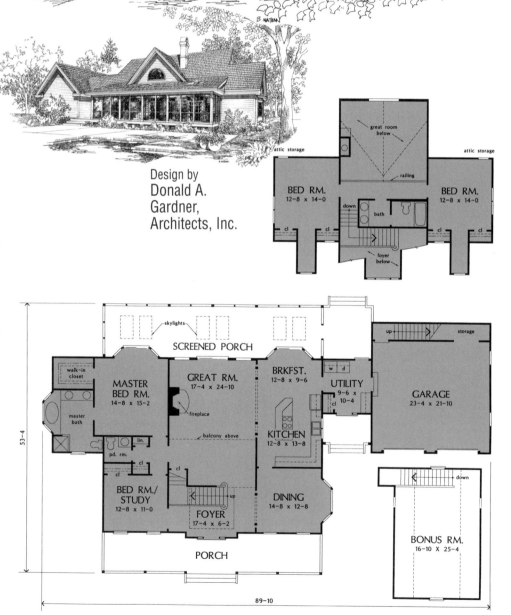

Design Q9761

First Floor: 1,907 square feet
Second Floor: 656 square feet
Total: 2,563 square feet

● Bay windows are located on all sides of this fine country home. The foyer leads to a bedroom, or if you prefer, a study to the left, and, through a columned entrance, to the formal dining room to the right. Straight ahead is the expansive great room with a cathedral ceiling and an overhead balcony. The large screened porch features skylights and may be accessed from the great room, the master bedroom and the breakfast area. The master suite features a bay window, a large walk-in closet and a lavish bath with a whirlpool tub. Two dormered family bedrooms share a full bath on the second floor.

Design by
Donald A.
Gardner,
Architects, Inc.

REAR

Design by
Donald A.
Gardner,
Architects, Inc.

GARAGE
20-4 × 20-4

DECK
36-8 × 10-0

covered
breezeway

SUN RM.
15-8 × 7-10

hot tub

GREAT RM.
20-0 × 15-6
(cathedral ceiling)

fireplace

UTILITY
9-0 × 5-4

wash
dry

bath

BED RM.
11-4 × 13-8

powder
rm.

lin.

master bath

walk-in
closet

rail

cl

BED RM.
14-8 × 11-0

MASTER
BED RM.
13-4 × 16-8

FOYER
4-6 × 12-4

DINING
12-0 × 12-0

KITCHEN
14-4 × 12-0

cl

cl

PORCH
19-2 × 5-0

BRKFST.
13-4 × 7-8

67-4

67-6

Design Q9619
Square Footage: 2,021

● Multi-pane windows, shutters,
dormers, bay windows and a
delightful covered porch grace the
facade of this country cottage.
Inside, the floor plan is no less
appealing. The great room has a
fireplace, a cathedral ceiling and
sliding glass doors with an arched
window above to allow for natural
illumination of the room. A sun
room with a hot tub leads to an
adjacent deck. This space can also
be reached from the master bath.
The generous master bedroom has
a walk-in closet and a spacious
bath with a double-bowl vanity, a
shower and a garden tub. Two
additional bedrooms are located at
the other end of the house for privacy. The garage is connected to
the house by a breezeway. Please
specify basement or crawlspace
when ordering.

FRONT

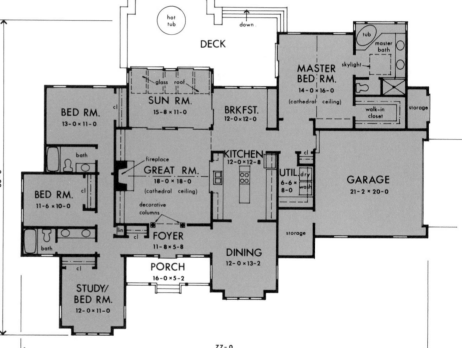

Design Q9647
Square Footage: 2,413

● Multi-paned windows, dormers, a covered porch and two projected windows with shed roofs offer a welcoming front exterior to this wonderful one-story home. The great room with cathedral ceiling, paddle fan, built-in cabinets and bookshelves has direct access to the sun room through two sliding glass doors. Columns between the foyer and great room create a dramatic entrance to the great room. The kitchen and cooking island serve both the dining room and breakfast area as well as the great room via a pass-through. The master suite has a double-door entrance and cathedral ceiling and overlooks the rear deck through a sliding glass door. Three family bedrooms and two baths are found at the other end of the house for privacy. The front bedroom could double as a study. The two-car garage contains ample storage space.

Design by
Donald A. Gardner, Architect, Inc.

Design Q9750

Square Footage: 1,575
Bonus Room: 276 square feet

● A covered porch and dormers combine to create the inviting exterior on this three-bedroom country home. The foyer leads through columns to an expansive great room with a cozy fireplace, built-in bookshelves and access to the rear covered porch. To the right, an open kitchen is conveniently situated to easily serve the bay-windowed breakfast area and the formal dining room.

Sleeping quarters are located on the left, where the master suite enjoys access to the covered porch, a walk-in closet and a relaxing master bath complete with double-bowl vanities, a whirlpool tub and a separate shower. A utility room, two secondary bedrooms and a full bath complete this plan.

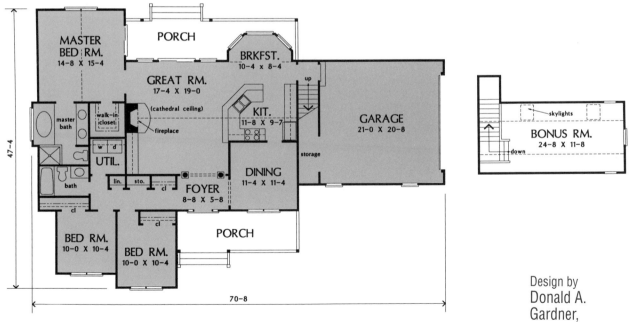

Design by
Donald A.
Gardner,
Architects, Inc.

Design Q9670
Square Footage: 2,046

● This three-bedroom country cottage projects an intriguing appearance with its bay windows, dormers and L-shaped layout. The great room has a cathedral ceiling along with an arched window above the exterior door leading to the deck. The sun room with operable skylights is accessible from the great room, kitchen and deck for maximum exposure. The centrally located kitchen allows direct access to eating and living areas. Three bedrooms include a master suite and a bedroom that might also be useful as a study.

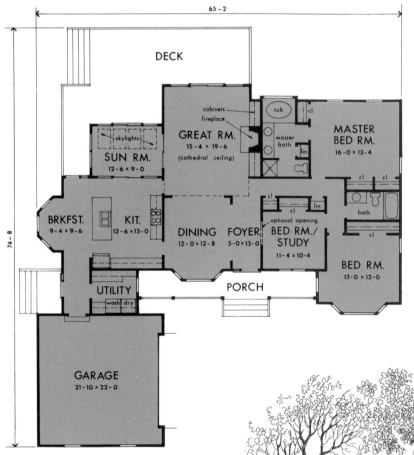

65 – 2

DECK

74 – 8

SUN RM.
12-6 × 9-0

skylights

GREAT RM.
15-4 × 19-6
(cathedral ceiling)

cabinets
fireplace

tub

master
bath

lin.

cl

MASTER
BED RM.
16-0 × 13-4

BRKFST.
9-4 × 9-6

KIT.
12-6 × 13-0

DINING
12-0 × 12-8

FOYER
5-0 × 13-0

BED RM./
STUDY
11-4 × 10-4

optional opening

cl

lin.

bath

cl

cl

cl

BED RM.
13-0 × 12-0

UTILITY

wash dry

PORCH

GARAGE
21-10 × 23-0

Design by
Donald A.
Gardner,
Architect, Inc.

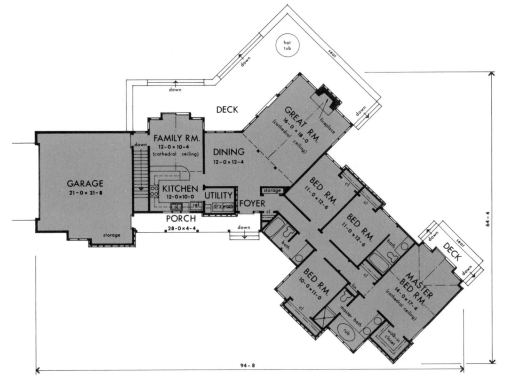

Design Q9601
Square Footage: 1,988

● This country-style ranch is the essence of excitement with its combination of exterior building materials and interesting shapes. Because it is angled, it allows for flexibility in design—the great room and/or the family room can be lengthened to meet family space requirements. The master bedroom has a cathedral ceiling, a walk-in closet, private deck and a spacious master bath with whirlpool tub. There are three family bedrooms, two of which share a full bath and one having a private bath. Expansive deck area with space for a hot tub wraps around interior family gathering areas. Both family room and great room have cathedral ceilings; the great room has a fireplace. For crawl-space foundation, order Design Q9601; for partial basement foundation, order Design Q9601-A.

Design by
Donald A.
Gardner,
Architect, Inc.

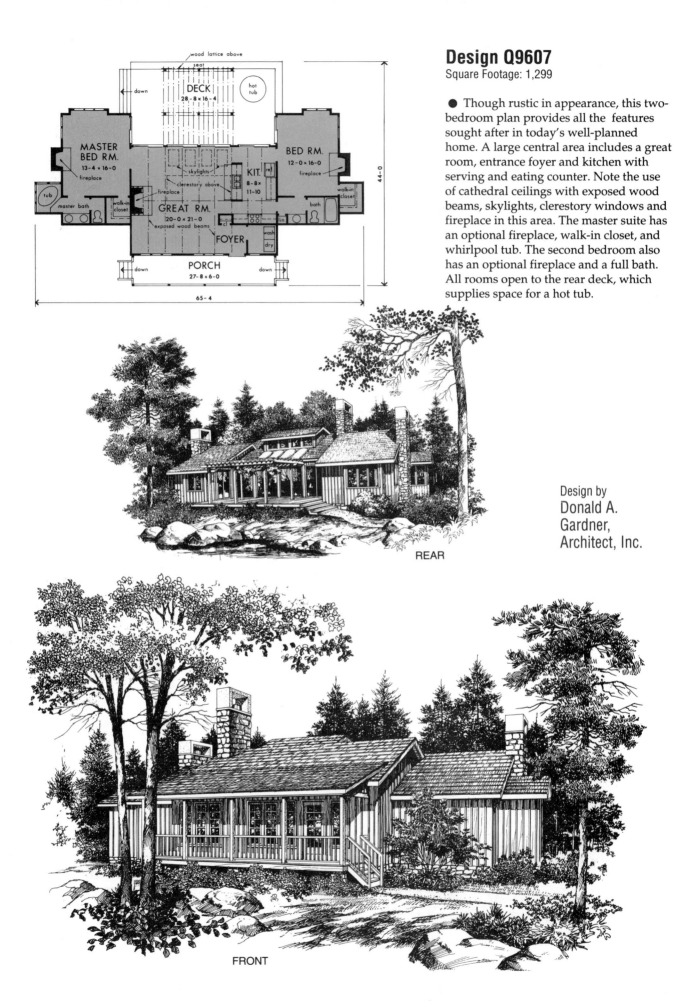

Design Q9607
Square Footage: 1,299

● Though rustic in appearance, this two-bedroom plan provides all the features sought after in today's well-planned home. A large central area includes a great room, entrance foyer and kitchen with serving and eating counter. Note the use of cathedral ceilings with exposed wood beams, skylights, clerestory windows and fireplace in this area. The master suite has an optional fireplace, walk-in closet, and whirlpool tub. The second bedroom also has an optional fireplace and a full bath. All rooms open to the rear deck, which supplies space for a hot tub.

Design by
Donald A.
Gardner,
Architect, Inc.

REAR

FRONT

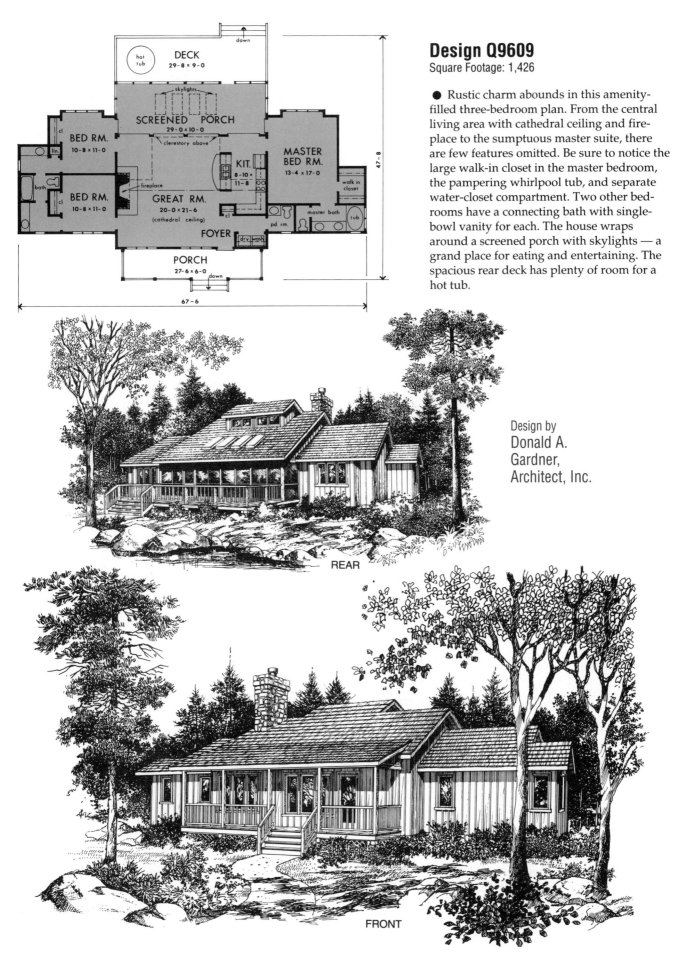

Design Q9609
Square Footage: 1,426

● Rustic charm abounds in this amenity-filled three-bedroom plan. From the central living area with cathedral ceiling and fireplace to the sumptuous master suite, there are few features omitted. Be sure to notice the large walk-in closet in the master bedroom, the pampering whirlpool tub, and separate water-closet compartment. Two other bedrooms have a connecting bath with single-bowl vanity for each. The house wraps around a screened porch with skylights — a grand place for eating and entertaining. The spacious rear deck has plenty of room for a hot tub.

Design by
Donald A.
Gardner,
Architect, Inc.

REAR

FRONT

209

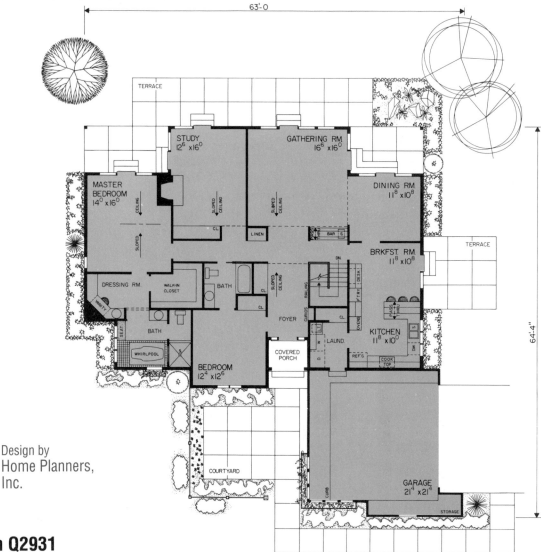

Design by
Home Planners,
Inc.

Design Q2931
Square Footage: 2,032

● Little details make the difference in this charming showplace: picket-fenced courtyard, carriage lamp, window boxes, shutters, muntined windows, multi-gabled roof, cornice returns, vertical and horizontal siding with corner board, front door with glass side lites, etc. Inside this appealing exterior there is a truly outstanding floor plan for the small family or empty-nesters. The master bedroom suite is long on luxury with a separate dressing room, private vanities, and whirlpool bath. An adjacent study, with warming fireplace, is just the right retreat. Other attractions: roomy kitchen and breakfast area, spacious gathering room, rear and side terraces, and an attached two-car garage with storage. For information on customizing this design, call 1-800-521-6797, ext. 800.

Design by
Home Planners, Inc.

QUOTE ONE™

Cost to build? See page 214
to order complete cost estimate
to build this house in your area!

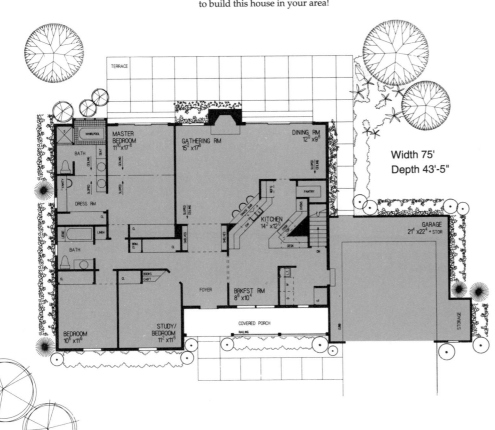

Width 75'
Depth 43'-5"

Design Q2947
Square Footage: 1,830

L **D**

● This charming one-story traditional home greets visitors with a covered porch. A uniquely shaped galley-style kitchen shares a snack bar with the spacious gathering room where a fireplace is the focal point. The dining room has sliding glass doors to the rear terrace as does the master suite. This bedroom area also includes a luxury bath with whirlpool tub and separate dressing room. Two additional bedrooms, one that could double as a study, are located at the front of the home. The two-car garage features a large storage area and can be reached through the service entrance to the home or from the rear terrace. For information on customizing this design, call 1-800-521-6797, ext. 800. California Engineered Plans and California Stock Plans are available for this home. Call 1-800-521-6797 for more information.

When You're Ready To Order . . .

Let Us Show You Our Home Blueprint Package.

Building a home? Planning a home? Our Blueprint Package has nearly everything you need to get the job done right, whether you're working on your own or with help from an architect, designer, builder or subcontractors. Each Blueprint Package is the result of many hours of work by licensed architects or professional designers.

QUALITY

Hundreds of hours of painstaking effort have gone into the development of your blueprint set. Each home has been quality-checked by professionals to insure accuracy and buildability.

VALUE

Because we sell in volume, you can buy professional-quality blueprints at a fraction of their development cost. With our plans, your dream home design costs only a few hundred dollars, not the thousands of dollars that custom architects charge.

SERVICE

Once you've chosen your favorite home plan, you'll receive fast, efficient service whether you choose to mail or fax your order to us or call us toll free at 1-800-521-6797.

SATISFACTION

Over 50 years of service to satisfied home plan buyers provide us unparalleled experience and knowledge in producing quality blueprints. What this means to you is satisfaction with our product and performance.

ORDER TOLL FREE 1-800-521-6797

After you've looked over our Blueprint Package and Important Extras on the following pages, simply mail the order form on page 221 or call toll free on our Blueprint Hotline: 1-800-521-6797. We're ready and eager to serve you.

· ·

Each set of blueprints is an interrelated collection of detail sheets which includes components such as floor plans, interior and exterior elevations, dimensions, cross-sections, diagrams and notations. These sheets show exactly how your house is to be built.

Among the sheets included may be:

Frontal Sheet
This artist's sketch of the exterior of the house gives you an idea of how the house will look when built and landscaped. Large ink-line floor plans show all levels of the house and provide an overview of your new home's livability, as well as a handy reference for deciding on furniture placement.

Foundation Plan
This sheet shows the foundation layout includ-

SAMPLE PACKAGE

ing support walls, excavated and unexcavated areas, if any, and foundation notes. If slab construction rather than basement, the plan shows footings and details for a monolithic slab. This page, or another in the set, may include a sample plot plan for locating your house on a building site.

Detailed Floor Plans

These plans show the layout of each floor of the house. Rooms and interior spaces are carefully dimensioned and keys are given for cross-section details provided later in the plans. The positions of electrical outlets and switches are shown.

House Cross-Sections

Large-scale views show sections or cut-aways of the foundation, interior walls, exterior walls, floors, stairways and roof details. Additional cross-sections may show important changes in floor, ceiling or roof heights or the relationship of one level to another. Extremely valuable for construction, these sections show exactly how the various parts of the house fit together.

Interior Elevations

Many of our drawings show the design and placement of kitchen and bathroom cabinets, laundry areas, fireplaces, bookcases and other built-ins. Little "extras," such as mantelpiece and wainscoting drawings, plus moulding sections, provide details that give your home that custom touch.

Exterior Elevations

These drawings show the front, rear and sides of your house and give necessary notes on exterior materials and finishes. Particular attention is given to cornice detail, brick and stone accents or other finish items that make your home unique.

Frontal Sheet

Foundation Plans

Detailed Floor Plans

Exterior Elevations

Interior Elevations

House Cross-Sections

*I*ntroducing nine important planning and construction aids

NEW

CUSTOM ENGINEERING

Our Custom Engineering Service Package provides an engineering seal for the structural elements of any Home Planners plan. This new Package provides complete calculations (except foundation engineering) from a registered professional, and offers many options invaluable to anyone planning to build. The Package includes: Structural framing plans for each horizontal framing area; Individual, certified truss designs; Specifications for all framing members; Calculation sheets detailing engineering problems and solutions concerning shear, bending, and deflections for all key framing members; Structural details for all key situations; Hanger and special connections specifications; Load and geometry information that may be used by a foundation design engineer and a Registered Professional Engineer's Seal for all of the above services. Home Planners also offers 3 Optional Engineering Services: Lateral load calculations and specifications for both wind and seismic considerations; Secondary Framing information for roofs, floors and walls; Light-gauge steel framing, providing details and cost comparisons for steel and wood.

SPECIFICATION OUTLINE

This valuable 16-page document is critical to building your house correctly. Designed to be filled in by you or your builder, this book lists 166 stages or items crucial to the building process. It provides a comprehensive review of the construction process and helps in making choices of materials. When combined with the blueprints, a signed contract, and a schedule, it becomes a legal document and record for the building of your home.

MATERIALS LIST

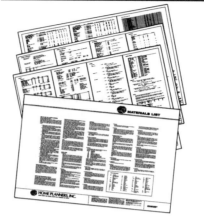

(Note: Because of the diversity of local building codes, our Materials List does not include mechanical materials.)

For many of the designs in our portfolio, we offer a customized materials take-off that is invaluable in planning and estimating the cost of your new home. This Materials List outlines the quantity, type and size of materials needed to build your house (with the exception of mechanical system items). Included are framing lumber, windows and doors, kitchen and bath cabinetry, rough and finish hardware, and much more. This handy list helps you or your builder cost out materials and serves as a reference sheet when you're compiling bids.

QUOTE ONE®

Summary Cost Report / Materials Cost Report

A new service for estimating the cost of building select designs, the Quote One® system is available in two separate stages: The Summary Cost Report and the Materials Cost Report.

The Summary Cost Report is the first stage in the package and shows the total cost per square foot for your chosen home in your zip-code area and then breaks that cost down into ten categories showing the costs for building materials, labor and installation. The total cost for the report (which includes three grades: Budget, Standard and Custom) is just $19.95 for one home, and additionals are only $14.95. These reports allow you to evaluate your building budget and compare the costs of building a variety of homes in your area.

Make even more informed decisions about your home-building project with the second phase of our package, our Materials Cost Report. This tool is invaluable in planning and estimating the cost of your new home. The material and installation (labor and equipment) cost is shown for each of over 1,000 line items provided in the Materials List (Standard grade) which is included when you purchase this estimating tool. It allows you to determine building costs for your specific zip-code area and for your chosen home design. Space is allowed for additional estimates from contractors and subcontractors, such as for mechanical materials, which are not included in our packages. This invaluable tool is available for a price of $110 ($120 for a Schedule E plan) which includes a Materials List.

To order these invaluable reports, use the order form on page 221 or call 1-800-521-6797.

CONSTRUCTION INFORMATION

If you want to know more about techniques—and deal more confidently with subcontractors we offer these useful sheets. Each set is an excellent tool that will add to your understanding of these technical subjects.

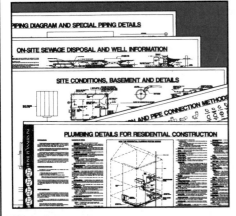

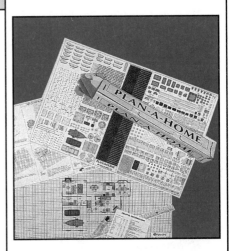

Plan-A-Home®

PLUMBING

The Blueprint Package includes locations for all the plumbing fixtures in your new house, including sinks, lavatories, tubs, showers, toilets, laundry trays and water heaters. However, if you want to know more about the complete plumbing system, these 24x36-inch detail sheets will prove very useful. Prepared to meet requirements of the National Plumbing Code, these six fact-filled sheets give general information on pipe schedules, fittings, sump-pump details, water-softener hookups, septic system details and much more. Color-coded sheets include a glossary of terms.

ELECTRICAL

The locations for every electrical switch, plug and outlet are shown in your Blueprint Package. However, these Electrical Details go further to take the mystery out of household electrical systems. Prepared to meet requirements of the National Electrical Code, these comprehensive 24x36-inch drawings come packed with helpful information, including wire sizing, switch-installation schematics, cable-routing details, appliance wattage, door-bell hookups, typical service panel circuitry and much more. Six sheets are bound together and color-coded for easy reference. A glossary of terms is also included.

Plan-A-Home® is an easy-to-use tool that helps you design a new home, arrange furniture in a new or existing home, or plan a remodeling project. Each package contains:

- **More than 700 reusable peel-off planning symbols** on a self-stick vinyl sheet, including walls, windows, doors, all types of furniture, kitchen components, bath fixtures and many more.

- **A reusable, transparent, 1/4-inch scale planning grid** that matches the scale of actual working drawings (1/4-inch equals 1 foot). This grid provides the basis for house layouts of up to 140x92 feet.

- **Tracing paper** and a protective sheet for copying or transferring your completed plan.

- **A felt-tip pen,** with water-soluble ink that wipes away quickly.

Plan-A-Home® lets you lay out areas as large as a 7,500 square foot, six-bedroom, seven-bath house.

CONSTRUCTION

The Blueprint Package contains everything an experienced builder needs to construct a particular house. However, it doesn't show all the ways that houses can be built, nor does it explain alternate construction methods. To help you understand how your house will be built—and offer additional techniques—this set of drawings depicts the materials and methods used to build foundations, fireplaces, walls, floors and roofs. Where appropriate, the drawings show acceptable alternatives. These six sheets will answer questions for the advanced do-it-yourselfer or home planner.

MECHANICAL

This package contains fundamental principles and useful data that will help you make informed decisions and communicate with subcontractors about heating and cooling systems. The 24x36-inch drawings contain instructions and samples that allow you to make simple load calculations and preliminary sizing and costing analysis. Covered are today's most commonly used systems from heat pumps to solar fuel systems. The package is packed full of illustrations and diagrams to help you visualize components and how they relate to one another.

To Order, Call Toll Free 1-800-521-6797

To add these important extras to your Blueprint Package, simply indicate your choices on the order form on page 221 or call us Toll Free 1-800-521-6797 and we'll tell you more about these exciting products.

▣ *The Deck Blueprint Package*

Many of the homes in this book can be enhanced with a professionally designed Home Planners' Deck Plan. Those home plans highlighted with a ▣ have a matching or corresponding deck plan available which includes a Deck Plan Frontal Sheet, Deck Framing and Floor Plans, Deck Elevations and a Deck Materials List. A Standard Deck Details Package, also available, provides all the how-to information necessary for building *any* deck. Our Complete Deck Building Package contains 1 set of Custom Deck Plans of your choice, plus 1 set of Standard Deck Building Details all for one low price. Our plans and details are carefully prepared in an easy-to-understand format that will guide you through every stage of your deck-building project. This page contains a sampling of 12 of the 25 different Deck layouts to match your favorite house. See page 218 for prices and ordering information.

SPLIT–LEVEL SUN DECK
Deck Plan D100

BI–LEVEL DECK WITH COVERED DINING
Deck Plan D101

WRAP–AROUND FAMILY DECK
Deck Plan D104

DECK FOR DINING AND VIEWS
Deck Plan D107

TREND–SETTER DECK
Deck Plan D110

TURN–OF–THE–CENTURY DECK
Deck Plan D111

WEEKEND ENTERTAINER DECK
Deck Plan D112

CENTER–VIEW DECK
Deck Plan D114

KITCHEN–EXTENDER DECK
Deck Plan D115

SPLIT–LEVEL ACTIVITY DECK
Deck Plan D117

TRI-LEVEL DECK WITH GRILL
Deck Plan D119

CONTEMPORARY LEISURE DECK
Deck Plan D120

⬛ *The Landscape Blueprint Package*

For the homes marked with an ⬛ in this book, Home Planners has created a front-yard landscape plan that matches or is complementary in design to the house plan. These comprehensive blueprint packages include a Frontal Sheet, Plan View, Regionalized Plant & Materials List, a sheet on Planting and Maintaining Your Landscape, Zone Maps and Plant Size and Description Guide. These plans will help you achieve professional results, adding value and enjoyment to your property for years to come. Each set of blueprints is a full 18" x 24" in size with clear, complete instructions and easy-to-read type. Six of the forty front-yard Landscape Plans to match your favorite house are shown below.

Regional Order Map

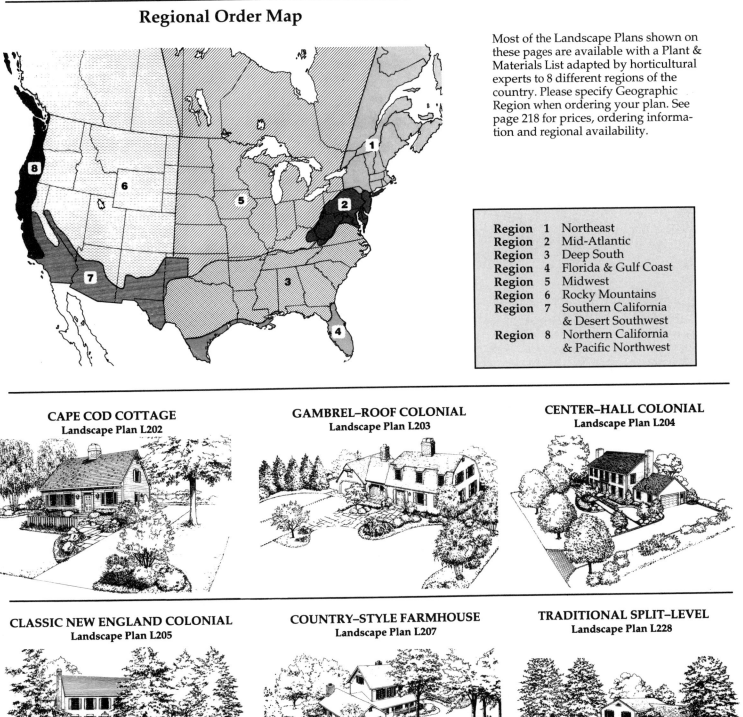

Most of the Landscape Plans shown on these pages are available with a Plant & Materials List adapted by horticultural experts to 8 different regions of the country. Please specify Geographic Region when ordering your plan. See page 218 for prices, ordering information and regional availability.

Region	**1**	Northeast
Region	**2**	Mid-Atlantic
Region	**3**	Deep South
Region	**4**	Florida & Gulf Coast
Region	**5**	Midwest
Region	**6**	Rocky Mountains
Region	**7**	Southern California & Desert Southwest
Region	**8**	Northern California & Pacific Northwest

CAPE COD COTTAGE
Landscape Plan L202

GAMBREL–ROOF COLONIAL
Landscape Plan L203

CENTER–HALL COLONIAL
Landscape Plan L204

CLASSIC NEW ENGLAND COLONIAL
Landscape Plan L205

COUNTRY–STYLE FARMHOUSE
Landscape Plan L207

TRADITIONAL SPLIT–LEVEL
Landscape Plan L228

Price Schedule & Plans Index

House Blueprint Price Schedule
(Prices guaranteed through December 31, 1998)

	1-set Study Package	4-set Building Package	8-set Building Package	1-set Reproducible Sepias	Home Customizer® Package
Schedule A	$350	$395	$455	$555	$605
Schedule B	$390	$435	$495	$615	$665
Schedule C	$430	$475	$535	$675	$725
Schedule D	$470	$515	$575	$735	$785
Schedule E	$590	$635	$695	$795	$845

Additional Identical Blueprints in same order ....$50 per set
Reverse Blueprints (mirror image) ....$50 per set
Specification Outlines..$10 each
Materials Lists (available only from those designers listed below):
- ▲ Home Planners Designs...$50
- ✳ Larry Garnett Designs...$50
- † Design Basics Designs...$75
- ✱ Alan Mascord Designs...$50
- ◆ Donald Gardner Designs..$50
- ■ Design Traditions Designs $50

Materials Lists for "E" price plans are an additional $10.

Deck Plans Price Schedule

CUSTOM DECK PLANS

Price Group	Q	R	S
1 Set Custom Plans	$25	$30	$35

Additional identical sets $10 each
Reverse sets (mirror image) $10 each

STANDARD DECK DETAILS
1 Set Generic Construction Details ....$14.95 each

COMPLETE DECK BUILDING PACKAGE

Price Group	Q	R	S
1 Set Custom Plans, plus 1 Set Standard Deck Details	$35	$40	$45

Landscape Plans Price Schedule

Price Group	X	Y	Z
1 set	$35	$45	$55
3 sets	$50	$60	$70
6 sets	$65	$75	$85

Additional Identical Sets...............................$10 each
Reverse Sets (mirror image)..........................$10 each

Index

To use the Index below, refer to the design number listed in numerical order (a helpful page reference is also given). Note the price index letter and refer to the House Blueprint Price Schedule above for the cost of one, four or eight sets of blueprints or the cost of a reproducible sepia. Additional prices are shown for identical and reverse blueprint sets, as well as a very useful Materials List for some of the plans. Also note in the Index below those plans that have matching or complementary Deck Plans or Landscape Plans. Refer to the schedules above for prices of these plans. All Home Planners' plans can be customized with Home Planners' Home Customizer® Package. These plans are indicated below with this symbol: 🏠 . See page 221 for information. Some plans are also part of our Quote One® estimating service and are indicated by this symbol: 🏠 . See page 214 for more information.

To Order: Fill in and send the order form on page 221—or call toll free 1-800-521-6797 or 520-297-8200.

DESIGN	PRICE	PAGE	CUSTOMIZABLE	QUOTE ONE®	DECK	DECK PRICE	LANDSCAPE	LANDSCAPE PRICE	REGIONS
▲Q1701	B	101	🏠		D117	S			
▲Q1956	A	105	🏠	🏠	D117	S			
▲Q2145	A	145	🏠	🏠			L209	Y	1-6,8
▲Q2146	A	146	🏠		D114	R	L203	Y	1-3,5,6,8
▲Q2174	C	176	🏠		D117	S	L220	Y	1-3,5,6,8
▲Q2188	C	97	🏠						
▲Q2223	B	190	🏠		D112	R	L205	Y	1-3,5,6,8
▲Q2538	B	115	🏠		D113	R	L201	Y	1-3,5,6,8
▲Q2542	D	185	🏠				L208	Z	1,2,5,6,8
▲Q2563	B	149	🏠		D114	R	L201	Y	1-3,5,6,8
▲Q2571	A	142	🏠		D114	R	L202	X	1-3,5,6,8
▲Q2596	B	147	🏠		D114	R	L201	Y	1-3,5,6,8
▲Q2614	C	177	🏠		D114	R			
▲Q2633	C	188	🏠						
▲Q2654	A	96	🏠						
▲Q2659	B	107	🏠	🏠	D113	R	L205	Y	1-3,5,6,8
▲Q2661	A	170	🏠	🏠	D113	R	L202	X	1-3,5,6,8
▲Q2680	C	135	🏠		D114	R	L224	Y	1-3,5,6,8
▲Q2681	B	26	🏠						
▲Q2682	A	140	🏠	🏠	D115	Q	L200	X	1-3,5,6,8
▲Q2694	C	6	🏠	🏠			L209	Y	1-6,8
▲Q2699	C	154	🏠	🏠			L211	Y	1-8
▲Q2774	B	7	🏠	🏠	D100	Q	L207	Z	1-6,8
▲Q2776	B	41	🏠	🏠	D113	R	L207	Z	1-6,8
▲Q2805	B	174	🏠	🏠	D113	R	L220	Y	1-3,5,6,8
▲Q2931	B	210	🏠						
▲Q2945	B	30	🏠						
▲Q2946	C	8	🏠		D114	R	L207	Z	1-6,8
▲Q2947	B	211	🏠	🏠	D112	R	L200	X	1-3,5,6,8
▲Q2970	D	88	🏠	🏠			L223	Z	1-3,5,6,8
▲Q2974	A	89	🏠	🏠			L223	Z	1-3,5,6,8
▲Q2976	C	189	🏠						
▲Q2981	D	60	🏠				L224	Y	1-3,5,6,8
▲Q2991	D	68	🏠	🏠	D111	S	L215	Z	1-6,8
▲Q2995	D	156	🏠	🏠	D106	S	L217	Y	1-8
▲Q2996	E	66	🏠	🏠	D111	S	L235	Z	1-3,5,6,8
▲Q2998	D	114	🏠	🏠	D103	R	L210	Y	1-6,8
▲Q3307	C	77	🏠	🏠	D111	S	L207	Z	1-6,8
▲Q3317	C	112	🏠						
▲Q3324	E	9	🏠		D114	R	L207	Z	1-6,8
▲Q3325	C	27	🏠		D100	Q	L238	Y	3,4,7,8
▲Q3327	C	109	🏠	🏠	D110	R	L217	Y	1-8

Before You Order . . .

Before filling out the coupon at right or calling us on our Toll-Free Blueprint Hotline, you may want to learn more about our services and products. Here's some information you will find helpful.

Quick Turnaround
We process and ship every blueprint order from our office within 48 hours. Because of this quick turnaround, we won't send a formal notice acknowledging receipt of your order.

Our Exchange Policy
Since blueprints are printed in response to your order, we cannot honor requests for refunds. However, we will exchange your entire first order for an equal number of blueprints at a price of $50 for the first set and $10 for each additional set; $70 total exchange fee for 4 sets; $100 total exchange fee for 8 sets . . . *plus* the difference in cost if exchanging for a design in a higher price bracket or *less* the difference in cost if exchanging for a design in lower price bracket. One exchange is allowed within a year of purchase date. **(Sepias are not exchangeable.)** All sets from the first order must be returned before the exchange can take place. Please add $15 for postage and handling via ground service; $20 via Second Day Air; $30 via Next Day Air.

About Reverse Blueprints
If you want to build in reverse of the plan as shown, we will include an extra set of reverse blueprints (mirror image) for an additional fee of $50. Although lettering and dimensions will appear backward, reverses will be a useful aid if you decide to flop the plan.

Revising, Modifying and Customizing Plans
The wide variety of designs available in this publication allows you to select ideas and concepts for a home to fit your building site and match your family's needs, wants and budget. Like many homeowners who buy these plans, you and your builder, architect or engineer may want to make changes to them. Some minor changes may be made by your builder, but we recommend that most changes be made by a licensed architect or engineer. If you need to make alterations to a design that is customizable, you need only order our Home Customizer® Package to get you started. As set forth below, we cannot assume any responsibility for blueprints which have been changed, whether by you, your builder or by professionals selected by you or referred to you by us, because such individuals are outside our supervision and control.

Architectural and Engineering Seals
Some cities and states are now requiring that a licensed architect or engineer review and "seal" a blueprint, or officially approve it, prior to construction due to concerns over energy costs, safety and other factors. Prior to application for a building permit or the start of actual construction, we strongly advise that you consult your local building official who can tell you if such a review is required.

About the Designers
The architects and designers whose work appears in this publication are among America's leading residential designers. Each plan was designed to meet the requirements of a nationally recognized model building code in effect at the time and place the plan was drawn. Because national building codes change from time to time, plans may not comply with any such code at the time they are sold to a customer. In addition, building officials may not accept these plans as final construction documents of record as the plans may need to be modified and additional drawings and details added to suit local conditions and requirements. We strongly advise that purchasers consult a licensed architect or engineer, and their local building official, before starting any construction related to these plans.

Local Building Codes and Zoning Requirements
At the time of creation, our plans are drawn to specifications published by the Building Officials and Code Administrators (BOCA) International, Inc.; the Southern Building Code Congress (SBCCI) International, Inc.; the International Conference of Building Officials; or the Council of American Building Officials (CABO). Our plans are designed to meet or exceed national building standards. Because of the great differences in geography and climate throughout the United States and Canada, each state, county and municipality has its own building codes, zone requirements, ordinances and building regulations. Your plan may need to be modified to comply with local requirements regarding snow loads, energy codes, soil and seismic conditions and a wide range of other matters. In addition, you may need to obtain permits or inspections from local governments before and in the course of construction. Prior to using blueprints ordered from us, we strongly advise that you consult a licensed architect or engineer—and speak with your local building official—before applying for any permit or beginning construction. We authorize the use of our blueprints on the express condition that you strictly comply with all local building codes, zoning requirements and other applicable laws, regulations, ordinances and requirements. **Notice:** Plans for homes to be built in Nevada must be re-drawn by a Nevada-registered professional. Consult your building official for more information on this subject.

Foundation and Exterior Wall Changes
Most of our plans are drawn with either a full or partial basement foundation. Depending on your specific climate or regional building practices, you may wish to change this basement to a slab or crawlspace. Most professional contractors and builders can easily adapt your plans to alternate foundation types. Likewise, most can easily change 2x4 wall construction to 2x6, or vice versa.

Disclaimer
We and the designers we work with have put substantial care and effort into the creation of our blueprints. However, because we cannot provide on-site consultation, supervision and control over actual construction, and because of the great variance in local building requirements, building practices and soil, seismic, weather and other conditions, WE CANNOT MAKE ANY WARRANTY, EXPRESS OR IMPLIED, WITH RESPECT TO THE CONTENT OR USE OF OUR BLUEPRINTS, INCLUDING BUT NOT LIMITED TO ANY WARRANTY OF MERCHANTABILITY OR OF FITNESS FOR A PARTICULAR PURPOSE.

Terms and Conditions
The terms and conditions governing our license of blueprints to you are set forth in the material accompanying the blueprints. This material tells you how to return the blueprints if you do not agree to these terms and conditions.

How Many Blueprints Do You Need?
A single set of blueprints is sufficient to study a home in greater detail. However, if you are planning to obtain cost estimates from a contractor or subcontractor—or if you are planning to build immediately—you will need more sets. Because additional sets are cheaper when ordered in quantity with the original order, make sure you order enough blueprints to satisfy all requirements. The following checklist will help you determine how many you need:

____ Owner

____ Builder (generally requires at least three sets; one as a legal document, one to use during inspections, and at least one to give to subcontractors)

____ Local Building Department (often requires two sets)

____ Mortgage Lender (usually one set for a conventional loan; three sets for FHA or VA loans)

____ TOTAL NUMBER OF SETS

Have You Seen Our Newest Designs?

Home Planners is one of the country's most active home design firms, creating nearly 100 new plans each year. At least 50 of our latest creations are featured in each edition of our New Design Portfolio. You may have received a copy with your latest purchase by mail. If not, or if you purchased this book from a local retailer, just return the coupon below for your FREE copy. Make sure you consider the very latest of what Home Planners has to offer.

Yes! Please send my FREE copy of your latest New Design Portfolio.

Offer good to U.S. shipping address only.

Name _____

Address _____

City_____State_____Zip_____

HOME PLANNERS, A Division of
Hanley-Wood, Inc.
3275 WEST INA ROAD, SUITE 110
TUCSON, ARIZONA 85741

Order Form Key

TB26

Toll Free 1-800-521-6797

Regular Office Hours:
8:00 a.m. to 8:00 p.m. Eastern Time, Monday through Friday
Our staff will gladly answer any questions during regular office hours. Our answering service can place orders after hours or on weekends.

If we receive your order by 4:00 p.m. Eastern Time, Monday through Friday, we'll process it and ship within 48 hours. When ordering by phone, please have your charge card ready. We'll also ask you for the Order Form Key Number at the bottom of the coupon.

By FAX: Copy the Order Form on the next page and send it on our FAX line: 1-800-224-6699 or 1-520-544-3086.

Canadian Customers
Order Toll-Free 1-800-561-4169

For faster service and plans that are modified for building in Canada, customers may now call in orders directly to our Canadian supplier of plans and charge the purchase to a charge card. Or, you may complete the order form at right, adding 40% to all prices and mail in Canadian funds to:

The Plan Centre 60 Baffin Place
Unit 5
Waterloo, Ontario N2V 1Z7

OR: Copy the Order Form and send it via our Canadian FAX line: 1-800-719-3291.

The Home Customizer®

"This house is perfect...if only the family room were two feet wider." Sound familiar? In response to the numerous requests for this type of modification, Home Planners has developed **The Home Customizer® Package**. This exclusive package offers our top-of-the-line materials to make it easy for anyone, anywhere to customize any Home Planners design to fit their needs. Check the index on page 218 for those plans which are customizable.

Some of the changes you can make to any of our plans include:

- exterior elevation changes
- kitchen and bath modifications
- roof, wall and foundation changes
- room additions and more!

The Home Customizer® Package includes everything you'll need to make the necessary changes to your favorite Home Planners design. The package includes:

- instruction book with examples
- architectural scale and clear work film
- erasable red marker and removable correction tape
- ¼"-scale furniture cutouts
- 1 set reproducible, erasable Sepias
- 1 set study blueprints for communicating changes to your design professional
- a copyright release letter so you can make copies as you need them
- referral letter with the name, address and telephone number of the professional in your region who is trained in modifying Home Planners designs efficiently and inexpensively.

The price of the **Home Customizer® Package** ranges from $555 to $795, depending on the price schedule of the design you have chosen. **The Home Customizer® Package** will not only save you 25% to 75% of the cost of drawing the plans from scratch with a custom architect or engineer, it will also give you the flexibility to have your changes and modifications made by our referral network or by the professional of your choice. Now it's even easier and more affordable to have the custom home you've always wanted.

New Custom Engineering Service

Through this exciting new service, you can now obtain an engineering seal for the structural elements of any Home Planners plan including complete calculations (minus foundation engineering) from a competent, registered professional. You'll receive a detailed analysis and engineering seal that will assist with the permit process, even in areas that normally require very specific calculations. For more complete information about this service, see page 214.

 For information about any of the above services or to order call 1-800-521-6797.

BLUEPRINTS ARE NOT RETURNABLE

ORDER FORM

HOME PLANNERS, A Division of Hanley-Wood, Inc.
SUITE 110, TUCSON, ARIZONA 85741

THE BASIC BLUEPRINT PACKAGE
Rush me the following (please refer to the Plans Index and Price Schedule in this section):

_____	Set(s) of blueprints for plan number(s) _____.	$_____
_____	Set(s) of sepias for plan number(s)_____.	$_____
_____	Home Customizer® Package for plan(s)_____.	$_____
_____	Additional identical blueprints in same order @ $50 per set.	$_____
_____	Reverse blueprints @ $50 per set.	$_____
_____	Custom Engineering Service for plan _____.	$_____
	_____ Lateral Load Calculations (add 25%)	$_____
	_____ Roof, Floors and Walls Framing (add 25%)	$_____
	_____ Steel Framing Options (add 50%)	$_____

IMPORTANT EXTRAS
Rush me the following:

_____	Materials List: $50	
	$75 Design Basics. Add $10 for a Schedule E plan Materials List.	$_____
_____	**Quote One®** Summary Cost Report @ $24.95 for 1, $14.95 for	
	each additional, for plans _____	$_____
	Building location: City _____ Zip Code _____	
_____	**Quote One®** Materials Cost Report @ $110 Schedule A-D; $120	
	Schedule E for plan _____	$_____
	(Must be purchased with Blueprints set.)	
	Building location: City _____ Zip Code _____	
_____	Specification Outlines @ $10 each.	$_____
_____	Detail Sets @ $14.95 each; any two for $22.95; any three	
	for $29.95; all four for $39.95 (save $19.85).	$_____
	❏ Plumbing ❏ Electrical ❏ Construction ❏ Mechanical	
	(These helpful details provide general construction	
	advice and are not specific to any single plan.)	
_____	Plan-A-Home® @ $29.95 each.	$_____

DECK BLUEPRINTS

_____	Set(s) of Deck Plan _____.	$_____
_____	Additional identical blueprints in same order @ $10 per set.	$_____
_____	Reverse blueprints @ $10 per set.	$_____
_____	Set of Standard Deck Details @ $14.95 per set.	$_____
_____	Set of Complete Building Package (Best Buy!)	
	Includes Custom Deck Plan _____.	
	(See Index and Price Schedule)	
	Plus Standard Deck Details	$_____

LANDSCAPE BLUEPRINTS

_____	Set(s) of Landscape Plan _____.	$_____
_____	Additional identical blueprints in same order @ $10 per set.	$_____
_____	Reverse blueprints @ $10 per set.	$_____

Please indicate the appropriate region of the country for
Plant & Material List. (See Map on page 217): Region _____

POSTAGE AND HANDLING	1-3 sets	4+ sets
DELIVERY (Requires street address - No P.O. Boxes)		
•Regular Service (Allow 4-6 days delivery)	❏ $15.00	❏ $18.00
•Priority (Allow 2-3 days delivery)	❏ $20.00	❏ $30.00
•Express (Allow 1 day delivery)	❏ $30.00	❏ $40.00
CERTIFIED MAIL (Requires signature)	❏ $20.00	❏ $30.00
If no street address available. (Allow 4-6 days delivery)		
OVERSEAS DELIVERY		
Note: All delivery times are from date Blueprint Package is shipped.	fax, phone or mail for quote	

POSTAGE (From box above) $_____

SUB-TOTAL $_____

SALES TAX (AZ 5%, CA & NY 8.25%, DC 5.75%, IL 6.25%,
MI 6%, MN 6.5%) $_____

TOTAL (Sub-total and tax) $_____

YOUR ADDRESS (please print)

Name _____

Street _____

City _____ State _____ Zip _____

Daytime telephone number (_____) _____

FOR CREDIT CARD ORDERS ONLY
Please fill in the information below:

Credit card number _____

Exp. Date: Month/Year _____

Check one ❏ Visa ❏ MasterCard ❏ Discover Card

Signature _____

Please check appropriate box: ❏ Licensed Builder-Contractor
❏ Homeowner

☎ ORDER TOLL FREE!
1-800-521-6797 or 520-297-8200

Order Form Key

TB26

Helpful Books & Software

Home Planners wants your building experience to be as pleasant and trouble-free as possible. That's why we've expanded our library of Do-It-Yourself titles to help you along. In addition to our beautiful plans books, we've added books to guide you through specific projects as well as the construction process. In fact, these are titles that will be as useful after your dream home is built as they are right now.

COUNTRY
1 200 country designs from classic to contemporary by 7 winning designers. 224 pages $8.95

BUDGET-SMART
2 200 efficient plans from 7 top designers, that you can really afford to build! 224 pages $8.95

MOVE-UP
3 200 stylish designs for today's growing families from 9 hot designers. 224 pages $8.95 NEW!

NARROW-LOT
4 200 unique homes less than 60' wide from 7 designers. Up to 3,000 square feet. 224 pages $8.95

REGIONAL BEST
5 200 beautiful homes from across America by 7 regional designers. 224 pages $8.95 NEW!

EXPANDABLES
6 200 flexible plans that expand with your needs from 7 top designers. 240 pages $8.95 NEW!

BEST SELLERS
7 NEW! Our 50th Anniversary book with 200 of our very best designs in full color! 224 page $12.95

NEW ENGLAND
8 260 of the best in Colonial home design. Special interior design sections, too. 384 pages $14.95

AFFORDABLE
9 430 cost-saving plans specially selected for modest to medium building budgets. 320 pages $9.95

LUXURY
10 154 fine luxury plans-loaded with luscious amenities! 192 pages $14.95

ONE-STORY
11 448 designs for all lifestyles. 860 to 5,400 square feet. 384 pages $9.95 NEW!

TWO-STORY
12 460 designs for one-and-a-half and two stories. 1,245 to 7,275 square feet. 384 pages $9.95

VACATION
13 345 designs for recreation, retirement and leisure. 312 pages $8.95 NEW!

MULTI-LEVEL
14 312 designs for split-levels, bi-levels, multi-levels and walkouts. 224 pages $8.95 NEW!

OUTDOOR
15 42 unique outdoor projects. Gazebos, strombellas, bridges, sheds, playsets and more! 96 pages $7.95 NEW!

DECKS
16 25 outstanding single-, double- and multi-level decks you can build. 112 pages $7.95

ENCYCLOPEDIA
17 500 exceptional plans for all styles and budgets—the best book of its kind! 352 pages $9.95

MODERN & CLASSIC
18 341 impressive homes featuring the latest in contemporary design. 304 pages $9.95

TRADITIONAL
19 403 designs of classic beauty and elegance. 304 pages $9.95

VICTORIAN
20 160 striking Victorian and Farmhouse designs from three leading designers. 192 pages $12.95

SOUTHERN
21 207 homes rich in Southern styling and comfort. 240 pages $8.95 NEW!

WESTERN
22 215 designs that capture the spirit and diversity of the Western lifestyle. 208 pages $9.95

EMPTY-NESTER
23 200 exciting plans for empty-nesters, retirees and childless couples. 224 pages $8.95

STARTER
24 200 easy-to-build plans for starter and low-budget houses. 224 pages $8.95

Landscape Designs

FRONT & BACK
25 The first book of do-it-yourself landscapes. 40 front, 15 backyards. 208 pages $14.95

BACKYARDS
26 40 designs focused solely on creating your own specially themed backyard oasis. 160 pages $14.95

EASY CARE
27 NEW! 41 special landscapes designed for beauty and low maintenance. 160 pages $14.95

Design Software

BOOK & CD ROM
28 NEW! Both the Home Planners Gold book and matching Windows™ CD ROM with 3D floor-plans. $24.95

3D HOME DESIGNER
29 Take home design to the next level. Windows™ compatible program automatically creates 3D views of any floor plan you draw. Includes bonus CD of 500 Designs. $49.95

Interior Design

HOME DECORATING
30 Special effects and creative ideas for all surfaces. Includes simple step-by-step diagrams. 96 pages $9.95

BATHROOMS
31 An innovative guide to organizing, remodeling and decorating your bathroom. 96 pages $8.95

KITCHENS
32 An imaginative guide to designing the perfect kitchen. Chock full of bright ideas to make your job easier. 176 pages $14 .95

Planning Books & Quick Guides

TRIM & MOLDING
33 Step-by-step instructions for installing baseboards, window and door casings and more. 80 pages $7.95

PAINTING
34 Tips from the pros on everything from preparation to clean-up. 80 pages $7.95

ROOFING
35 Information on the latest tools, materials and techniques for roof installation or repair. 80 pages $7.95

WALLS & MORE
36 A clear and concise guide to repairing or remodeling walls and ceilings. 80 pages $7.95

FLOORS
37 All the information you need for repairing, replacing or installing floors in any home. 80 pages $7.95

PATIOS & WALKS
38 Clear step-by-step instructions take you from the basic design stages to the finished project. 80 pages $7.95

WINDOWS & DOORS
39 Installation techniques and tips that make your project easier and more professional looking. 80 pages $7.95

PLUMBING
40 Tackle any plumbing installation or repair as quickly and efficiently as a professional. 160 pages $12.95

ADDING SPACE
41 Convert attics, basements and bonus rooms to useful living space. 160 pages $14.95

HOME REPAIR
42 An owner's manual for your home. Sound advice on home maintenance and improvements. 256 pages $9.95

TILE
43 Every kind of tile for every kind of application. Includes tips on use installation and repair. 176 pages $12.95

WALLPAPERING
44 Use the book the pros use. Covers tools and techniques for every type of wallcovering. 136 pages $12.95

BASIC WIRING
45 A straight forward guide to one of the most misunderstood systems in the home. 160 pages $12.95

HOUSE CONTRACTING
46 Everything you need to know to act as your own general contractor...and save up to 25% off building costs. 134 pages $12.95

VISUAL HANDBOOK
47 A plain-talk guide to the construction process; financing to final walk-through, this book covers it all. 498 pages $19.95

CONTRACTING GUIDE
48 Loaded with information to make you more confident in dealing with contractors and subcontractors. 287 pages $18.95

FRAMING

49 For those who want to take a more-hands on approach to their dream. 319 pages $19.95

- -

Additional Books Order Form

To order your books, just check the box of the book numbered below and complete the coupon. We will process your order and ship it from our office within 48 hours. Send coupon and check (in U.S. funds).

YES! Please send me the books I've indicated:

☐	1:FH $8.95		☐	26:BYL $14.95
☐	2:BS $8.95		☐	27:ECL $14.95
☐	3:MU $8.95		☐	28:HPGC $24.95
☐	4:NL $8.95		☐	29:PLAN3D $49.95
☐	5:AA $8.95		☐	30:CDP $9.95
☐	6:EX $8.95		☐	31:CDB $8.95
☐	7:HPG $12.95		☐	32:CKI $14.95
☐	8:NES $14.95		☐	33:CGT $7.95
☐	9:AH $9.95		☐	34:CGP $7.95
☐	10:LD2 .... $14.95		☐	35:CGR $7.95
☐	11:VO $9.95		☐	36:CGC $7.95
☐	12:VT $9.95		☐	37:CGF $7.95
☐	13:VH $8.95		☐	38:CGW $7.95
☐	14:VS $8.95		☐	39:CGD $7.95
☐	15:YG $7.95		☐	40:CMP $12.95
☐	16:DP $7.95		☐	41:CAS $14.95
☐	17:EN $9.95		☐	42:CHR $9.95
☐	18:EC $9.95		☐	43:CWT $12.95
☐	19:ET $9.95		☐	44:CW $12.95
☐	20:VDH $12.95		☐	45:CBW $12.95
☐	21:SH $8.95		☐	46:SBC $12.95
☐	22:WH $9.95		☐	47:RVH $19.95
☐	23:EP $8.95		☐	48:BCC $18.95
☐	24:ST $8.95		☐	49:SRF $19.95
☐	25:HL $14.95			

Canadian Customers
Order Toll-Free 1-800-561-4169

Additional Books Sub-Total $_____
ADD Postage and Handling $ _3.00_
Sales Tax: (AZ 5%, CA & NY 8.25%, DC 5.75%,
      IL 6.25%, MI 6%, MN 6.5%) $_____
YOUR TOTAL (Sub-Total, Postage/Handling, Tax) $_____

YOUR ADDRESS (Please print)

Name _____

Street _____

City _____ State_____ Zip _____

Phone (_____) _____—_____

YOUR PAYMENT
Check one: ☐ Check ☐ Visa ☐ MasterCard ☐ Discover Card
Required credit card information:

Credit Card Number_____

Expiration Date (Month/Year) _____/ _____

Signature Required _____

 Home Planners, A Division of Hanley-Wood, Inc.
3275 W Ina Road, Suite 110, Dept. BK, Tucson, AZ 85741

TB26

Design Q9621

OVER 3 MILLION BLUEPRINTS SOLD

"We instructed our builder to follow the plans including all of the many details which make this house so elegant... Our home is a fine example of the results one can achieve by purchasing and following the plans which you offer... Everyone who has seen it has assured us that it belongs in 'a picture book.' I truly mean it when I say that my home 'is a DREAM HOUSE.'"

S.P.
Anderson, SC

"We have had a steady stream of visitors, many of whom tell us this is the most beautiful home they've seen. Everyone is amazed at the layout and remarks on how unique it is. Our real estate attorney, who is a Chicago dweller and who deals with highly valued properties, told me this is the only suburban home he has seen that he would want to live in."

W. & P.S.
Flossmoor, IL

"Your blueprints saved us a great deal of money. I acted as the general contractor and we did a lot of the work ourselves. We probably built it for half the cost! We are thinking about more plans for another home. I purchased a competitor's book but my husband wants only your plans!"

K.M.
Grovetown, GA

"We are very happy with the product of our efforts. The neighbors and passersby appreciate what we have created. We have had many people stop by to discuss our house and kindly praise it as being the nicest house in our area of new construction. We have even had one person stop and make us an unsolicited offer to buy the house for much more than we have invested in it."

K. & L.S.
Bolingbrook, IL

"The traffic going past our house is unbelievable. On several occasions, we have heard that it is the 'prettiest house in Batvia.' Also, when meeting someone new and mentioning what street we live on, quite often we're told, 'Oh, you're the one in the yellow house with the wrap-around porch! I love it!'"

A.W.
Batvia, NY

"I have been involved in the building trades my entire life... Since building our home we have built two other homes for other families. Their plans from local professional architects were not nearly as good as yours. For that reason we are ordering additional plan books from you."

T.F.
Kingston, WA

"The blueprints we received from you were of excellent quality and provided us with exactly what we needed to get our successful home-building project underway. We appreciate your invaluable role in our home-building effort."

T.A.
Concord, TN